# Distant Early Warning

# DISTANT EARLY WARNING

## Marshall McLuhan and the Transformation of the Avant-Garde

ALEX KITNICK

The University of Chicago Press Chicago and London

The University of Chicago Press, Chicago 60637
The University of Chicago Press, Ltd., London

Published 2021
Printed in the United States of America

30 29 28 27 26 25 24 23 22 21 1 2 3 4 5

ISBN-13: 978-0-226-75331-7 (cloth)
ISBN-13: 978-0-226-75345-4 (paper)
ISBN-13: 978-0-226-75359-1 (e-book)
DOI: https://doi.org/10.7208/chicago/9780226753591.001.0001

Library of Congress Cataloging-in-Publication Data
Names: Kitnick, Alex, 1981– author.
Title: Distant early warning : Marshall McLuhan and the transformation of the avant-garde / Alex Kitnick.
Other titles: Marshall McLuhan and the transformation of the avant-garde
Description: Chicago ; London : The University of Chicago Press, 2021. | Includes bibliographical references and index.
Identifiers: LCCN 2021009504 | ISBN 9780226753317 (cloth) | ISBN 9780226753454 (paperback) | ISBN 9780226753591 (ebook)
Subjects: LCSH: McLuhan, Marshall, 1911–1980—Aesthetics. | Avant-garde (Aesthetics) | Art, Modern—20th century—Philosophy. | Art criticism—History—20th century.
Classification: LCC N7483.M39 K58 2021 | DDC 709.04—dc23
LC record available at https://lccn.loc.gov/2021009504

♾ This paper meets the requirements of ANSI/NISO Z39.48-1992 (Permanence of Paper).

**Fools lament the decay of criticism. For its day is long past. Criticism is a matter of correct distancing. It was at home in a world where perspectives and prospects counted and where it was still possible to take a standpoint. Now things press too closely on human society.** Walter Benjamin, *One-Way Street*

# Contents

# Introduction

**Art ceases to be a form of self-expression in the electric age. Indeed, it becomes a necessary kind of research and probing.** Marshall McLuhan and Harley Parker, *Through the Vanishing Point: Space in Poetry and Painting* (1968)

In 1976, Harry Benson, a photographer of presidents and movie stars, made a portrait of Marshall McLuhan.[1] At that point in his career McLuhan was equal parts professor and celebrity. A public intellectual and culture hero, he appeared on television shows, and his articles ran in wide-circulation magazines—the next year he would take his star turn in *Annie Hall* (1977). (When an overzealous moviegoer rhapsodizes about media theory, McLuhan retorts: "You know nothing of my work!") In the Benson photograph, McLuhan displays a toothy charisma, leaning over a table covered with piles of paper, open folders, books, and newspapers ("View of Canada: never a believer in happy ending," a headline reads). His hands are balled into fists. With sleeves rolled up, pen in shirt pocket, glasses low on the nose, McLuhan is outfitted with all the insignia of the intellectual—and he is smiling so as to let us know the pleasure he takes in his enterprise. Behind him hangs a large painting: a sprawling canvas by the French artist René Cera, *Pied Pipers All*, completed seven years before, in 1969, for the inauguration of McLuhan's Centre for Culture and Technology at the University of Toronto.[2] Incorporating abstract forms and figurative motifs in a complex whole, it is a large canvas, both mythological and technological in subject matter, with strange creatures, some blaring horns, immersed in the lines of a pulsing network. A rectangle resembling a television screen hovers at the center of the canvas. In the photograph, Benson has posed McLuhan so that his head is directly in its middle: beatific icon and talking head at once.

This portrait is no accident. Over the course of his career, McLuhan made art central to his self-presentation and claimed it as a constant

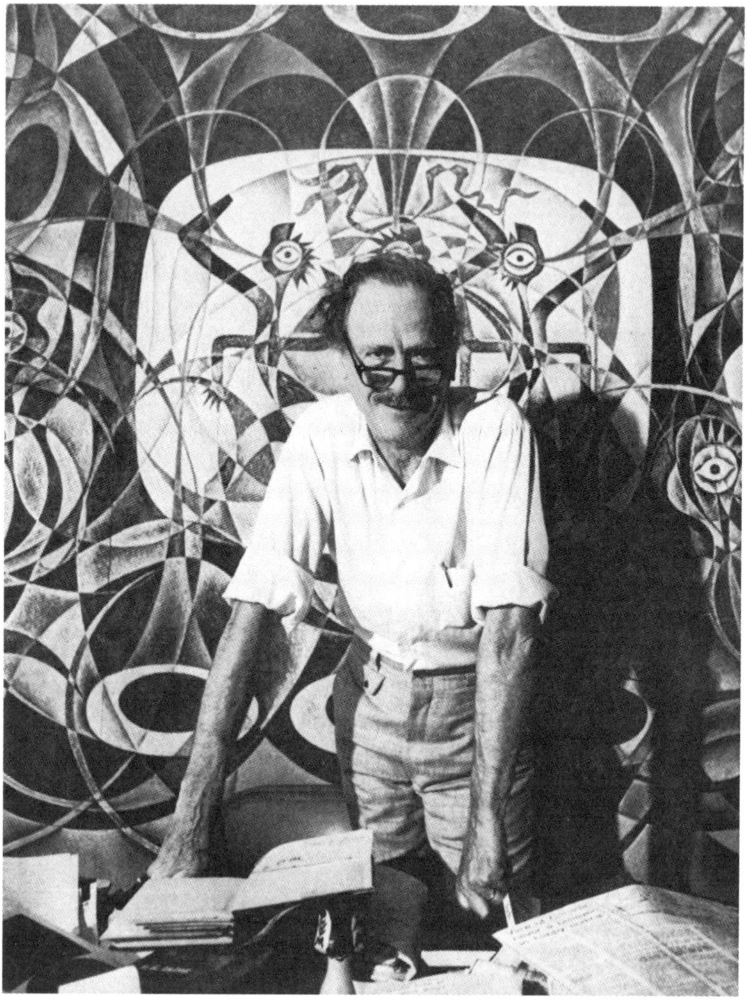

**1** Harry Benson, *Portrait of Marshall McLuhan* (1976), in *People*, September 20, 1976.

touchstone in his thought: art provided for him the most direct way of both gauging and affecting the powers of media, which he famously made his project to understand. "The power of the machine to transform the character of work and living strongly invites us to transform every level of existence by art," he wrote in 1954.[3] Since the machine's impact on living invited one to view it in an aesthetic register, art, too,

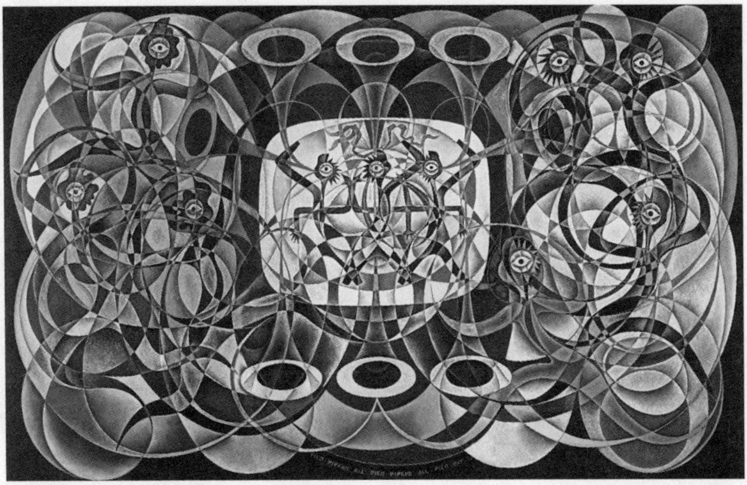

**2** René Cera, *Pied Pipers All* (1969). Estate of Elizabeth and René Cera. Photo: Michael McLuhan.

could transform life. Historically aware but future oriented, McLuhan did not celebrate art for its powers of self-expression, nor did he view it as a fixed canon or "blood bank" by which the present moment accesses the past. For him, art offered a means of cultural exploration and environmental change.[4] While McLuhan spent most of his life—which ran the better part of the twentieth century, from 1911 to 1980—in the halls of university English departments and, as his star rose, corporate conference rooms and packed auditoriums, art—in some expanded sense—remained his constant topic.[5]

Cutting across the twentieth century, this book introduces McLuhan's theory of art and parses the relationship between McLuhan and the arts of his time. It positions him alongside contemporary artistic developments rather than simply as an inspiration behind them, and, in so doing, it tries to reimagine the relationship between theory and practice, criticism and art. While such binaries are often structured in terms of before and after or cause and effect, with McLuhan they form a feedback loop, a discourse native to his time. Here, ideas and forms migrate from one field to another, influencing each other's behavior in turn: Art provides a template for how McLuhan will act in the world, just as McLuhan would later set an example for artists. My first chapter, "The Age of Mechanical Reproduction," explores how McLuhan's interest in the French-American artist Marcel Duchamp allowed him to innovate a wry brand of cultural criticism that would in turn influence artists such as Richard Hamilton and others affiliated with London's Independent Group.

McLuhan took what he needed from the past, and, in doing so, he pushed an earlier generation's cultural projects into line with developments in the wider culture. Returning to the historical avant-garde in light of the postwar world's technological and economic shifts, he laid a groundwork for how artists might operate in a changed media situation, insisting that they think in terms of environments and bodies politic rather than such traditional disciplines as painting and sculpture. Indeed, the relationship between the artwork and the body politic formed a central tenet of his thought. "Ever since Burckhardt saw that the meaning of Machiavelli's method was to turn the state into a work of art by the rational manipulation of power, it has been an open possibility to apply the method of art analysis to the critical evaluation of society," he wrote in his 1951 *The Mechanical Bride*. "The Western world, dedicated since the sixteenth century to the increase and consolidation of the power of the state, has developed an artistic unity of effect which makes artistic criticism of that effect quite possible." If tyranny and violence transformed the state into a work of art, one might analyze it with the tools of art criticism. Furthermore, it might be criticized with artistic devices: "Today we are in a position to criticize the state as a work of art, and the arts can often provide us with the tools for analysis for that job."[6] Artworks were not only "tools for analysis," however; they also proposed alternative ways of being.

There are many rich stories to be told here. Too often McLuhan is reduced to the mantras that seized the popular imagination—"the medium is the message," "the global village," and so forth—and, while these phrases disseminated his thought, repetition has hollowed them out.[7] We have heard them so many times that they have nearly lost their meaning. One way to save these expressions is to look at them from a different perspective. Changing the terms of McLuhan's story and tilting it toward art might be one way of casting his thought in a new light. Artists after all were some of his most sympathetic readers as well as his most penetrating interpreters. Though he engaged many of them directly, his ideas just as often reached them through text and TV. "McLuhan's relevance to art and literature is in fact what his literary detractors have notably failed to come to grips with," the critic Richard Gilman opined in 1967, at the height of McLuhan's fame.[8] This relevance and this failure are central to the story this book aims to tell.

**Each of the** book's chapters reads McLuhan in relation to an artist's practice, though not every artist McLuhan touched appears here—his reach was too vast.[9] Rather, this book locates concrete points of contact: it focuses on the Anglo-American tradition from which McLuhan sprang and the North American reality with which he wrestled. Each chapter fastens on a key word that is equal parts technological paradigm and social formation (*mechanization*, *electricity*, *electronics*, *information*, *corporation*, etc.), with two exceptions: chapter 2 establishes McLuhan's relationship to the avant-garde, while chapter 5 considers his concept of massage. Following a paper trail, many chapters focus on a particular book or article of McLuhan's, which allows the reader both to track concepts and to focus on questions of design. Indeed, the appearance of McLuhan's work is often central; numerous publications foster an awareness of their material structure in order to see what can be done between two covers. Dedicated to thinking through the viability and vitality of different technologies in relation to their historical moments, McLuhan wrote with wonderful attention to form.[10] He often compared his writing to a *mosaic*—a term he also used to describe the composite nature of the TV image—because of the way he sutured shards of text into a tense whole and because *mosaic* related his own labor to artistic work.[11] While his patchwork style can make difficult reading, it also grapples with the fate of the printed word in a time of technological change when new claims were made on attention.[12] Ultimately, it was human faculties—and their attendant technologies—that McLuhan set out to explore.

McLuhan's first two books, *The Mechanical Bride: Folklore of Industrial Man* (1951) and *Counterblast* (1954),[13] each offer evidence of his novel ideas about design and typography and serve as the key texts of my first two chapters. They also demonstrate his connections to the visual arts: where *The Mechanical Bride* owes a debt to Duchamp and his consideration of the body—often the female body—under modernity, *Counterblast* responds to Wyndham Lewis's 1914 Vorticist publication *Blast*, which imagined a new synthesis of the arts. While McLuhan's subsequent *The Gutenberg Galaxy: The Making of Typographic Man* (1962) and *Understanding Media: The Extensions of Man* (1964) are more sober in design, their organization into short chapters suggests yet another engagement with the book form, fragmenting it into something more like a magazine.[14] The latter title is discussed in relation to Robert Rauschenberg's work in chapter 3, "Lights On," which explores McLuhan's relationship to the neo-avant-garde and Pop art. McLuhan's experimentation reached a fever pitch when he partnered with the book producer Jerome Agel and the graphic designer Quentin Fiore on the 1967 *The Medium Is the Massage: An Inventory of Effects*,[15] a delirious montage of image and text packaged in the relatively new format of the mass-market paperback and, subsequently, an LP record and a television documentary. The story of this project is the subject of my fifth chapter, "Massage, ca. 1966," which also examines Claes Oldenburg's happenings.

While McLuhan is well-known as a theorist of media, this book claims that he should also be understood as a theorist of art. One of my primary aims is to demonstrate that his theory of art and his theory of media were integral to each other. Indeed, he understood media as technologies that had become so pervasive as to create their own environments, thus evoking the powers of art in their ability to inform creation and control. While he understood media as art forms that shape perception, he also thought art played a distinctive role in a wider field of media, which comprised everything from telephones to television, photography to film. Where media often engaged in civil war with one another, art could draw awareness to this situation and even push against it. "Art as anti-environment becomes more than ever a means of training perception and judgment," he wrote in *Understanding Media*.[16] The *anti-* here is important; art challenges the dominant environment in order to shed new light on it, a topic discussed in chapter 6, "Information Environment," which surveys the landmark exhibitions *The Machine* and *Information* at New York's Museum of Modern Art

(MoMA) and *Software* at the Jewish Museum in relation to McLuhan's reboot of *Counterblast* in 1969.[17]

At the moment of the art market's ascension, McLuhan advocated for art's ability to raise awareness. ("Art offered as consumer commodity rather than as a means of training perception," he maintained, "is as ludicrous and snobbish as always.")[18] Only art, he believed, could stand up against a numbing, habitual environment and show what was really going on. In this regard, he remained very much a modernist; the idea that art offers an opportunity to hone one's vision aligns him with Bauhaus figures such as László Moholy-Nagy, on whom he wrote in 1949.[19] That said, his work proved of greatest interest to postmodern artists, such as the Korean video artist Nam June Paik, whose complicated relationship with McLuhan's work forms the kernel of chapter 4, "Electronic Opera." (The impact of *Understanding Media* is felt here, too.) For these artists, "training perception" was not enough. They wanted to modulate the environment itself, and this, too, was a position to which McLuhan returned throughout his career: perception was valuable only as long as it brought about change. It is this neo-avant-garde position that put him in conversation with the artists of his moment. For McLuhan, following Lewis, to be avant-garde meant not simply to criticize culture but to control it, and as such his investigation of media must be read in relation to artists who were also imagining a new relationship between art and life. Where Rauschenberg's "combines" acted in the "gap" between them and Allan Kaprow "blurred" the two with his "assemblages, environments, and happenings," McLuhan collapsed them, taking life as the new material for art. He argued that, rather than simply reflecting their moment, artists must aim for environmental control.

But if art pushes against media, shifts in media also generate art. As each new technological development threatens to make the previous one obsolete (or, at least, less dominant), McLuhan argued, it also transforms it into an art form, making us aware of the world just past and its difference from the present: TV granted film art status, just as today, in the age of the Internet, television appears comfortably in the museum. Art for McLuhan cast a strange light on the present, illuminating environments that might otherwise remain invisible. Fittingly, he believed that artists provided insight into the future. Imagining them alternately as antennae, thermometers, satellites, and DEW lines (Distant Early Warning lines were a Cold War radar system, a bit of nomenclature that draws attention to McLuhan's Cold War moment), he believed they signaled what was to come. Some, however, found this an inconsistency in his thought. "McLuhan has a paradoxical attitude toward the 'modern' arts," the journalist Tom Wolfe wrote in a 1965 profile. "On the one hand, he says artists are geniuses who serve as 'early warning systems' for changes in society's sensory balance. But at the same time, he says so-called 'modern' art is always one technology behind."[20] But is this as much of a paradox as it seems? To designate something obsolete raises awareness about what might come after. It also allows artists to explore what might be done with ostensibly outmoded forms. Flagging technologies as dated enables them to come to grips with new ones and assume a constructive role. Ultimately, this was what McLuhan wanted from artists. In 1967, he wrote: "We have now become aware of the possibility of arranging the entire human environment as a work of art."[21]

Certainly, Wolfe was not the first of McLuhan's detractors. From the beginning of his career, many believed him to be more of a media darling than a media savant. Few academics found him sufficiently academic, while others considered his relationships with business and his emphasis on form over content unseemly. (I take up the question of McLuhan's corporate relationships, which both extend and transform his concept of the avant-garde, in chapter 7, "Culture Was His Business," in which I discuss the "corporate" work of the Canadian collective General Idea through the lens of the 1970 volume *Culture Is Our Business*.)[22] McLuhan's technological optimism has been another source of complaint, but close analysis shows him to be ambivalent about technological change. While not a fatalist, McLuhan also refused a naive boosterism: he set himself to figuring out what might be done with the conditions before him.[23] In recent years, his "body-humanism," his belief that media extend from human abilities, has led many to dismiss him tout court.[24] Though his understanding of the body as a source of media is one of the more questionable aspects of his thought (certainly it is increasingly difficult to trace today's prosthetic technologies back to our bodily faculties), his declarative statements gave artists something to think about—and push against—given that so many examined the relationship between the body and technology as well.[25] The project of this book, however, is not to evaluate his claims on their merits—many would be difficult to substantiate—but rather to understand how they affected the arts with which they were contemporaneous and vice versa. Part of the force of his writing comes from how seriously he took art, which had the effect of gathering artists around his ideas. In a way that may seem overly heroic today, he put the weight of the world on artists' shoulders. He wanted artists to take control, and in this he was not alone: his was a time of utopian all-or-nothing pronouncements. But, while we may not agree with all of his claims (indeed, he had too much faith in art), the impetus to think about art in relation to the future—and future peril—still weighs on us today.[26]

That said, much of what draws me to McLuhan is not simply what he wrote but how he wrote it. He frequently borrowed ideas from others, occasionally citing them, but often not.[27] Part of his work involved trimming ideas into slogans and preparing them for circulation.[28] Studying McLuhan might help us think not only about the relationship between art and media, then, but also about the status and function of criticism and the various ways it might be practiced. ( John Cage once told Richard Kostelanetz: "I do not know of any instance where what a critic has done has changed what I do." "You don't, then, consider Marshall McLuhan a critic?" Kostelanetz asked. Cage responded: "If you do, then I'd have to change my mind because I find him very illuminating.")[29] It is commonplace today to say that there is no outside—that all critical distance has been foreclosed—but McLuhan was one of the first to follow through on this insight and imagine a critical position that would do its work from within or alongside its object of study. He coined the term *allatonceness* to describe a condition, similar to sonic experience, in which information hits an individual at every angle; for him, it suggested a new world that challenged the linear regime of the eye.[30] His criticism sought to respond to this condition. Not only did he collaborate with the subjects he covered, but he also borrowed their very forms and styles for critical work, a fact that can be seen in the crazed fonts of his 1954 zine *Counterblast*, lifted from Lewis, as well as his 1967 multimedia project *The Medium Is the Massage*, which made conscious links to the counterculture. Making one's way through McLuhan's work, one finds not only an expanded notion of art, then, but also an expanded form of criticism. Criticism, too, transformed in his hands: It is no longer a practice of judgment but, as McLuhan considered art, a new means of exploration. It emitted distant early warnings. It was a DEW line, too.

# 1

# The Age of Mechanical Production

**A mechanized world is always in the process of getting ready to live.**
Marshall McLuhan, *Understanding Media: The Extensions of Man* (1964)

Throughout the 1940s, McLuhan traveled between schools working as a junior professor. He struggled to define his positions. He tried to write a book, but his subject kept changing. He wrote drafts and reorganized material. He reedited essays and tried different styles of writing. His archive from these years is full of tables of contents written out in longhand. Potential chapter titles include "The New American Vortex," "The Cubist Artist and the Encyclopaedic Spectator," and "Strategies for the Vorticist." Clearly, he saw himself working in an avant-garde tradition, but he could not quite figure out his innovation. Eventually he hit on his idea.

For years, McLuhan had been cutting advertisements out of newspapers and magazines and saving them in files with names like "Sex and Technology," "New Woman," and "Sensate Mores." Questions about gender and sexuality guided much of his research, and he made notes about the patterns connecting his tear sheets that he worked up into lectures for his students and, later, into essays. On June 30, 1948, he wrote to the poet Ezra Pound, whom he had recently visited at St. Elizabeth's Hospital in Washington, DC, describing "one job on current ads, comics, gallup polls, press, radio, movies etc. etc."[1] Three years later, his first book, *The Mechanical Bride*, appeared and with it a new form of cultural criticism that cut deeply into contemporary life. (His description of the book as a "job" starts to get at its nature.) The book is composed of fifty-nine short essays, each paired with an advertisement, newspaper page, or comic strip. Running no longer than a page or two, the essays employ close reading to draw far-out conclusions. McLuhan reads the world of fashion, for example, in relation to "stockmarket operations" and "weather predictions." As the book's title indicates, he sought to size up mechanization, but his purview was wider than the world of machines; he saw the power of mechanization operating not only in bodies displayed in advertisements but also in the language of contemporary prose that framed them. (While the bride in the book's title points to the female body, he makes clear that mechanization has repercussions for men, too: it leaves them unsure of what to do.) The book's genesis in identifying patterns in the media, of cutting and organizing, analyzing and commenting, comes across in the final product. It is a montage of observations that gets at the heart of the mechanical world.

Concerned primarily with ads and magazines, *The Mechanical Bride* pushes at the limits of the conventional book. The writer Jonathan Miller calls it a "cyclorama of commercial exhibits" and "a merry-go-round of specimens from the mass media," which gives some sense of its circular feeling, its lack of a clear beginning or end.[2] Many find it difficult to read from start to finish and opt to skim it, as one might a magazine, until an exciting title catches the eye. Its form lies somewhere between *Wunderkammer* and filing cabinet, but it also resembles an anthropological collection (as suggested by the *folklore* in the book's subtitle), while its method takes after fieldwork, collecting specimens for exhibition and analysis. Unlike traditional anthropology, however, which typically looks *elsewhere*, McLuhan's method was to use his own culture's signs and symbols as material, the cultural artifacts of the so-called industrial man.[3] But McLuhan does not celebrate their vitality as much as he holds them up for scrutiny, placing them in a book to make them foreign and funny.[4] "I discovered that when you take anything out of the daily newspapers and put it on the screen, people go into a fit of laughter," he later explained.[5] Dropped between book covers as if in a vitrine, artifacts lay before the reader for analysis, amusement, and critique.

The book's chapters form a constellation of pantyhose and germ killers. An essay on *Esquire* follows one on the 1938 film *Blondie*; a spot for blended whiskey rubs up against an ad for Clark Grave Vaults. The mystery is how all these things relate to one another. Though the body is a constant theme (everything from bodybuilding manuals to corsets operates in the name of corporeal management and the "cult of hygiene"), McLuhan makes clear that the media do their work through the psyche first and foremost. "Ours is the first age in which many thousands of the best-trained individual minds have made it a full-time business to get inside the collective public mind," he writes. "To get inside in order to manipulate, exploit, control is the object now."[6]

Finding the "collective public mind" under siege by admen, McLuhan mounts a counterattack in hopes of "reversing the process." His antidote is "critical vision," which is the only device that "can mitigate the unimpeded operation of the automatic." He declares: "The only practical answer to the 'storm of triviality and propaganda' is that it be brought under control by being inspected."[7] Critical vision and inspection—the traditional tools of the literary critic—become the tackle of the media critic as well. Though many contemporary reviewers found McLuhan's voice dour, today one finds a surprising lack of moralism in his tone; while he disagreed with the culture in front of him, he refused simply to denounce it.[8] Setting aside censoriousness, McLuhan meets admen on their own turf with humor, wit, and play, though some also detected indifference.[9] Arguing that mass culture trades in "experience," that it delivers "a direct wallop to the nervous system, unmediated by judgment or reflection," McLuhan seeks to generate an equally affective response.[10]

## Practical Criticism

If *The Mechanical Bride* plays with the traditional form of the book, it is a textbook at heart, albeit one that veers far from academic norms. "For a book by a professor, let alone a first book, it could not be less academic," the critic Greil Marcus has written, and, in addition to its novel structure, *Bride* lacks the notes and lengthy excurses characteristic of the trade.[11] Yet McLuhan was keen to expand the possibilities of education. He often complained that classrooms remained nineteenth-century disciplinary structures and that they were unfit to cope with the demands of the modern world; to him, they did more to inhibit learning than to facilitate it. School, he often said, curtailed a child's education, owing, in part, to its insistence on book learning. "The effectiveness of the classroom has diminished with the decline of the monopoly of book-culture," he wrote in 1954.[12] "What we have to see is that the new media have created classrooms without walls," he wrote in another essay that same year, suggesting that educational opportunities existed outside, too, and that the whole world could serve as a school.[13] Classrooms set up a false dichotomy between education and entertainment, inside and out; one had to open them up so as to address the media with an educator's eye.[14] "The time has come to put the questions inside the school, rather than the answers," McLuhan proposed. "In other words, it is now possible to make the schools not a place for packaged information, but a place for dialogue and discovery."[15] He first tested this hypothesis at the University of Wisconsin in the mid-1930s by analyzing ads in his English courses instead of canonical texts.[16] He also found this a helpful method for connecting with students. "I was confronted with young Americans I was incapable of understanding," he recounted in a 1967 *Newsweek* profile. "I felt an urgent need to study their popular culture in order to get through."[17] While his incomprehension was partially generational, it also had a national component: McLuhan frequently attributed his critical insights to his Canadian identity. Hovering just outside American culture (in spirit, if not in body), Canada provided a perfect spot from which to survey capitalism's terrain.[18]

McLuhan's brand of media criticism followed the tradition of close reading established by the Cambridge literary critic I. A. Richards. A partisan of the New Criticism, Richards militated against intentionality and generally challenged authorship; he assigned his students poems with writers' names omitted so they could concentrate on their form and not rely on a writer's reputation for guidance. His 1929 *Practical Criticism* organized the responses to these tests with the goal of "present[ing] an instructive collection of contemporary opinions, presuppositions, theories, beliefs, responses and the rest, but also . . . mak[ing] some suggestions towards a better control of these tricksy components of our lives."[19] He wanted to control "tricksy" opinions and responses by training individual perception. His work emphasized literature's psychological and physiological effects, focusing on what aesthetic constructions *do* to readers over what they mean. Describing painting in his *Principles of Literary Criticism*, Richards wrote: "All depends upon the purpose, the total response to which form and colour are merely means."[20] While works of art are material, in other words, their real work is to generate effects, which is to some extent what the reader had to guard against.

In 1933, another Cambridge critic, F. R. Leavis, the voice behind the journal *Scrutiny*, expanded on Richards's investigations in his *Culture and Environment: The Training of Critical Awareness*, written with Denys Thompson. The book extended Richards's project. As Terry Eagleton has noted, criticism at Cambridge offered something "more than merely 'literary'": "Criticism was to venture forth from the academies into the lurid regions of advertising and popular culture."[21] Here, Leavis transferred Richards's brand of analysis from "prose and verse . . . to the analysis of advertisements (the kind of appeal they make and their stylistic characteristics)" with the hopes of teaching students a "critical habit" that would help them navigate a deleterious culture. "The great agent of change, and, from our point of view, destruction, has been the machine—applied power," he declared. He offered a capacious conception of the machine, with advertising its most malevolent manifestation. He encouraged students to read widely and to study the effects of what they read. The book's final section lists ninety-three lessons for strengthening critical acumen. Lesson 10 instructs the reader to "explain and illustrate the use of valets, butlers and 'superior'-looking manservants in advertisements," while lesson 58 encourages one to "compare the bungalow quarter in *Star-Dust in Hollywood* with Sturt's Village before it changed." Leavis also suggests that students collect newspaper clippings in order to analyze their layouts, the project being a kind of consumer analysis in which students played both researcher and subject at once: "As 'field-work,' pupils might, besides observing and collecting types of advertisement, look for and note the effects of advertising on themselves and their friends." The idea was to train "taste and sensibility" in order to constitute a public sphere that could stand up against machinic mass culture.[22] By attending closely to the media's effects, one might form antibodies to withstand them, a kind of moral resistance to one's objects of study. While Leavis imagined himself a crusader, his project, as Terry Eagleton has noted, betrayed a certain melancholy: It knew deep down that it could not reform society but only keep a few dutiful adherents out of harm's reach.[23]

Clearly, McLuhan borrowed from both Richards and Leavis, whose lectures he attended while a student at Cambridge in the mid-1930s, but he employed their techniques with different ambitions.[24] Despite his desire to engage the outside world, Leavis maintained a fundamentally conservative position. He mourned the loss of England's "organic community" and believed that "it is on literary tradition that the office of maintaining continuity must rest."[25] Ultimately, he hoped to banish advertisements and turn back to the world of great books. McLuhan, on the other hand, sought to move forward, believing that new media contained novel possibilities. He saw how the newspaper, for instance, broke up provincial views and created a new form of "human solidarity." Though he understood mass media's negative aspects, he refused simply to dig in his heels and pine for an earlier time. "The aim of this book is not to rouse 'sales resistance,'" he wrote in an early draft of *The Mechanical Bride*. "That would be a frivolous expenditure of effort which would only land the reader deeper than ever in the emotional morass of irrational reactions."[26] His goal was not to go against but, striking a Nietzschean chord, to emphasize the importance of "self-preservation" and "self-defense" in the face of change. McLuhan realized that one could no longer return to a great tradition—one had to rely on oneself. While critical vision was crucial to such an undertaking, one could not simply reject mass culture. One had to read actively, practicing something like what Michel de Certeau would later call "reading as poaching": "Like a hunter in the forest, [the reader] spots the written quarry, follows a trail, laughs, plays tricks."[27] Where Leavis longed for an organic community "with the living culture it embodied,"[28] McLuhan prepared for a brave new world, both artificial and mass-produced, that one might navigate but not fight.[29]

## Anonymous History

To say that McLuhan focused on the present is not to suggest that he turned his back on history. He was trying to write a new kind of history, a history of his own time. Indeed, *The Mechanical Bride* forms an "anonymous history" similar to the one laid out by the architectural historian Sigfried Giedion in his 1947 *Mechanization Takes Command: A Contribution to Anonymous History*, which McLuhan frequently cites in his own book.[30] In *Mechanization Takes Command*, Giedion cataloged an encyclopedic array of practices, including bread making, cattle slaughtering, and lock making, as part of an attempt to gauge "the effects of mechanization upon the human being" and better understand "the things that shape . . . life."[31] McLuhan, too, was interested in "the interrelation of disparate activities." Understanding such relationships, he claimed in *Bride*, "is indispensable to modern man living in an era of specialization, change and expansion."[32]

In his method Giedion strayed far from the scholar's typical path. He approached history through "humble objects" and "modest things" rather than the stories of great minds and heroic events. He studied operating manuals and instructions rather than theoretical treatises and architectural plans. His research trips included a visit to a "modern bread factory [in Philadelphia] with its hourly output of 30,000 loaves."[33]

Giedion presents a catalog or inventory. He typically refused to judge mechanization—"Affirmation or mere negation leads nowhere. . . . Everything depends on how, and for what purposes, mechanization is used"—though he did occasionally lament life's new pattern. For him, supply creates demand, and, in what is one of his most memorable examples, he claims that the invention of white bread lowered standards of public taste. He compares this situation with "the painters of the ruling taste [who] set out to satisfy public demand more and more, thus securing a market and rewards."[34] The moral is that both bread manufacturers and "painters of the ruling taste" weakened public taste by giving people what they ostensibly wanted. (An illustration of a Wonder Bread advertisement is offered as proof of the dire result.) One of Giedion's great talents as a historian is his ability to find common ground between cynical painters and corporate bakers; both take advantage of the public for the sake of profits. His writing, however, betrays a particular anxiety about "anonymous corporations [that] penetrate nearly every province of living."[35] Anything but innocuous, anonymity effaces subjectivity and lowers taste. Anonymous history, on the other hand, aims to counter such forces by contending with the deprivations of an anonymous age.

In a 1951 review of *Mechanization Takes Command*, McLuhan wrote that Giedion sharpened "contemporary awareness" through "alert and prolonged attention to a great range of things and activities."[36] It was precisely this great range of anonymous forces—not the grand designs of a single artist but the proliferating processes and artifacts of everyday life—that McLuhan wanted to explore, yet he found Giedion lacking in one crucial respect, namely, Giedion's "mysterious question" of why one desires artificial things in a technological society. "In his masterly account of the mechanization of the bread industry [Giedion] expressed bewilderment at the fact that European immigrants accustomed to excellent bread were in America eager for the ersatz loaf," he writes.

> The answer lies in the fact that we are also eager for ersatz dreams, blondes, houses and entertainment. Is it not the sheer magical power of the technological environment which leads us to prefer the artificial to the natural? . . . When the entire economy is on an artistic or magical basis, sparked by the magical appeals and promises of the ads (visual ads are in themselves magical in their habit of transforming ordinary objects and situations) is it not repugnant to the total pattern and promise of the new life to accept "natural" effects even at the level of physical taste?[37]

It is not simply bread that is ersatz, in other words. All life is. Bread is only one component in a technological system that created a new "total pattern" of life. The cumulative effect of such a system was difficult to resist.[38]

In order to respond to the "sheer magical power of the technological environment," McLuhan updated Giedion's method of study. Where Giedion focused on production—for him the key to mechanization lay in the assembly line—McLuhan examined consumption: the products that mechanization produces, their marketing, and psychic effects. Where Giedion's book is stocked with machinic illustrations and diagrams—"*Nikola Tesla's small motor with three-blade fan*" or an "*automatic hog-weighing apparatus*"—*The Mechanical Bride* contains ads for Lysol Germ-Killer and Palomino stockings. McLuhan's hilarious tone, moreover, is a far cry from Giedion's monotonous inventory. *Bride*'s witty analyses giddily take on the rhetoric of ad copy, teaching one how to deconstruct with irony and style. "Does your Butler yearn for a mustache?" McLuhan asks in an entry on Emily Post. "Are you shaky about the logistics of birth, marriage, and death?"[39]

At this point in his career, McLuhan wanted less to change the world than to survive it. (In the next chapter, we will see his thinking shift as he inches closer to Wyndham Lewis's understanding of the artist as an agent for change and transformation.) For him, the ad world presented a mixed blessing—it was a culture industry with positive aspects. While, in his 1947 "American Advertising," he noted American market research's "strong totalitarian squint," he also claimed that ads provide "a common experience and a common language for a country [the United States] whose sectional differences and technological specialisms might easily develop into anarchy." Postwar politics clearly weighed on his mind: "Viewed merely as an interim strategy for maintaining hope, tolerance, and good-humour in an irrational world, this orgy of irrationalism may not be without its cathartic function," he wrote.[40] *Interim* is key. An orgy of irrationalism cannot go on forever. Advertising, for McLuhan, will not provide a new world order, just a stopgap until a better plan takes shape. At least, that is how he felt in 1947; advertising offered social cohesion by offering a new myth yet threatened to tip over into "psychological bureaucracy."[41]

If McLuhan displayed ambivalence about advertising, he piled scorn on the editorial efforts of mass-market publications. Again and again he goes after *Time*, at one point calling it "a nursery book in which the reader is slapped and tickled alternately": "It is full of predigested pap, spooned out with confidential nudges."[42] The popular press infantilized its readers by failing to treat them as adults. Still, mere condemnation would not suffice for navigating the maelstrom of commercial media, and in the protagonist of Edgar Allan Poe's "A Descent into the Maelstrom" McLuhan found a model for his approach. "Poe's sailor saved himself by studying the action of the whirlpool [in which he was drowning] and by co-operating with it," he writes in *The Mechanical*

*Bride*. "The present book likewise makes few attempts to attack the very considerable currents and pressures set up around us today by the mechanical agencies of the press, radio, movies, and advertising."[43] The mechanical is synonymous with the automatic and unthinking, but McLuhan's project is less to undo or "attack" these forces than to find ways in which to inhabit this new world while holding onto something of one's self. It could be said that McLuhan wrote with a sense of humility and scale or that he wrote from the point of view of the consumer. Skeptical of Marx, he did not advocate seizing the means of production in order to overcome alienation but rather aspired to withstand its "considerable currents." His was less a critique than a practice of everyday life. In this regard he followed Richards, who championed *navigation*, "the art of knowing where we are wherever, as mental travellers, we may go."[44] These were personal projects, in other words—imaginative ones. Solutions came from digging deep inside one's person rather than through collective work. If, for McLuhan, flexibility provided the key to longevity, it also seemed the only way one might push one's old self through the maelstrom of modernity.

## Brides and Bachelors

Though *The Mechanical Bride* is composed of artifacts from popular culture, its method and position—indeed, its dandy spirit—owes much to art practice. For McLuhan, art brought modernity's pressures to light and offered tips on how to navigate them.[45] *Bride*, for example, frequently mentions Picasso's collage and its relationship to the newspaper. In an article on radio market research, McLuhan writes that, "as in cubist painting, the spectator is placed in the center of the picture," and, in its emphasis on paper scraps, one could argue, *Bride* relies heavily on Cubism as well.[46] The book, however, owes its true debt to Marcel Duchamp, especially the artist's most canonical works: the 1912 canvas *Nude Descending the Staircase* (itself a Cubistic comment) and his glassy magnum opus, *The Bride Stripped Bare by Her Bachelors, Even* (1915–23). McLuhan's title borrows the bride from the latter work and joins her to the mechanical matrix depicted in the former.

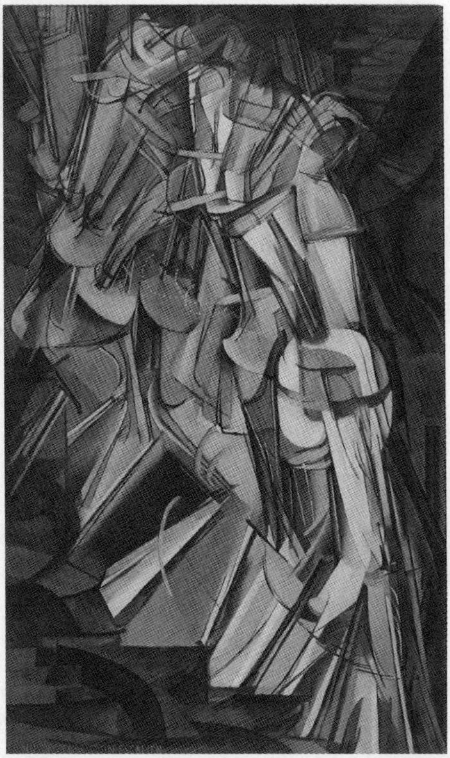

**1.1** Marcel Duchamp, *Nude Descending a Staircase (No. 2)* (1912). Philadelphia Museum of Art, The Louise and Walter Arensberg Collection, 1950-134-59. © Association Marcel Duchamp/ADAGP, Paris/Artists Rights Society (ARS), New York 2021.

A hallmark of modern art since its display at the 1913 Armory Show, *Nude* provided a touchstone for McLuhan's cohort. In *Mechanization Takes Command*, Giedion triangulated it with Eadweard Muybridge's *Athlete Descending a Staircase* (ca. 1880) and Étienne-Jules Marey's "Oscillations of the Leg in Running," tying Duchamp's painting to developments in physiology and bodily discipline. If Marey imagined the body as a mechanism, with chronophotography depicting its working, for Giedion the work provided an example of "how deeply mechanization penetrated man's inner existence."[47]

Duchamp himself stressed the connection with such precedents. "In one of Marey's books, I saw an illustration of how he indicated

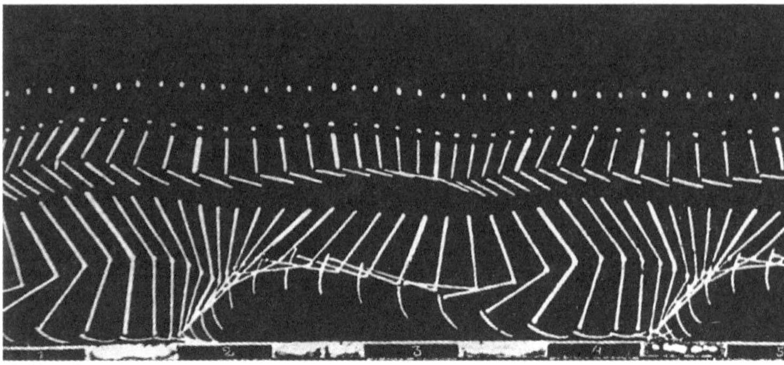

**1.2** Étienne-Jules Marey, *Man Running* (ca. 1880). Science History Images/Alamy Stock Photo.

people who fence, or horses galloping, with a system of dots delineating the different movements," he told Pierre Cabanne. "That's what gave me the idea for the execution of the *Nude Descending a Staircase*."[48] But, if Marey abstracted the body to its barest movements, transforming it into a graphic effusion of white lines against a black background, *Nude* lays abstraction back atop the body—importantly, the female body—in order to show its effects. The human sensorium but also the Western tradition of the nude would never be the same. Effaced and distorted, the body appears as a lost object: a Caucasian-flesh-toned time-lapse image. Duchamp's nude is fragmented, even ghostlike, a strange amalgamation of abstract movement reattached to the singularity of a body. In *Mechanization Takes Command*, Giedion claims Duchamp's work met a negative reception owing to "the deeply ingrown fallacy that problems of feeling have nothing to do with problems of science."[49] While some believed that science could be kept in the laboratory, Giedion and McLuhan knew its effects always broke into the outside world—onto the consuming body, which they consistently gendered female.

Despite these stakes, McLuhan treats Duchamp's painting with a surprisingly light touch in *The Mechanical Bride*. "The famous portrait of a 'Nude Descending a Staircase,' with its resemblance to an artichoke doing a striptease, is a cleansing bit of fun intended to free the human robot from his dreamlike fetters," he writes.[50] The nude's robot quality evokes the viewer's own robot nature, making one momentarily self-conscious. Years later, McLuhan viewed the painting through a darker lens, claiming: "[It] reveals the fragmented, analytic abstraction of the industrial process as a skeletal charade, a retrieval of the ancient rituals of *le danse macabre*. The dance of the machines during the past two centuries represents the most violent and lethal expression of human somnambulism and self-hypnotism. Duchamp's nude is a comic mime of the descent of a somnambulist robot world, via the stages of a precisely etiolated rational pattern of relentless progress." The painting depicts a "robot world"—a space of mechanical sleepwalkers revealing the dark side of rationality and progress. Both texts, however, stress the work's "comic" aspects; comedy wakes people up.[51] McLuhan often enlisted humor to deal with the mechanical. "The writing of this book, for example, was 'fun' and it is intended to provide fun," he wrote on one of the *Bride*'s manuscript pages. "Fun through intelligibility."[52] This line also propelled the book's marketing. "A practical joke on modern life—perpetrated by one with true satiric insight!" the ad copy reads. Critical laughter shakes off the robot world in order to bring the viewer back to life.

Designed by Ernst Reichl, the cover of *Bride* depicts a robot world close in spirit to Duchamp's. Statuesque legs sourced from an advertisement for Gotham Gold Stripe Beautiful Stockings constitute the cogs of a machine.[53] Body parts fuse with systems of production, but they appear less as laboring limbs than as finished products. An ad featured in the essay "Love-Goddess Assembly Line" makes the point explicit: four girdled women lined up as if at a factory workbench, each holding an empty picture frame in front of her torso, present a hybrid of production and product. Where Giedion understood that under Taylorism "human movements become levers in the machine,"[54] McLuhan saw how mechanization served the regime of consumption. Production, he recognized, has aesthetic effects, not only for the manufactured object, but also for the consuming subject, and here, as is so often the case, the subject is gendered female. If, for Giedion, Taylorism studied "the human body . . . to discover how far it can be transformed into a mechanism,"[55] McLuhan saw the body changed into a commodity. "Did you notice the Model-T bodies of the women in that revived 1930

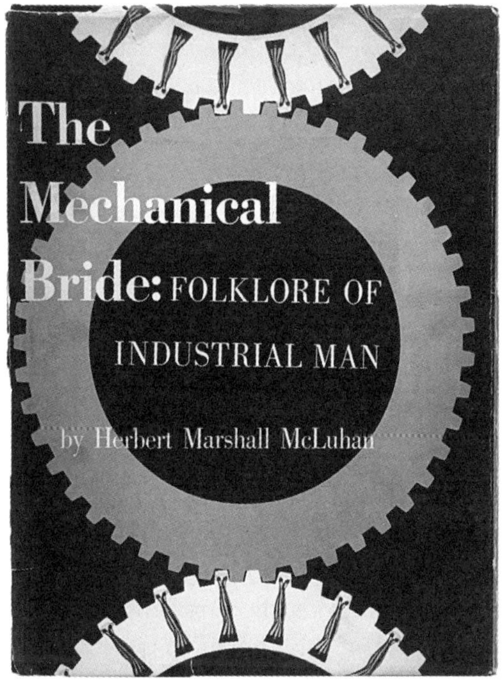


**1.3** Cover of Marshall McLuhan, *The Mechanical Bride: Folklore of Industrial Man* (1951). Photo: Kevin Sell.

movie last night?" he asks. "Can the feminine body keep pace with the demands of the textile industry?"[56] Industry is demanding, but, while McLuhan read the effects of modernity through the female body, he rarely accounted for the patriarchal structures that prepared the ground for his analysis. Indeed, his prose often repeats the sexual objectification of women in the advertising and movies he references. Yet, while his tone is coy and hardly feminist, it conveys how industry presented female bodies as consumable products. (At the same time, women were increasingly figured as consumers as well.)

McLuhan was not the first to ask questions about bodies and capitalist production. In the *Grundrisse*, Marx wrote: "The worker's activity . . . is determined and regulated on all sides by the movement of the machinery, and not the opposite."[57] Several thinkers in the early twentieth century considered the machine's ability to shape the body off the clock as well. McLuhan's musings are close in spirit to those of Siegfried Kracauer about the "mass ornament," which he developed in 1920s Germany. Kracauer, too, focused on the aesthetics of production and how capitalist modes insinuated themselves into cultural forms. Writing about the Tiller Girls, a troupe of dancers, he noted how their routines—"products of American distraction factories"—resembled modes of production and, by extension, transformed ideas about sexuality: "The hands in the factory correspond to the legs of the Tiller Girls." As a result: "The Tiller Girls can no longer be reassembled into human beings after the fact." The whole body no longer counts; only its individual parts and functions matter. For Kracauer, this breakup reconfigures erotic life. The "sexless bodies in bathing suits" form "a linear system that no longer has any erotic meaning but at best points to the locus of the erotic," he concludes.[58]

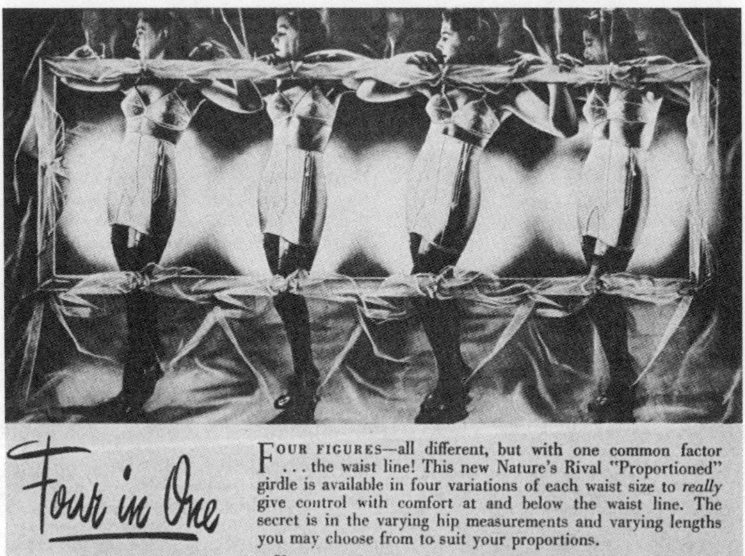


**1.4** Advertisement from Marshall McLuhan, *The Mechanical Bride: Folklore of Industrial Man* (1951).

Some thirty years later, McLuhan investigated a similar transformation of female sexuality. (Men are often banished from his analysis, perhaps because the book's reader is imagined as male, though in the final pages McLuhan admits: "Men flounder in such times.") As the female body is finessed and polished like a machine, treated more like a "slick object" than a human being, McLuhan, like Kracauer, sees its sexual energies migrating elsewhere. The girdle ad, for example, "insists on the close relation of motorcar glamour to sex just as the feminine glamour ads and the modern beauty chorus insist on their relation to the machine." Cars provide one comparison, but McLuhan also likens bodies to the abstraction of finance, building on Kracauer's idea that the locus of the erotic lies in the interstices of a "linear system." "There is some sort of relation between the dynamo of abstract power which imparts motion to 'the line,'" he writes of the Ziegfeld Girls, an update of the Tiller Girls, "and the dynamo of abstract finance and engineering which moves the passions of the tired businessman idolatrously seated in front of that line."[59] What tempts the businessman, in other words, is not any particular girl but the link between bodies that echoes the rhythm of finance. Not only are women replaceable in this model, but their parts can be traded in as well. A woman's legs as pictured in the media, McLuhan observes, "are not intimately associated with her taste or with her unique self but are merely display objects like the grill work on a car."[60] Such language is deeply misogynistic, but it is also diagnostic, distilling the painful message contained in these ads.[61] McLuhan reads representations of women's bodies as a barometer of social change, with femininity and consumption explicitly linked. Though the image of the mechanical bride was fashioned through the patriarchal structures of industrial man, McLuhan did not seek to remedy the situation, nor did he seem to understand the ways in which women challenged this totalizing message on an everyday basis. In *The Mechanical Bride*'s last sentence, he insists that the divisions between men and women "cannot be mended until their fullest extent is perceived."[62] Here, again, the goal is perception: he wants to see—and understand—how the human and human relations are broken down and reformatted, but he refuses antidotes, leaving it to others to imagine solutions from the groundwork he laid.[63]

## Independent Group

*The Mechanical Bride* was a message in a bottle; McLuhan did not know who would pick it up. Though it was widely reviewed, few knew what to make of it. Artists, however, soon made good on its implications. In London, it quickly became a key text of the Independent Group (IG), a band of artists and critics who, like McLuhan, dedicated themselves to picking apart the topography of postwar culture.[64] Somewhat similar to McLuhan's position in Canada, the IG's location in London offered sufficient distance from which to look at America and measure the difference. The group had other books, too—Giedion's *Mechanization Takes Command* was also an important title—but the *Bride*'s temperament and tone and its penchant for illustrations jibed with the IG's sensibilities, which looked quite different from the high-modernist ideas ruling London's advanced art circles at the time.[65] The group met from 1952 to 1955, and, over the course of those years, it discussed topics ranging from information theory to car design, Dada to science fiction. Gathering at the Institute of Contemporary Arts, which opened in 1951, the IG imagined itself less as a prewar ism and more as an educational program; it was a think tank set on responding to a new postwar culture.[66] McLuhan, of course, sought to do something similar. "*The Mechanical Bride*, with its Duchamp-derived title, was one of the first primers on how to read the 'Pop' environment—when most of the academics had not quite caught up with abstract expressionism," John McHale, one of the group's key conveners, later wrote.[67] As the painter Richard Hamilton recalled: "It didn't take long, with [the curator Lawrence] Alloway's influence, for the discussion to turn to Marshall McLuhan's *The Mechanical Bride*."[68]

We don't know exactly how the group got its hands on the book. Alloway recalls seeing an ad for it in the back pages of *View*, Charles Henri Ford's avant-garde literary magazine, but the journal ceased publication in 1947, making that impossible.[69] That year, however, McLuhan published "TIME, LIFE, and FORTUNE" in *View*'s spring issue, its cover featuring Pavel Tchelitchew's finely rendered drawing of a man's face, his red veins creating a worried, even wired portrait.[70] The article

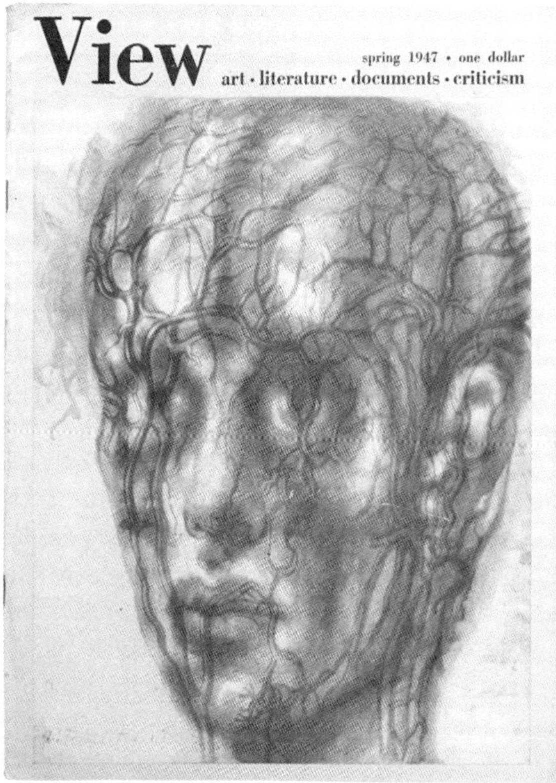


**1.5** Pavel Tchelitchew, *Interior Landscape*, as featured on the cover of *View*, Spring 1947.

has a similarly nervous tone, especially when compared to the irony and play of *The Mechanical Bride*. Full of high-minded disdain, McLuhan assails Henry Luce, the publisher of the three magazines, for his "passion for glossy mediocrity and stereotypical order which derives from his obsession with mechanism."[71] Luce's publications reveal the rationale of the machine by attempting to manufacture opinion, McLuhan suggests; they are "the best imitation of thought and feeling that the machine can produce." Confronted with such a sorry state, McLuhan calls on "artists and intellectuals" (a telling combination) to remedy the situation—something that he would do many times over the course of his career. "Because the areas in which perception is cultivated or even tolerated have been ever more rapidly circumscribed," he writes, "the artist and intellectual have had to turn to unmasking clichés and the mass mechanisms of sensibility as part of the business of survival." Pulling back the surface of contemporary life to show the machine beneath, artists and intellectuals unravel clichés to open up the possibility for genuine thought. It is a tall order and one made more difficult by the power structure McLuhan encountered. "Even in this role of the enemy of bloated inanities and glossy fakes," he proclaims, "the artist and intellectual find the ultimate enemies of the human to be extremely elusive." Power resides in traditional seats of government no longer but in mysterious new quarters, having shifted from state politics to mediatic spaces. As McLuhan puts it: "The centers of political initiative today are as inaccessible as the accusers of a Kafka character." He does not see how one can intervene. In 1947, he hit an impasse and advocated a boycott of media. "The process of renewal can't come from above," he argues.

> It can only take the form of reawakened critical faculties. The untrancing of millions of individuals by millions of individual acts of the will. Psychological decentralization. A merely provisional image of how it might (not how it should) occur could be formed by supposing every mechanical agency of communication in the world to be suspended for six months. No press. No radio. No movies. Just people finding out who lived near them. Forming small communities within big cities. It would be agony. All psychological drugs cut off. No capsulated thoughts or memories. To say that anything like this could never happen, or that it should never be allowed to happen is a remark worthy of those mesmerized practical men who are efficiently arranging for the obsequies of our world's mind and body alike. If something like this doesn't happen it is quite plain what will happen.[72]

McLuhan's tone at the end of this passage is worried, if not apocalyptic. He sees anarchy on the horizon and suggests that it can be countered only with community. The type of community he fathoms, however, is not yet a *global village* (a term that crystallized in 1962, in *The Gutenberg Galaxy*, to suggest the interconnection and intimacy created by new media) but rather a series of emphatically local ones, determined by people who know each other, not powers on high. Imagining a group of "decentralized" individuals steeped in human contact, he refuses the media's power over everyday life. Instead of fantasizing about an electrically connected mass audience, he imagines "every mechanical agency of communication in the world . . . suspended for six months." While, at this moment, he could still fathom "dropping out," in a few years, as evidenced in *Bride*, he would find such a position untenable. When everything is instantaneous and connected, there is no going back. One has to swim with the current.

## Pop before Pop

**Mass production advertising is establishing our whole pattern of life—principles, morals, aims, aspirations, and standard of living. We must somehow get the measure of this intervention if we are to match its powerful and exciting impulses with our own.** Alison Smithson and Peter Smithson, "But Today We Collect Ads," 1956

In retrospect, it is easy to see the proto-Pop tendencies at work in *The Mechanical Bride*, such as the emphasis on appropriation and the ambivalence about mass culture, and many of these characteristics determined the practices of IG members as well. The architects Alison and Peter Smithson embraced McLuhan's ideas about the domination of mass culture in their 1956 "But Today We Collect Ads," stating: "One of the traditional functions of fine art, the definition of what is fine and desirable for the ruling class, and therefore ultimately that which is desired by all society, has now been taken over by the ad-man."[73] That same year, Lawrence Alloway published "Technology and Sex in Science Fiction: A Note on Cover Art" (1956), which built on McLuhan's insights about the relationship between sex and technology in the *View* article. ("The extravagant sexy covers also have a social function, that of entertaining our erotic appetites," Alloway wrote.)[74] A year before, another IG convener, the architectural historian Reyner Banham, also picked up on McLuhan's idea about the intermingling of sex and technology. In "Vehicles of Desire," he examined advances in automotive styling, noting how cars had become bodily and full of feeling. "The top body stylists," he wrote, "aim to give their creations qualities of apparent speed, power, brutalism, luxury, snob-appeal, exoticism, and plain common-or-garden sex."[75] Fighting to replace modern architecture's calcifying ideals with stylish, expendable ones (in other words, to switch out Le Corbusier's Delage for a Chevy Camaro), Banham offered a take on popular culture that is more celebratory than McLuhan's: he puts the latter's nascent tone into overdrive. (Writing in 1959, McHale noted that while *The Mechanical Bride* was a "classic of its kind . . . its strong moral overtones render many conclusions outmoded.")[76] Calling ads "dreams that money can buy" (which is also the title of Hans Richter's 1947 Surrealist film and a frequent McLuhan slogan), Banham insisted that they are best when most like Broadway shows, with "maximum glitter and maximum impact."[77]

Soon Banham's writing made a visible impact on Richard Hamilton, who, in certain works, transformed McLuhan's analyses into painted essays. Paintings such as *$he* (1958), in which a disembodied woman simultaneously dovetails with kitchen appliances and dissolves into Taylorist dots, could have appeared in *The Mechanical Bride* itself. "I could see that there was a relationship between the object and the kind of woman that could be associated with the appliance," Hamilton later said, evoking one of McLuhan's key insights.[78] Something similar happens in *Hommage à Chrysler Corp.* (1957), a haunting palimpsest of woman and car in which breasts and headlights appear to be shared by the same—nearly invisible—body. (The title, as many have noted, is a double entendre: the work pays homage to both the Chrysler Corporation as well as the Chrysler *body*.) Hamilton sourced many of the pictorial elements from advertising images, and one feels that each figure has been crafted according to the industry's techniques.[79] (The form of the woman's right breast is rendered topographically, while the front fender is lovingly polished.)[80] If these works strip bare and expose advertising's promises, they also remain faithful to its seductive techniques. If there is critique here, in other words, there is also complicity—not only with the advertising industry but also with the patriarchal idea that women's bodies can be made and remade as men see fit.

While McLuhan's influence is present, one should note that Hamilton also diligently studied Duchamp. We are witnessing a constellation

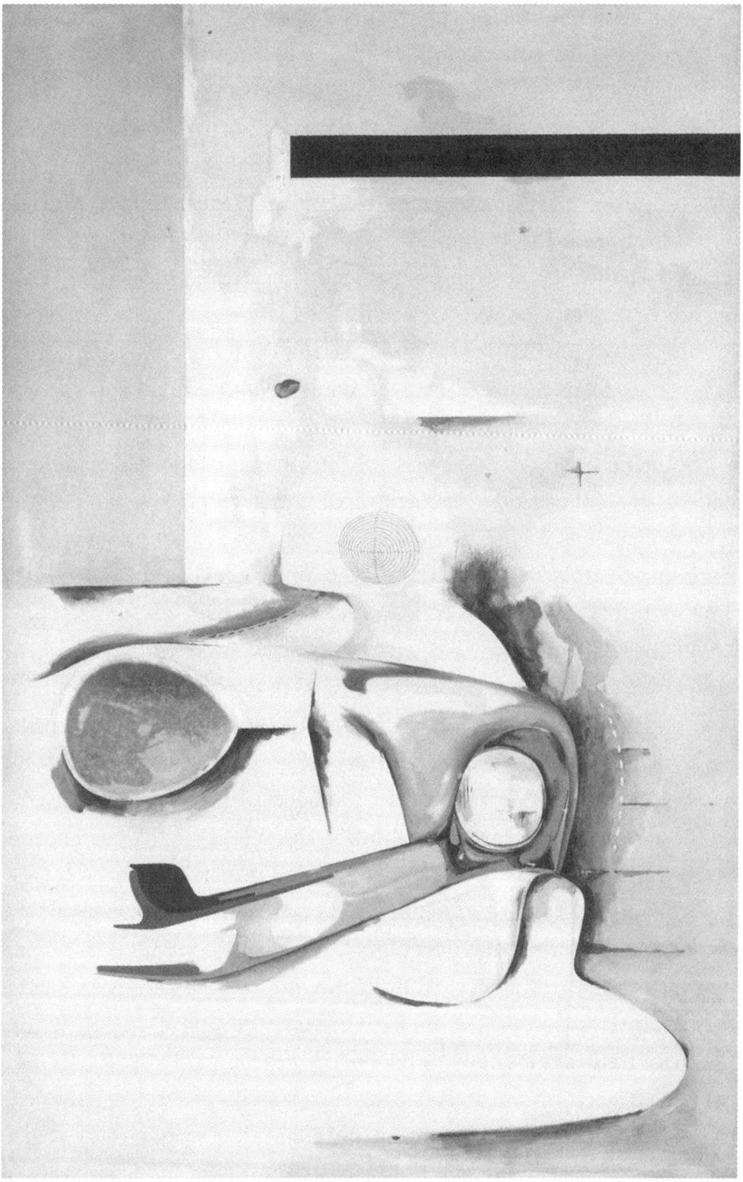

**1.6** Richard Hamilton, *Hommage à Chrysler Corp.* (1957). © R. Hamilton. All Rights Reserved, DACS and ARS 2021. Photo © Tate.

of interests, not a causal chain. Beginning in the late 1950s, Hamilton pored over the notes in Duchamp's *Green Box* and translated its innuendos and sexual mechanics into iconic works of art. If he and McLuhan worked along parallel tracks, Hamilton ultimately made his mark in painting, turning to genres such as the nude, and rendering his subjects in oil on canvas (though he added cellulose and lenticulars, too). At the same time, he insisted that his work mapped a new territory that he dubbed "Pop-Fine-Art" or "positive Dada." In his 1960 "For the Finest Art Try—POP," he wrote that his art displayed "a respect for the culture of the masses and a conviction that the artist in 20th century urban life is inevitably a consumer of mass culture and potentially a contributor to it."[81] If he sought to contribute, he did so by creating paintings that might trickle down into the common culture or hold their own within it.[82] McLuhan, on the other hand, dreamed that artists might make a larger impact. Rather than hole up in an ivory tower, they had to enter the wider world. One had to engage head-on, but the question was how. For many, the answer pointed away from painting toward a wider field of media.

# 2

# What It Means to Be Avant-Garde

**The Artist, like Narcissus, gets his nose nearer and nearer the surface of Life.**
Wyndham Lewis, *Blast* (1914)

McLuhan always imagined himself as a scion of the avant-garde. For him, however, *avant-garde* did not simply designate the early twentieth-century movements of Dada, Futurism, Surrealism, and Constructivism, which sought to merge art and life under the sign of politics. Rather, the term signaled a way of working that challenged convention in a much broader sense. In his 1962 *The Gutenberg Galaxy*, McLuhan calls the fifteenth-century painters Masaccio and Jan Van Eyck *avant-garde* for introducing the hard rules of perspective into a pictorially amorphous world. To earn the epithet one had to be technically inventive, but innovation was also "politically daring": for McLuhan the rethinking of form had political effects.[1] "The Charleston, with its aspect of a mechanical doll agitated by strings, appears in Russia as an avant-garde form," he wrote in 1964, describing the effect of the jittery dance on a society accustomed to the elegance of ballet.[2] The avant-garde rubs against society by introducing foreign elements, and by doing so it throws dominant tendencies into relief, even disarray. (In McLuhan's Cold War example, dance has the power to shake up even the most authoritarian states.) For McLuhan, being avant-garde depends on context—one has to work against and within prevailing conditions to upset them—and, as such, nothing can be avant-garde in a vacuum or stay avant-garde forever. "Rimbaud's *avant-garde* world of montage and transparency had become the old environment by 1911," McLuhan wrote in 1967, which is to say that the modern world had caught up with the poet's techniques.[3] The avant-garde must constantly

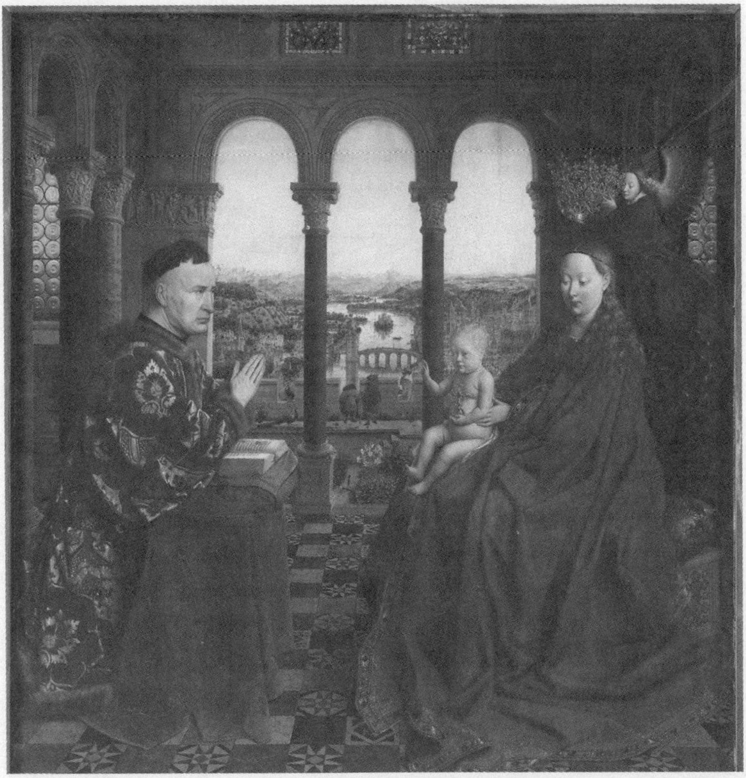

**2.1** Jan van Eyck, *Madonna of Chancellor Rolin* (ca. 1435). From the collegiate church of Notre-Dame in Autun. Photo: Gérard Blot. Musée du Louvre. © RMN-Grand Palais/Art Resource, NY.

reinvent itself and search out new ways of working. As Asger Jorn put it in a 1962 painting, *L'avant-garde ne se rend pas.*

Despite his expansive definition, McLuhan cherished a canon of traditionally avant-garde figures. Trained as a scholar of medieval English literature at Cambridge—he submitted his dissertation on Thomas Nashe's trivium in 1943—he wrote at length about modernist writers such as James Joyce, Wyndham Lewis, and Ezra Pound.[4] While he invoked these authors as much as he analyzed them, sprinkling their best phrases throughout his books like talismans, they clearly had a deep effect on his thinking, especially in terms of art. Their main contribution, he reasoned, had to do with the way they understood their work alongside other branches of culture and how they poached these realms for their energies. "James Joyce was the first to exploit the multiple revolution of telegraph, press, radio, cinema, and TV," McLuhan wrote in 1954, prizing Joyce's wordplay for the way it communicated the "verbi-voco-visual" reality of new media by jamming together different sensory modes.[5] Similarly, Pound's importance stemmed from the way he used the typewriter to set the parameters of his work, thereby communicating the spirit of "technological America."[6] On a related note, McLuhan observed that T. S. Eliot's poetry "pointed to the effects of the internal combustion engine on poetic rhythms."[7] What united these writers, in other words, was the attention they paid to the technologies they used and the way their use of these technologies threw previous ways of writing into relief. Their work focused on the way language got to the page and how it looked when it got there, not simply on what it meant. While modernist critics like Clement Greenberg insisted that such work self-critically examined the discipline of literature, McLuhan saw it in relation to a wider field of technical media. For him, these writers compared their work to extraliterary print forms, such as the newspaper and the magazine, in order better to grasp not only the changing status of the book but also broader networks of communication.[8] Always looking to draw connections, he saw these writers as part of a wider cultural project, one that included modernist artists, including Paul Cézanne, Marcel Duchamp, and Pablo Picasso. For McLuhan, this double trinity belonged to a formalist avant-garde tradition that showed "intense concern for technique." If the writers communicated the disjunctive logic of the newspaper through their play with type and spacing, Picasso did something similar in his *papiers collés*, gluing down newspaper scraps in order to stress how print media influenced perception. As McLuhan wrote in *The Mechanical Bride*, the newspaper is "front page cubism," bringing together a multiplicity of events under the rubric of a dateline.[9] McLuhan was often at his best when he "interfaced" literary and plastic forms against one another.[10] He prized this ability in artists as well, which is perhaps why it was Lewis, both painter and prose artist, an avant-garde of one, who provided McLuhan with the model of what an avant-garde artist might do.[11]

A provocateur working at the fulcrum of various media and social worlds, Lewis put his energies to work on many different fronts. Over the course of his career, he published magazines, wrote novels, churned out critical studies, and made paintings and drawings. It was this swirl of activity, wrapped in an arch social posture (his biographer Jeffrey Meyers writes of his "strident Byronic *persona*—mad, bad, and dangerous to know"), which helped him make his mark in London.[12] In early 1914, after breaking with Roger Fry's Omega Workshops, a design guild dedicated to the beautification of everyday life, Lewis founded the Rebel Art Centre and launched the Vorticist movement, England's response to the international avant-gardes.[13] Where Fry dedicated his workshop to the decorative arts, Lewis placed himself on a more caustic path. While influenced by Marinetti's Futurism, Lewis's movement did not chase the future as much as it drilled down into the present, hoping to find its essence by pushing against the grain. Lewis viewed himself as an extreme individualist, which for him meant not simply being singular but also having the ability to mold popular opinion.[14] He imagined himself as a hardened figure fighting "against the flaccid conventions of Victorian taste."[15] Nowhere was this more apparent than in the pages of his short-lived journal *Blast*.

Though McLuhan read all Lewis's work, *Blast* provided the base on which he would stake his position. Printed in an edition of seventeen hundred and published in 1914, just before the outbreak of World War I, *Blast* is a mishmash of proclamations and ideas. Billed as the "Review of the Great English Vortex," it anthologizes a movement that was just beginning to cohere and would just as rapidly peter out (a second and final issue, the "War Number," came out in July 1915). Paul Edwards calls the publication Vorticism's "shifting foundation," and, indeed, much of *Blast*'s shiftiness has to do with the diverse positions it contained.[16] Weighing in at some 160 pages, it combines poems by Ezra Pound, plays by Lewis, and woodcuts by Edward Wadsworth in addition to Lewis's own theoretical tracts. Lewis later referred to it as a "mass of propaganda," channeling the feeling of a political campaign.[17] Its sans serif title spread diagonally across the pink cover communicates the tilt of its mission, like a lance aiming at an enemy. The "energy of the diagonal," as Hugh Kenner has noted, exudes an unnatural, inhuman

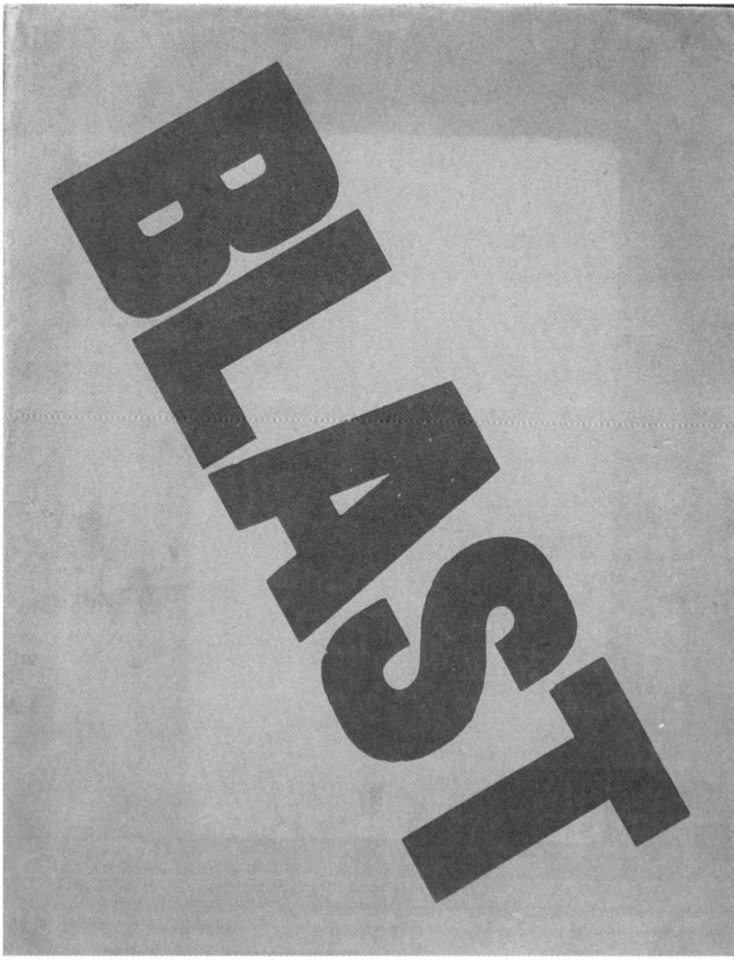


**2.2** Cover of *Blast* (1914). © Wyndham Lewis Memorial Trust/Bridgeman Images, New York 2021.

nature, with the implication of strident opposition. By contrast, "the directions of French abstraction tended to be horizontal and vertical, like water and trees."[18]

"We stand for the Reality of the Present—not for the sentimental Future, or the sacripant Past," Lewis states in "Long Live the Vortex," *Blast*'s excited preface. (Like Poe's maelstrom, Lewis's vortex presents another forceful gust, but, here, the artist has the opportunity to harness its powers.) The subsequent "manifesto" offers up a variety of "Blast" and "Bless" exclamations celebrating and chastising a great many things. The blast is not only the sound of modernity but also the act of negation. France gets blasted for its "poodle temper" but blessed for its "masterly pornography" and "combativeness." Ports and hairdressers receive blessings, while "Rousseauisms (wild Nature cranks)" get blasted. On the whole, artifice is held high (one thinks of Baudelaire on cosmetics), while nature is degraded. The proclamations appear in outsize type and undergo rapid shifts in size, scale, and spacing; according to Lewis, an old printer published the issue in exchange for drink. Perhaps not surprisingly, the thing looks agitated, self-consciously inelegant, with wonky towers of sans serif text: rather than a literary magazine, it brings to mind a newspaper or a carnival poster, and, in fact, much of literary London broke ranks with Lewis after the journal came out. Just as important as what *Blast* said, in other words, was how it said it—an idea that would later provide a cornerstone for McLuhan's thought (think "the medium is the message").

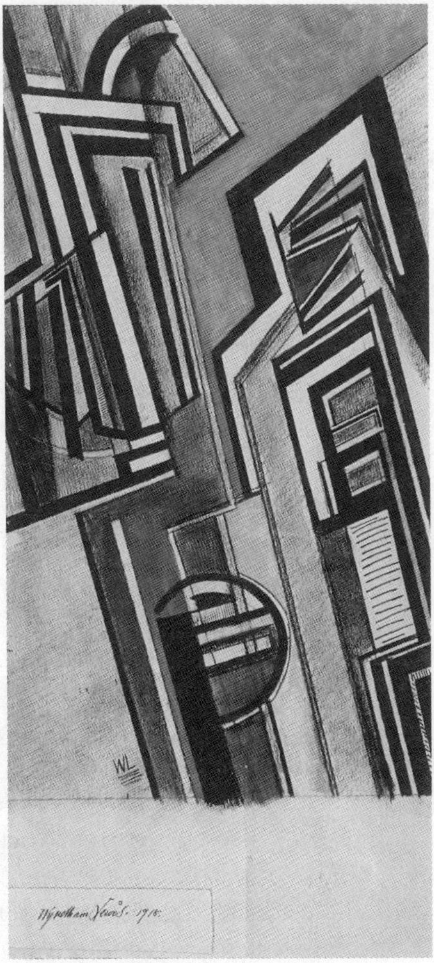

**2.3** Wyndham Lewis, *Vorticist Composition* (1915). © Wyndham Lewis Memorial Trust/ Bridgeman Images, New York 2021. Photo © Tate.

Among its cantankerous proclamations, *Blast* also takes positions on visual art, with Lewis's paintings—hardened geometries, "forms locked in passionate stases"—serving as illustrations.[19] Lewis claimed that his style, which he described as "dogmatically anti-real," stemmed from a desire to "exclude from painting the everyday visual real altogether." "Another thing to remember," he continued, "is that I considered the world of machinery as real to us, or more so, as nature's forms, such as trees, leaves, and so forth."[20] Lewis wanted to find the true form of things, the pure expression of his age, and for him that meant stripping away appearances to expose the hard core beneath. "In contrast to the jelly-fish that floats in the center of the subterranean stream of the 'dark' Unconscious," he wrote, "I much prefer, for my part, the shield of the tortoise, or the rigid stylistic articulations of the grasshopper."[21] For him, hardness meant permanence and solidity; he championed the Platonic consistency of pyramids and valued the heavyset forms of the Vorticist sculptor Henri Gaudier-Brzeska over the French flux of Auguste Rodin. The artist, he believed, had to "manipulate matter and existence" by pulling them out of the instability of time and into the solidity of space.[22] This had the effect of stopping life and capturing its essence but also of controlling it. For all his talk about the present, as Kenner notes, much of Lewis's imagery belongs to a "cemetery-world."[23] If his painting is "sprung like a steel trap to capture what he considers to be the essential in life," it often stops it dead in its tracks.[24] For Lewis, this fidelity to order, this desire to fix and freeze the world, was gendered as well. As Hal Foster has noted: "Lewis calls on artists to mold this flaccid feminine modernity into an armored masculine modernism."[25]

Lewis arrived at his theory of the avant-garde through the German aesthetician Wilhelm Worringer and his English disciple T. E. Hulme, who understood "primitive" art as an abstraction of the external world.[26] Following their ideas rather literally, Lewis imagined himself as a primitive in the new land of technology, eager and anxious to take control of seemingly unknowable forces. "The artist of the modern movement is a savage (in no sense an 'advanced,' perfected, democratic, futuristic individual of Mr. Marinetti's limited imagination): this enormous, jangling, journalistic, fiery desert of modern life serves him as Nature did more technically primitive man," he wrote in *Blast*.[27] The fiery desert of modern life was frightening; the artist had to control it and make it fit his needs. The "urge to abstraction," Worringer

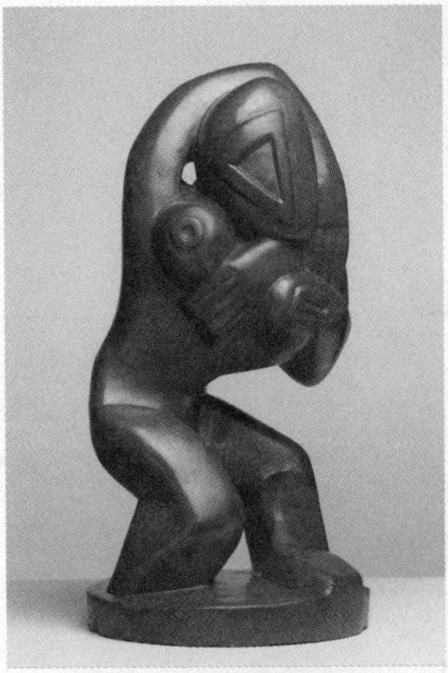

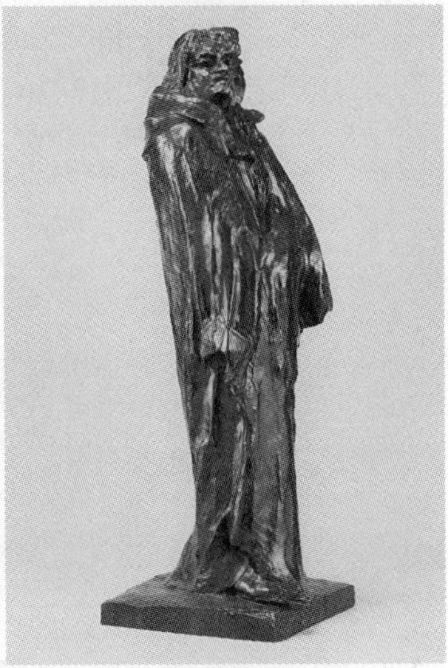

**2.4** (left) Henri Gaudier-Brzeska, *Red Stone Dancer* (1913). Photo © Tate.

**2.5** (right) Auguste Rodin, *Final Study for the Monument to Balzac* (modeled 1897, cast 1972). The Metropolitan Museum of Art, New York.

wrote in his 1908 *Abstraction and Empathy*, "emerged from spiritual dread of space." In such a situation one had "to wrest the object . . . out of the unending flux of being, to purify it of all its dependence upon life, i.e. of everything about it that was arbitrary, to render it necessary and irrefragable, to approximate it to its *absolute* value."[28] Lewis claimed this idea as the function of the artist, as did McLuhan in turn. In his 1953 "Wyndham Lewis: His Theory of Art and Communication," McLuhan wrote: "It is presumably the view of Lewis that the role of the artist in society is to energize it by establishing such intellectually purified images of the entelechy of nature."[29] It is the artist's task, in other words, to present society with new forms rather than copy what is already there. "Making rather than matching" is the artist's work.[30] Or as Ezra Pound put it in 1915: "Vorticism means that one is interested in the creative faculty as opposed to the mimetic."[31] This is yet another definition of what it means to be avant-garde.

Despite his talk of solidity, Lewis thought he was living in the midst of a breakdown—and he wanted things to break down further.

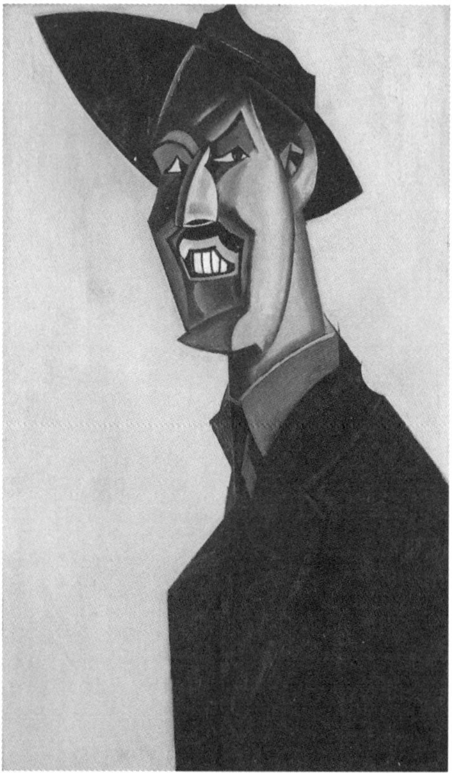

**2.6** Wyndham Lewis, *Wyndham Lewis as a Tyro* (1920–21). Ferens Art Gallery, Hull Museums, UK. © Wyndham Lewis Memorial Trust/Bridgeman Images, New York 2021.

In "Orchestra of Media," a brief essay in *Blast*, he argues that, in order to remain relevant, art must incorporate that which traditionally falls outside its borders. Artists now had to make their work out of new media. "Painting, with the Venetians, was like pianoforte playing as compared to the extended complicated orchestra aspired to by the Artist to-day," he wrote. "The reflection back on the present, however, of this imminent extension—or, at least the preparation for this taking in of other media—has for effect a breaking up of the values of beauty, etc., in contemporary painting." Limited to a single instrument, Venetian painting could do only so much, but artists now had a variety of media at their disposal, and "values of beauty" would transform in time. "Sculpture of the single sententious or sentimental figure on the one hand, and painting as a dignified accomplished game on the other, is breaking up and caving in," Lewis wrote.[32] The old disciplines would give way to something new. Hulme went so far as to call it "the final break-up of the Renaissance."[33] But Lewis did not think artists were doing enough to further their cause. Unfortunately, he concluded, "few to-day have forsaken [the medium of oil paint] for the more varied instruments, or orchestra of media, but have contented themselves with violating it." Never mind that Lewis was a lifelong painter. The point is that most artists remained content simply to disturb the old conventions of art—or *épater la bourgeoisie*—rather than produce something genuinely new And the new is what the artist, in Lewis's view, should seek to master.

## Masters and Masses

Though Vorticism was short-lived, Lewis continued to publish and paint. In a 1920 self-portrait, he depicted himself as a tyro with an arch, angled face. In 1926, he published *The Art of Being Ruled*, a massive, quixotic tome.[34] Though his tone always verged toward the hyperbolic, he burned bridges with his 1931 *Hitler*, the first English-language examination of the German leader. "It is as an exponent—not as critic nor yet as advocate—of German Nationalsocialism, or Hitlerism, that I come forward," he wrote at the beginning of the book, which gathered together a series of newspaper articles dispatched from Berlin. Claiming a position of impartiality, he cataloged Hitler's "wildly 'idealistic' nationalsocialist proposals for the 'conquest of the Western soul,' and for the founding of a peaceful confederacy of 'aryan' states" while also noting the cult of personality that surrounded him. While much of the book seeks to understand the economic roots of Hitlerism, casual mentions of "the extremely bad manners and barbaric aggressiveness of the eastern slum-Jew immigrant" make it clear that Lewis was no impartial observer, yet he stressed England's anti-Semitism as well.[35] Despite his professed wariness regarding Hitler's "nationalist" tendencies, Lewis's racist, jingoistic language offended contemporaries: People spat at the window of a London bookshop showcasing the book.

While Fredric Jameson claims that fascism functioned "as the political (and libidinal) embodiment of Lewis's chronic negativity, his oppositionalism, his stance as the Enemy," his positions were clearly more than rhetorical provocations: they still shock today.[36] On September 2, 1939, the day before Britain declared war on Germany, Lewis left the country, wisely sensing he was no longer welcome. Sailing for Canada, the country of his birth (legend has it that he was born off the coast of Nova Scotia on his father's yacht), he spent the war years in financial duress, writing novels, and searching for portrait commissions (something McLuhan aided him in obtaining), returning to England only after the Allied victory in 1945.[37]

The year he left England, Lewis wrote a follow-up to *Hitler* entitled *The Hitler Cult* in an attempt to put his previous arguments into perspective.[38] A wry and detached volume, it is similar to his other screeds. He claims that no one took Hitler seriously in 1931; by the same token, he argues, no one should have taken him too seriously either. "The great leaders of today were then perspiring nobodies," he declares, half-heartedly pleading with readers to absolve him. "To foresee *all* that has happened since, I should have had to have been a very exceptional seer." In the book's conclusion, however, he undermines his apology by admitting: "I find it extremely difficult, I confess, to be serious about what is happening just now."[39]

Lewis's combination of false modesty and levity is noxious, but it also obscures his lifelong interest in order and power. *Hitler* did not drop out of the ether. Though Germany's "passion" and "conviction" affected him, Lewis had long been interested in the relationship between leaders and masses.[40] "The Vorticist is not the Slave of Commotion, but it's [*sic*] Master," he claimed in *Blast*, and, like the "savage" who seeks to control his environment, the figure of the master would serve him throughout his career. "People, in Lewis's view, are never politically free," the critic Hugh Kenner, a former student of McLuhan's, wrote in 1954. "Somebody is always ruling them, and the illusion of freedom may be one of its anaesthetics." As such, Lewis thought it better to speak truth not *to* but *of* power. "Somebody has to herd [people]," Kenner wrote, "and since power is the ubiquitous principle of human affairs, Lewis, though he never persuaded himself that it was either beneficent or lovely, preferred the man who exercised it openly and hence with some show of responsibility."[41]

For Lewis, this "responsibility" fell to the artist. As the art historian Eric Michaud has shown, many modernist figures believed it was the task of a hybrid artist-dictator to shape amorphous masses.[42] Dictators would carry out artistic work—their politics a form of aesthetic activity—with the masses as their medium. The end result imagined the state as a kind of *Gesamtkunstwerk*, or total work of art. Lewis's fable "The Caliph's Design" (1919), which tells the story of a ruler who gives his architects one night to design a new city or be put to death, offers some idea of how Lewis thought this power might be "responsibly" wielded.[43] Hitler, an architecture aficionado and former watercolorist, must have appeared to Lewis as the realization of his thought—an artist who had put down his brushes in order to take control.[44] ("For Hitler, true art consists in revealing the heroic race, the heroic body, and bringing it to power," the critic Boris Groys insists.)[45] Not surprisingly, in his 1937 memoir, *Blasting and Bombardiering*, Lewis claimed that his career as a soldier in World War I and his work as an artist were one and the same—both were attempts at shaping the body politic.[46]

## *Counterblast*

Though McLuhan read Lewis at Cambridge in the 1930s, he first met him in 1943, during the writer's time in Canada.[47] (In 1944, Lewis drew a portrait of McLuhan as a plaid jacket, his head and legs disappearing into the whiteness of the page.) Their relationship, which included a long correspondence, proved formative, and McLuhan credited Lewis as a major influence throughout his career, often returning to and rephrasing his ideas. Significantly, he celebrated Lewis's early avant-garde work, putting aside the problematic aspects of his oeuvre that came after. (That McLuhan knew of this material is not in question. His annotated copies of *Hitler* and *The Hitler Cult* are held in his library collection at the Thomas Fisher Rare Book Library at the University of Toronto.) In many ways, in fact, McLuhan tried to channel the esprit of the early Lewis, and in 1954, at the age of forty-three, he

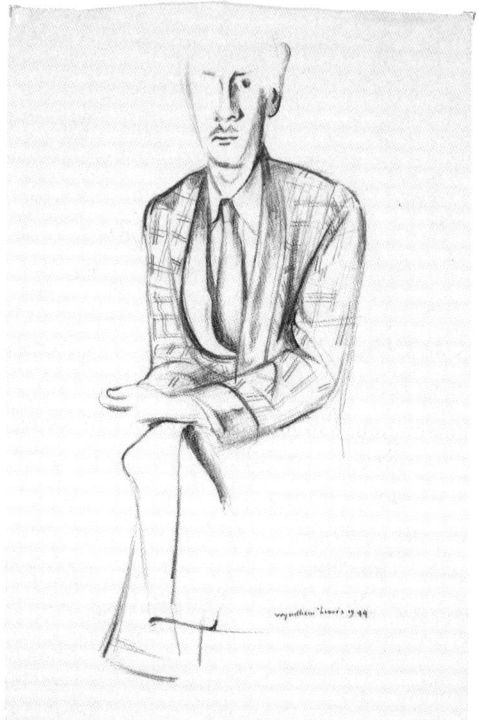

**2.7** Wyndham Lewis, *Marshall McLuhan* (1944). © Wyndham Lewis Memorial Trust/Bridgeman Images, New York 2021. Photo: Michael McLuhan.

published a small pamphlet—eighteen pages, stapled down the side, run off on a mimeograph machine—titled *Counterblast,* a clear riff on Lewis's *Blast* (and a rather artistic effort for an academic). It was a do-it-yourself job, and legend has it that he distributed it in front of a cigar store in Toronto.[48]

Mimicking its source publication in font and declamatory style, *Counterblast* also breaks with it. McLuhan replaces Lewis's hot pink cover with a cool baby blue one, and his title runs straight across, not on the diagonal. The topic changes, too. "As theme for *Blast* forty years later I have taken in place of abstract art and industrial culture, the new media of communication and their power of metamorphosis," McLuhan wrote to Lewis in December of that year.[49] Transposing *Blast*'s

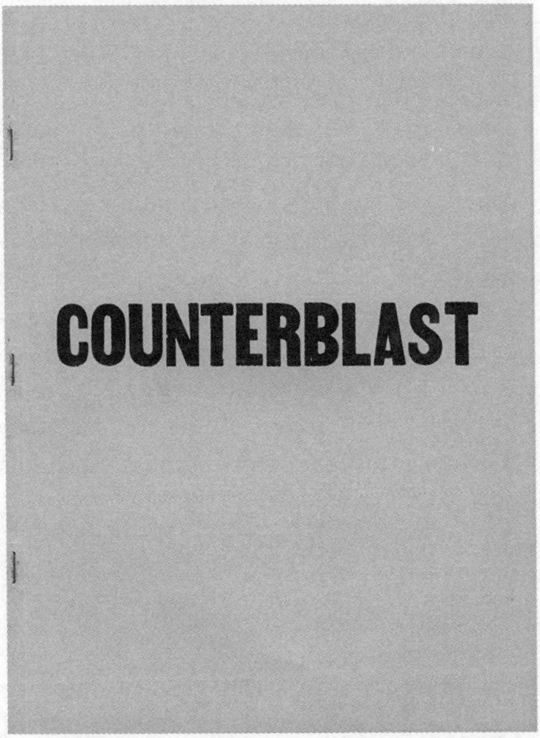


**2.8** Cover of Marshall McLuhan, *Counterblast* (1954).

Eurocentric points to postwar North America, McLuhan leveraged Lewis's invective to launch a tirade against the small-mindedness of Canadian life. Published just three years after *The Mechanical Bride*, this new title strikes a more aggressive position; rather than simply navigate the world with wit and dandyish esprit, McLuhan now presents the possibility of pushing back. Maintaining the Blast/Bless structure of the original, he fires off at "the woodcraft of all beaver minds devoted to CANADIAN PONDS AND STREAMS" and "the canadian BEAVER, submarine symbol of the SLOW UNHAPPY subintelligentsias." While *Counterblast* is provincial in its targets, one quickly realizes that McLuhan's forays into the local speak to the global and that the two are linked through new media. Dropping the names of television networks—"CBC BBC NBC CBS nets of the BIG GAME hunters"—

McLuhan defines his moment in terms of the reach of American (and British) communications: Canada is caught in its net. In addition to television, he also targets magazines, including "THE NEW YORKER whimsical sycophant of CREAM PUFF culture," though McLuhan's bête noire, the *Time* publisher "Henry Goose on the Luce"—who christened the "American Century"—is called out for special scrutiny.[50] What is important, however, is that TV and magazines work together; they both belong to a larger project of boxing in the Canadian mind.

In *Counterblast*'s "Media Log," the second of the tract's three sections, McLuhan makes increasingly programmatic claims about the relationship between media and society, writing: "Technological culture in the newspaper form structures ordinary unawareness in patterns which correspond to the most sophisticated manoeuvers of mathematical physics." Media create complicated pattern languages, in other words, and McLuhan wants to understand their grammar, how they reorganize the mind. He wants to look at the big picture rather than the individual part, believing that one can gain perspective only from such a vantage point.

But, if the newspaper was one technology of control, it was not the most pressing or the most pervasive. Other, newer media had taken its place. In fact, in *Counterblast*'s final section, "Five Sovereign Fingers Taxed the Breath," its title borrowed from Dylan Thomas's poem "The Hand That Signed the Paper Felled a City," McLuhan claims that print has died.[51] So, too, has the city: it is a "cultural ghost for tourists," a museum that one visits to survey bygone urban life. Now that magazines circle the globe and TV beams out to millions of homes, "any highway eatery with its tv set, newspaper, and magazine is as cosmopolitan as New York or Paris." Older vertical models of centralization give way to new horizontal networks. "The INSTANTANEOUS global coverage of radio-tv makes the city form meaningless, functionless," McLuhan writes. The globe had been reorganized: "The new media are not ways of relating us to the old 'real' world; they are the real world and they reshape what remains of the old world at will." New media do not show us pictures of the old world, in other words; they reformat our lived experience. Thus, it was with these media that McLuhan decided he had to engage.

One of the most powerful lessons McLuhan gleaned from Lewis is that artists must take control of this new situation; they, too, must play the orchestra of media, even if the instruments are different now. Like Lewis, McLuhan believed that new media had eclipsed painting and sculpture and surpassed the machine as well. "All the new media," he argued, "including the press, are art forms which have the power of imposing, like poetry, their own assumptions." One might ask how much of Lewis's authoritarian vision informs McLuhan's idea of the "imposing" artist. Clearly, McLuhan's version is softer than Lewis's artist-dictator shaping the masses, but he still believes that artists must take control of media in order to remake the world and that they are capable of doing so. Certainly, it is a moral failure that he never commented on Lewis's activities after *Blast*,[52] but what is perhaps more significant is how Lewis's thought infected the work of a thinker so closely associated with the countercultural project of the 1960s: McLuhan, too, had dreams of control. That said, he also spotted the artist's vulnerabilities. In a preemptive swipe against the corporate admen who would soon knock at his door and whom he would answer affirmatively, he argues that new media cannot be entrusted to just anyone: "The media are not toys; they should not be in the hands of Mother Goose and Peter Pan executives. They can be entrusted only to new artists, because they are art forms."

For McLuhan, this new artist would no longer be a maker of objects but an expert in communications, helping "imagine the Earth City" (not yet the global village) and "the new spaces created by the new media." This means not that artworks will be made of new media (newspaper, TV, etc.) but that media will be used to shape life itself into a work of art. "Technological art takes the whole earth and its population as its material, not as its form," McLuhan writes. This idea that the world had become raw material for artists would dominate his thinking on art, and, interestingly, it is a concept closer to artistic avant-gardes than literary ones (for more on this, see chapter 6, "Information Environment," below). McLuhan, however, gave it a unique—one might say neo-avant-garde—spin; he understood that the historical conditions that brought about early twentieth-century avant-gardism—World War I, the political climate of Germany, the Bolshevik revolutions, etc.—

differed from the forces animating his own Cold War moment. As such, art could not simply repeat old maneuvers. It ceased to be critical; it sought control instead. If there is an authoritarian glimmer to McLuhan's thought—though *elitist* might be the better word—this is where we find it.

For all his debts to Lewis, then, the *counter-* in *Counterblast* demands attention. McLuhan wanted to blast back at Lewis, who had, he thought, missed his moment. He wanted to make the most of his. "The English have lived longer with technological change than anybody else, but they lost their chance to shape it when the ship yielded to the plane," McLuhan wrote in *Counterblast*'s opening salvo. The Industrial Revolution lacked the proper cultural component, and this failure led to the advent of war:

> In 1914, a few weeks before the War, Wyndham Lewis the painter put out blast. He set out to create a new vortex of thought and feeling consistent with the changed conditions of life, work, and society. He was too late. The imbalance of thought and feeling in the new technological world of England and Europe was extreme. The explosion of 1914 did not do the work of blast. blast was full of energy, hope and new vision. Those who crept back from the battlefields had none of these. The work of reorientation of technological man was left to America in the twenties. America was not ready. America botched it.

So far artists had failed to align thought and feeling with their technological moment, but perhaps this time they might get it right. Artists, however, would have to control technology in order for such a thing to happen; media managers and businessmen, lacking the proper feeling, were not capable of doing it themselves. The insistence on reorienting "technological man" was not simply a cultural project, then, but also a political one, formulated in the wake of World War II and in the midst of the Cold War. Under such conditions, McLuhan thought politics had to be carried out via cultural means (a kind of soft power), and so it was on the cultural field, as we will see in the next chapter, where he did his work and where he was most embraced.

3

# Lights On

**Every step is change.** Robert Rauschenberg, *Random Order* (1963)

The first issue of the "little magazine" *Location* appeared in the spring of 1963. The artist Larry Rivers drew a cover featuring a map of New York City with a wide blue circle hovering over Greenwich Village. Surely, this is the location referenced in the journal's title, and most of the articles came from artists and writers based in New York. The painter Willem de Kooning contributed a short essay called "Content Is a Glimpse," the novelist Saul Bellow submitted the story "Sono and Moso," the illustrator Saul Steinberg published a series of drawings titled "The Nose Problem," and the artist Robert Rauschenberg offered a photo collage titled "Random Order." There is also an article by McLuhan, who, based in Toronto, is the outlier in the group but still someone to reckon with: his byline claims that "his new book, *The Gutenberg Galaxy*, has aroused considerable controversy in this country and abroad."

In a letter dated March 10, 1962, Donald Barthelme, one of the magazine's managing editors and himself a distinguished fiction writer, encouraged McLuhan to submit an essay on "the corruption of the imagination."[1] Imagination does not seem to have excited him, however, and instead he sent an essay on electricity and human extensions called "The Agenbite of Outwit," its title a play on "agenbite of inwit," a recurring phrase in Joyce's *Ulysses*.[2] Electricity served as a cornerstone of McLuhan's thought in the 1960s; he believed that it transformed the mechanical, linear world of print—the so-called the Gutenberg galaxy—into something complex and multidirectional that played on the body in different ways.[3] "With the telegraph Western man began a process of putting his nerves outside his body," he wrote, naming a messaging technology that put electricity to use. "Previous technologies had been extensions of physical organs: the wheel is a putting outside

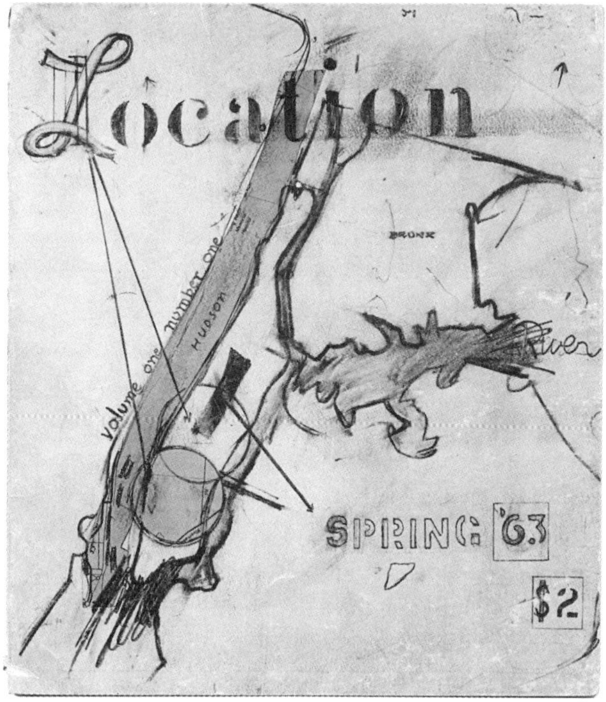


**3.1** Cover of *Location*, vol. 1 (Spring 1963). © 2021 Estate of Larry Rivers/Licensed by VAGA at Artists Rights Society (ARS), NY.

ourselves of the feet, the city wall is a collective outering of the skin. But electronic media are, instead, extensions of the central nervous system, an inclusive and simultaneous field. Since the telegraph we have extended the brains and nerves of man around the globe. As a result, the electronic age endures a total uneasiness, as of a man wearing his skull inside and his brain outside." That technologies formed extensions of man was fundamental to McLuhan's thought, and, while such a transformation had utopian potential, it also made "man" vulnerable by turning him inside out. Electricity's "inclusive and simultaneous field" created a dangerous situation of "total uneasiness." McLuhan, however, believed that artists might ameliorate this situation, and he ended his text in much the same way he concluded *Counterblast* twelve years before: "I believe that artists in all media, respond soonest to the challenges of new pressures. I would like to suggest that they also show

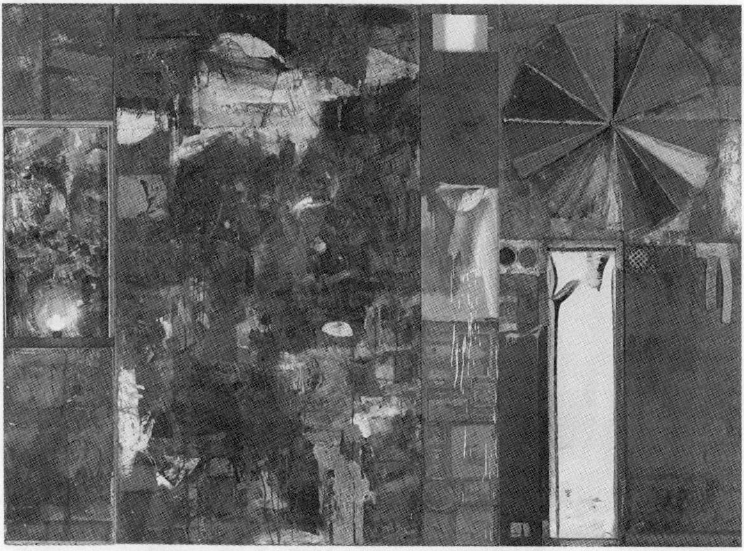

**3.2** Robert Rauschenberg, *Charlene* (1954). Collection Stedelijk Museum Amsterdam. © 2021 Robert Rauschenberg Foundation/licensed by VAGA at Artists Rights Society (ARS), NY.

us ways of living with new technology without destroying earlier forms and achievements. The new media, too, are not toys; they should not be in the hands of Mother Goose and Peter Pan executives. They can be entrusted only to new artists."[4]

McLuhan's article found good company in *Location*. Rauschenberg shared similar concerns, even if he did not phrase them as heroically. His "Random Order," a taped-together array of photographs, emphasizes quotidian, quasi-infrastructural aspects of life: the snapshots offer glimpses of a truck, a toilet, a sink, a window, and a water tower, among other objects. A network of notes, written in the artist's crude hand, frames the photographs, and, while many have the quality of Zen koans (at one point we read, "Every step is change"; further down the page we are asked, "Looking again?"), in the context of McLuhan's electric article one phrase jumps out: "A light bulb in the dark cannot show itself without showing you something else too."[5] Rauschenberg's technological observation is astute: by its very nature, a light bulb incorporates everything around it. There is no way for it to be alone.

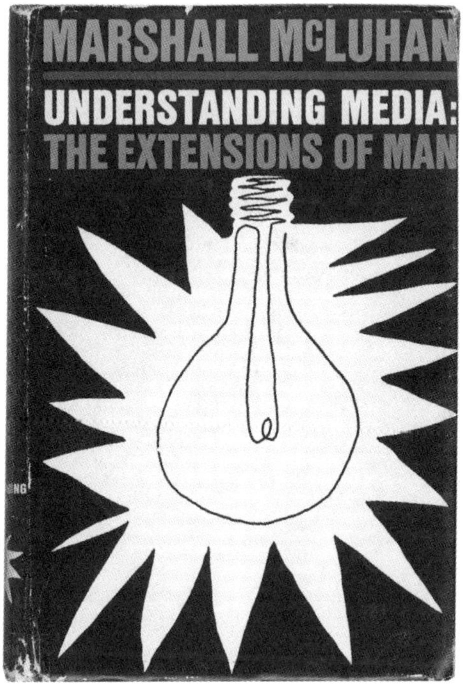


**3.3** Cover of the first hardback edition of Marshall McLuhan, *Understanding Media: The Extensions of Man* (1964).

Rauschenberg had been concerned with similar thoughts for some time; he, too, thought art had to plug into the wider world. In 1954, he placed a flashing bulb in *Charlene*, a massive combine painting replete with fun-house mirror, umbrella, T-shirt, and newspaper. He would return to the technology of electric light throughout his career. "Well, in my paintings, almost from the very beginning, I observed that painting changed from one kind of light to another," he said in 1967. "Then I started incorporating lights into my painting."[6] He took up light, in other words, after recognizing the importance of context. Realizing that his work was subject to environmental conditions and changing surroundings and thus lacked a consistent identity, he incorporated the environment into it, by hooking up his paintings to electrical technologies, including fans, motors, and radios. *Charlene*'s mirror worked toward much the same end.

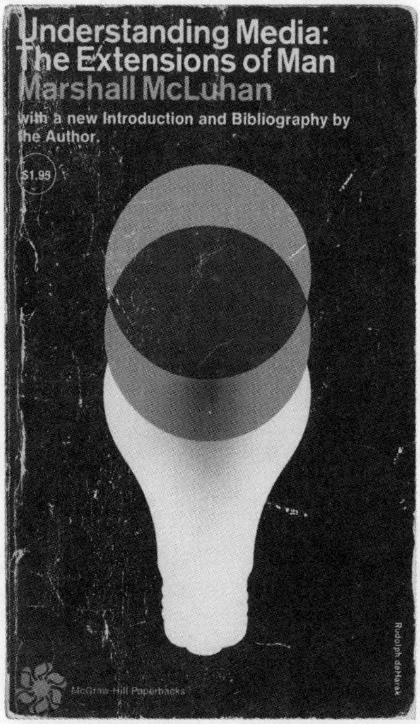


**3.4** Cover of the first paperback edition of Marshall McLuhan, *Understanding Media: The Extensions of Man* (1964).

Clearly something was in the air. Rauschenberg's "Random Order" appeared a year before the publication of McLuhan's *Understanding Media* (1964), which has a lot to say about light bulbs. Early editions feature bulbs on the cover—one has an almost Expressionist filament, the other a modish contour—while inside McLuhan turns to the light bulb to illustrate his famous mantra "the medium is the message," a phrase he first used in 1954 to debunk the "gratuitous assumption that communication is a matter of transmission of information, message or idea."[7] "The electric light is pure information," McLuhan wrote. "It is a medium without a message . . . unless it is used to spell out some verbal ad or name. This fact, characteristic of all media, means that the 'content' of any medium is always another medium."[8] Film footage, for example, provides the content for television just as TV now serves as material for YouTube. But, for McLuhan, content was beside the point;

it distracts one from the real work a technology does, a view even more apparent today with the exponential multiplication of *stuff* to watch. As McLuhan put it: "The 'content' of a medium is like a juicy piece of meat carried by the burglar to distract the watchdog of the mind."[9] Content, in other words, draws one's mind away from the issue at hand, while McLuhan wants to focus on the question of *medium—the actual experience of technology*. "Whether the light is being used for brain surgery or night baseball is a matter of indifference," he continued. "It could be argued that these activities are in some way the 'content' of the electric light, since they could not exist without the electric light. This fact merely underlines the point that 'the medium is the message' because it is the medium that *shapes* and *controls* the scale and form of human association and action."[10]

McLuhan's interest in media, then, was a concern with the wider forces that shape and control; to understand their effects he examined the kinds of activities different media made possible. In his review of *Understanding Media*, the *New Yorker* critic Harold Rosenberg suggested that this analysis was also helpful in understanding contemporary art. McLuhan's thesis "provides a suggestive description of much contemporary art—for example, that of Rauschenberg," Rosenberg wrote, "who through photographs and silk-screen reproductions makes news the content of his painting."[11] The individual meaning of Rauschenberg's images, he argued, was less important than the way the artist handled them and the media through which they passed. Photography and silk screen, in other words, trumped the informational value of any particular image. Rauschenberg himself echoed this idea in Emile de Antonio's 1972 documentary *Painters Painting*. "It doesn't really matter what's inside," he quips. "You begin with the possibilities of the material."

McLuhan eagerly marked this convergence of his ideas and those of contemporary artists, and others also took note. Bruce Bacon's 1967 documentary *Picnic in Space*, made during McLuhan's tenure as Schweitzer Professor at New York's Fordham University, offers one key example of this imbrication of theory and art. Outfitted in shirt and tie, McLuhan sits in a grassy field with the artist Harley Parker, ruminating on aesthetic questions.[12] Parker, a former student at Black Mountain College and one of McLuhan's closest allies, worked as the head designer at Toronto's Royal Ontario Museum, where he attempted to put McLuhan's theories into practice: In one case, he transformed the museum's Hall of Fossil Invertebrates into a multisensory space, replete with scents, touchable reproductions of fossils, and information-spouting telephones.[13] (The display served as the setting for Yousuf Karsh's famous portrait of McLuhan, pencil in hand, a book of medieval mosaics opened before him.) In another instance, in conjunction with the 1967 McLuhan-led museum conference "Exploration of the Ways, Means, and Values of Museum Communication with the Viewing Public," Parker outfitted the Dutch Gallery at the Museum of the City of New York with "several slide projectors, including one that hung from the ceiling and revolved, a movie projector, tape recordings, and a few artifacts," so as to transform it into an environment.[14] "The museum as a retrieval system for classified objects is not going to be acceptable for very long," McLuhan claimed at the conference. "People now feel the need to have a sense of the total surround of these objects and the total environment that produced them. And the sort of culture that produced them."[15] Posters hung from the ceiling, and costumed mannequins stood in the center of the room. Parker and McLuhan wanted to rid the museum of didactic labels so that one could experience artwork without a story line. It was all part of what one museum official called "total museology."[16] In the spirit of Alexander Dorner's "atmosphere room," which sought to reconstruct the native context of artworks, Parker wanted not simply to present objects but to re-create the environments in which objects originate and thus engage visitors on a physical rather than simply a visual level.[17] The notion of the environment was, as we will see, also becoming increasingly central to contemporary art.

McLuhan and Parker's conversations in *Picnic in Space* are extemporaneous and wandering. Scenes repeat. Voices echo. Morton Subotnick's electronic compositions provide an eerie soundtrack. Both erudite and aloof, McLuhan contradicts nearly every idea his interlocutor puts forward. But the dialogue is also interrupted by a montage of artworks by Roy Lichtenstein, Piet Mondrian, and Andy Warhol. Jasper Johns's *Light Bulb* (1958), however, makes a special impression.[18] One

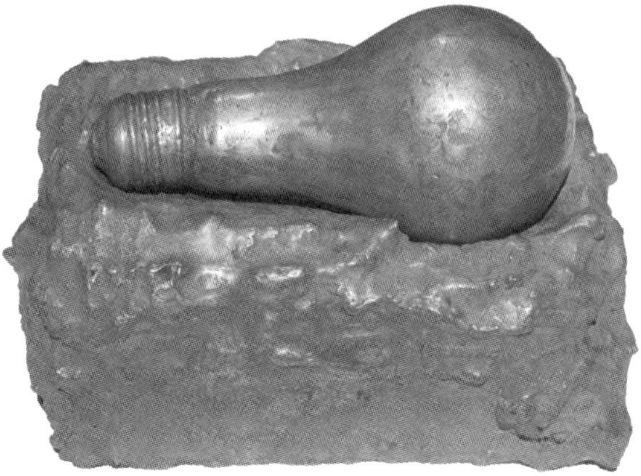

**3.5** Jasper Johns, *Light Bulb I* (1958). Museum of Contemporary Art San Diego, California. © 2021 Jasper Johns/Licensed by VAGA at Artists Rights Society (ARS), NY.

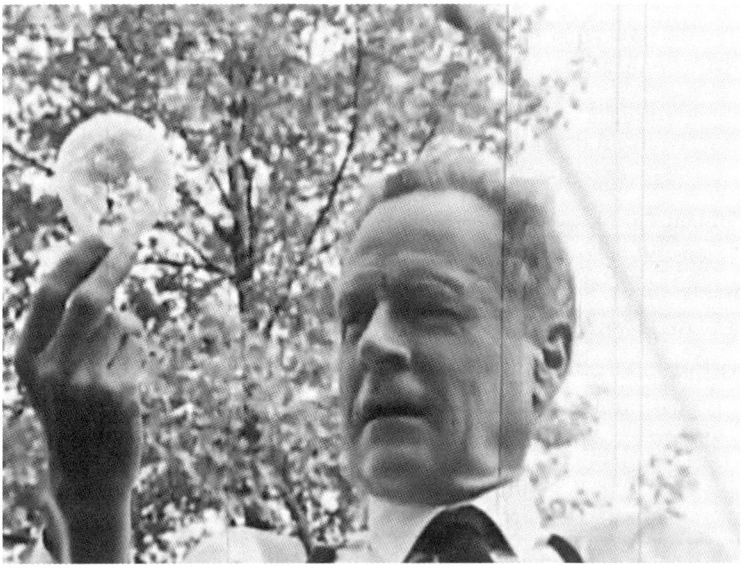

**3.6** Still from Bruce Bacon, *Picnic in Space* (1967).

of the artist's first proto-Pop objects (he made a flashlight earlier that same year), the work is a life-size replica of a light bulb crafted from gray sculpmetal that rests on a molten hunk of the same material. Replacing glass, filament, and soldered metal with a homogeneous piece of hobbyist's gunk, *Light Bulb* creates "a new thought for that object," transforming an item with illuminating and environmental implications into something dense and dysfunctional, thereby inviting the viewer to pay attention to something typically taken for granted.[19] Where a proper light bulb brightens and edges outward, *Light Bulb* is dark and solid, coterminous with itself. Where a functional light bulb is hooked up, connected, and wired to power, *Light Bulb* is pulled out, untwisted, and cut off. (In a sense, it is both companion to and inversion of Rauschenberg's *Charlene*.)[20] The art historian Joshua Shannon describes its "ancient, fossil-like" quality,[21] while Max Kozloff calls it "a death mask of light bulb."[22] "If artists in recent years have been interrupting this flow of information and interring it in magnetic petrifications of their own," Kozloff wrote, "they owe to Johns the signal model for such maneuvers. As illuminated by Marshall McLuhan, whose two tracts *The Gutenberg Galaxy* and *Understanding Media* were early read by the painter and his circle, the peculiarities of current communications are revealed to be provocative in relation to modern art." He added: "Precisely because a message is not transmitted the way one expects it to be, physiologically, emotionally, or symbolically, the medium gains identity and, as McLuhan would imply, accrues content."[23]

Later in *Picnic in Space*, McLuhan contemplates a small glass light bulb as if he were an artist gauging the qualities of his model. As he does so, he muses about how artists help society navigate technological change. "In order to make anything noticeable, you have to yank it out of its original context," he says as an image of *Light Bulb* flashes onto the screen. One quickly realizes that this "yanking," this displacement from context and environment, which he specifies as the artist's key task, is what he is up to as well. "All this genius stuff and so on is rather useless categorizing," he continues. "There are people who just happen to notice what's going on around them. Why the hell call them geniuses? They're awake." McLuhan was not belittling artists by stripping them of genius status; rather, he was expanding the idea of what an artist might be. "The artist is the man [*sic*] in any field, scientific or humanistic, who grasps the implications of his actions and of new knowledge in his own time," McLuhan wrote in *Understanding Media*.[24] Or as the 1967 *Newsweek* profile of him put it: "Few people are alert. Mostly they are the avant-garde poets, artists and sleuths—McLuhan includes himself in these categories—who have consciously sharpened their perceptions, realized the phoniness of the rearview mirror and forced themselves to look ahead and see the environment as it really is."[25] *Newsweek* got it pretty close to right: artists no longer create artworks but instead practice perception in the hopes of changing what they see. Theorists could do something similar, too.

By considering McLuhan in a constellation of neo-avant-garde artists, one can perhaps better see the social implications of the art of this time. Counter to Peter Bürger's argument that the neo-avant-garde institutionalized the avant-garde in the museum and thus rendered it historical, seen through McLuhan's eyes it becomes deeply enmeshed in questions of social and technological change. While Bürger is correct to claim that the neo-avant-garde lacks the spirit of protest typical of its forebearers, he misses the fact that many of its artists sought to use their art programmatically in the wider world, albeit in a largely postpolitical vein.[26] This art was not disinterested, in other words; it sought to make sense of and affect—indeed, *control*—technological change. One only need look at organizations like Experiments in Art and Technology (EAT), founded by Rauschenberg, the artist Robert Whitman, and the engineers Billy Klüver and Fred Waldhauer in 1966, to understand the extent to which artists at this moment dedicated themselves to research about and the development of the contemporary world. Based in a loft at 9 East Sixteen Street in Manhattan, the group supplied technological expertise to artists so that they might facilitate collaborative projects "outside art." (The group involved itself in everything from a Pepsi Pavilion in Osaka for Expo '70 to an agricultural project in India, assisting farmers with milk production via satellite communications.)[27] Rauschenberg's emphasis on the *gap* between art and life, however, is worth remembering: just as the collaboration between art and industry was, the collaboration between art and technology was perhaps most generative when a space existed between the two—a fact that

McLuhan's environmental determinism often elided. In many ways, Pop art, which followed the path set by Johns and Rauschenberg and which McLuhan also engaged, similarly functioned through its difference with the most contemporary forms of media.

## Pop Art

Many referred to McLuhan as a "Pop philosopher."[28] Certainly, he possessed a Pop persona, showing up on TV shows and in the pages of mass-circulation magazines in addition to panel discussions with Pop artists. (In September 1966, he interviewed the painter James Rosenquist, decked out in a paper suit, at the Art Gallery of Ontario in Toronto. Rosenquist gifted him a flyswatter.)[29] Harold Rosenberg went so far as to call *The Mechanical Bride* "a kind of early pop art, with a layout like a museum catalog and with headlines, clips of advertising art, comic-strip boxes."[30] McLuhan touched on Pop art in his writings. We might speak, too, of his Pop criticism, which shifts from the pronouncement of judgment to the probing of ideas. We have seen how he influenced London's Independent Group (IG). With the next generation of Pop artists, the relationship would be more symbiotic.

McLuhan had a novel take on Pop art. While many saw it as a study of the popular image, he considered it a form of environmental research. For him it functioned as an "anti-environment," a counterforce that trained perception and focused awareness on the wider environment.[31] "The world of so-called Pop Art has been handed down to us, as it were, by the new satellite environment," he wrote in 1966. "Pop Art is not a new environment of electric information, but the old mechanical environment suddenly observable as an art form."[32] Popular imagery was available to art, something to gaze at and contemplate, because it no longer served as the most contemporary form of communication; rather, it had become content for the new medium of satellite transmission. In McLuhan's eyes, Pop art was not a present-tense "electric" art but a visible remnant of the just-past mechanical world. "Pop Art is an indication that as the whole planet goes inside a new satellite-and-information environment made by man, we can no longer afford to

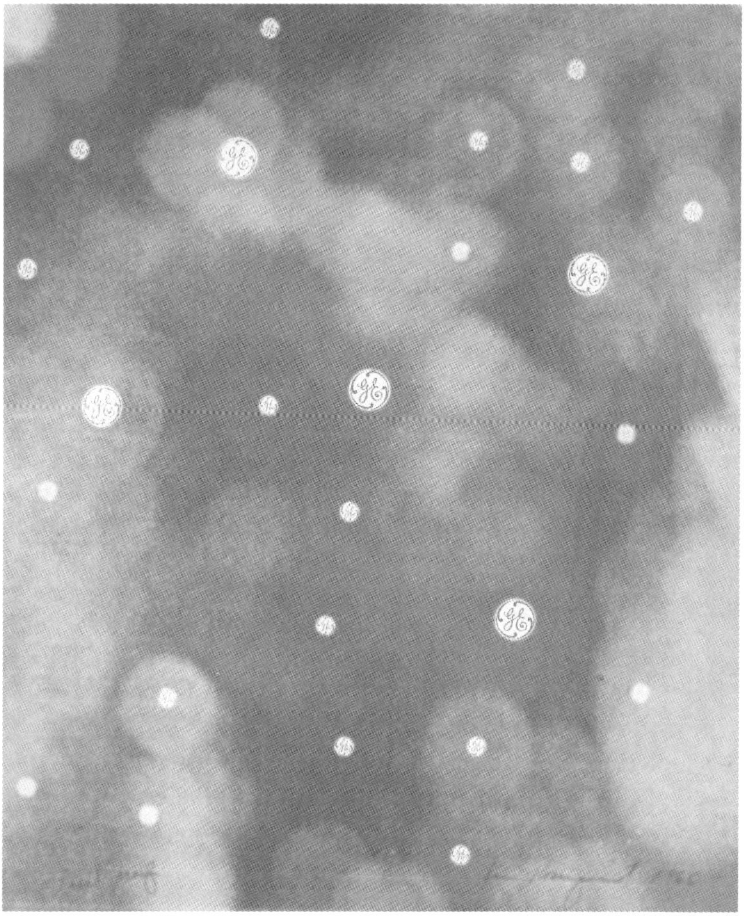

**3.7** James Rosenquist, *Circles of Confusion* (1965), from *11 Pop Artists, Volume I* (1966). © 2021 Estate of James Rosenquist/licensed by VAGA at Artists Rights Society (ARS), NY. Used by permission. All rights reserved.

deal with the human habitat as something given to us by Nature," he claimed. "We have now to accept the fact and responsibility that the entire human environment is an artifact, an art form, something that can be staged and manipulated like showbiz."[33]

Art and showbiz stand in dialectical relationship in this formulation: each is a form of manipulation, but art, McLuhan hoped, would do showbiz one better by programming the environment in a responsible

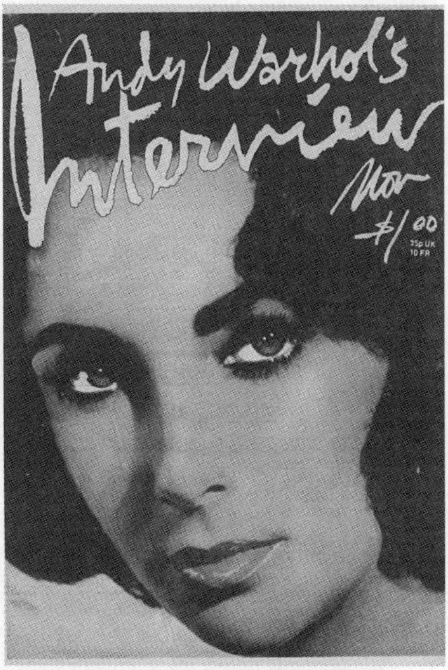


3.8 Cover of Andy Warhol's *Interview*, November 1976. © Interview Magazine, New York.

fashion. "In our time we can see that pop art consists in taking the outer environment and putting it in the art gallery, or indoors somewhere," he wrote in 1967, "suggesting that we have reached the stage where we have begun to process the environment itself as an art form."[34] For McLuhan, the next step was to reach back out and manipulate the media environment. Andy Warhol, the Pop artist par excellence, had similar ideas, even if he did not see his work as a responsibility. "Pop Art took the inside and put it outside, took the outside and put it inside," he wrote in *POPism*, his memoir of the 1960s.[35] For every painting Warhol produced depicting a commercial object, he also stepped out of the gallery and into the media at large—the magazine stand, the publishing industry, the movie theater. The two sides of art and commerce worked in each other's service, with Warhol leveraging one against the other to create a hybrid enterprise that was neither art nor showbiz but somehow a nebulous gap world of its own.

If McLuhan suggested a working schema for artists, he also offered a model of how one might move in the world. "There were two types of people doing counterculture-type things," Warhol wrote of the 1960s. "The ones who wanted to be commercial and successful and move right up into the mainstream with their stuff, and the ones who wanted to stay where they were, outside society. The way to be counterculture and have mass commercial success was to say and do radical things in a conservative format. Like have a well-choreographed, well-scored, anti-Establishment 'hippie be-in' in a well-ventilated, well located theater. Or like McLuhan had done—write a book saying books were obsolete." At first glance, Warhol's comments seem to cast McLuhan in a derogatory light and portray him as opportunistic, a square cashing in on fashion. But Warhol struggled with these issues, too: he worried about the transformations in "Pop culture" as it moved from the "primitive period" to the "Early Slick" and how one might work in a changed environment.[36] Many in the counterculture wondered whether to stay outside and drop out or go inside and clean up (consider the 1968 slogan for the antiwar presidential candidate Eugene McCarthy, "Get Clean for Gene"). Surely, Warhol, who often donned a coat and tie, took the latter, McLuhanesque tack, not only in his self-presentation as a "personality," but also in his work.[37] Pop art shared much with the phenomenon he describes. It was radical content (or at least content traditionally foreign to art) dropped into a conservative format: Campbell's soup cans on canvas; a Pop wedding at the Michigan State Fair. Its embrace of conventions is what allowed it to enter the common culture. In this regard, McLuhan appears as a Pop artist alongside Warhol, a con man smart enough to know that he had to present in a certain way to have the impact he desired. But the comparison goes the other way, too. In a 1970 essay, the critic Gregory Battcock wrote: "Warhol was, during the sixties, a visual Marshall McLuhan."[38] Both men, in other words, mastered media analysis and invention. Or, to put it slightly differently, both knew that one had to be "cool" to be involved. (That said, Warhol was underwhelmed when he met McLuhan. "One night in April 1973," Bob Colacello tells us, "Andy passed up dinner with Joan Crawford for dinner with Marshall McLuhan, and was furious with himself for making the wrong choice.")[39]

Warhol's idea that an artist's work and life would be networked together, that the studio would be only one site of production alongside the gallery, the magazine, and the nightclub, jibes closely with McLuhan's idea that people would increasingly turn toward roles—and away from goals—in the new media environment. "What is taking the place of the job is role-playing," McLuhan wrote in "The End of the Work Ethic." "When you are moonlighting and starlighting, that is role playing; and most people are doing this in some degree or other. The job-holder drops out and the consultant drops in."[40] This all sounds rather slick, and, as it turned out, the "tribal man" that McLuhan envisioned emerging from the electric world (now the global village) would not take root.[41] Rather, as the artist-critic and former IG convener John McHale suggested in his 1967 review of *Understanding Media*, the "hip artificer"—a master of surfaces quick to recognize fluctuations in technology and style—would set the future's course.[42] No longer an artist but an artificer: it was going to take an agile type of person to adapt to—and, indeed, command—the brave new world. It would take someone who would not simply foresee the future but determine its shape as well.

4

# Electronic Opera

**"Electronics" has been the catch-phrase since 1950, in science and society, in music and stock-market . . . why not in art?** Caption in *Electronic Art*, Nam June Paik's 1965 Galeria Bonino catalog (November 23–December 11, 1965)

If the light bulb captured information in its purest form, television, McLuhan thought, presented its most powerful possibilities. Where a light bulb is electric, television is electronic: the former only regulates energy; the latter allows the manipulation of information. A light bulb alternates between light and dark, but a television tells us about weather and war. McLuhan, however, thought television had an even greater complexity: though it was typically considered a visual medium, its effects, he insisted, extend far beyond the eyes. For him, watching television was a bodily experience. In *Understanding Media*, he likens the "TV viewer" to a "skin-diver" who slips into the screen. "The TV image requires each instant that we 'close' the spaces in the mesh by convulsive sensuous participation that is profoundly kinetic and tactile," he continues.[1] In his hands, the experience of watching the nightly news is sensuous and far-out—a radical break from the linearity of print and type.[2] "That theme of touch . . . is so basic now with the TV generation," he wrote in 1969, as if the connection between television and tactility were obvious to all. TV viewers have "been X-rayed by the TV image from early childhood, [and] now feel the need of handling all things in depth."[3] The real effect of television was not simply on eyeballs, in other words, but on bodies. It created a new environment.

At a time when many found TV superficial, McLuhan insisted that its powers extend far beyond the surface, an idea that he derived, in part, from the medium's technical properties: TV's relatively low definition in the 1960s required an active viewer to connect the dots. Like a high-tech mosaic, it aggregated beams of light on a smooth surface. "Marshall McLuhan's famous formulations of the sixties," the art his-

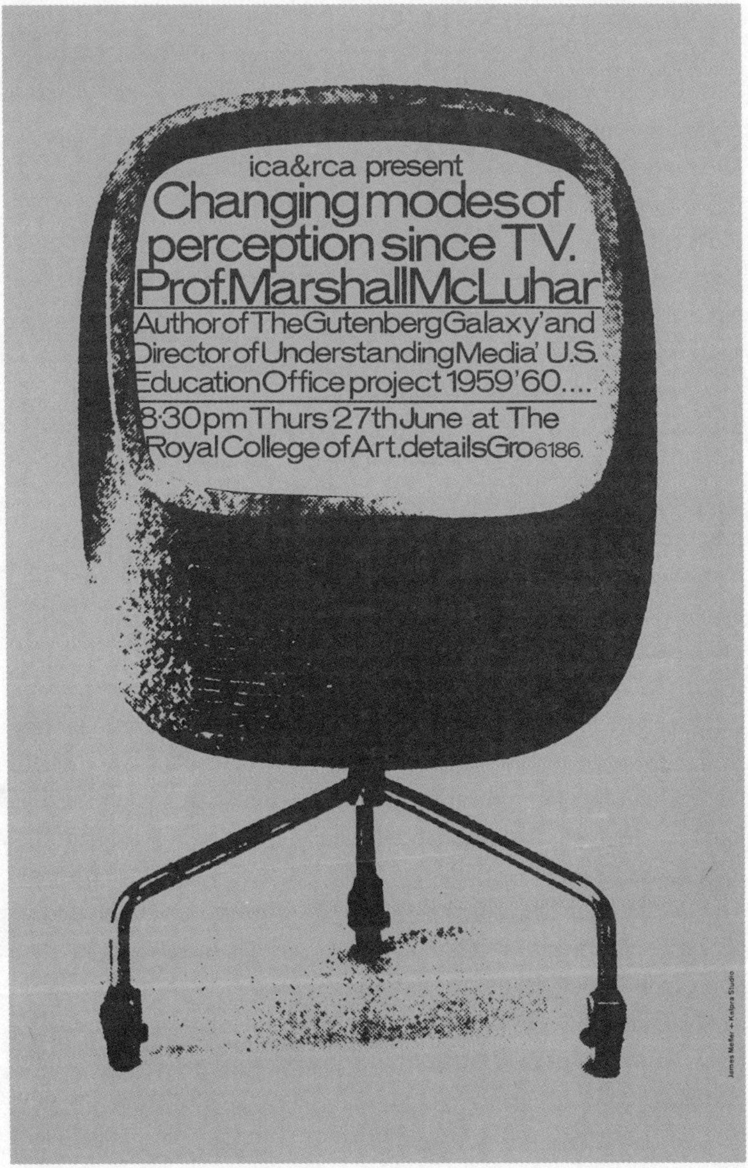


**4.1** Poster for a lecture by Marshall McLuhan at the Royal College of Art, London, 1963.

torian Jonathan Crary has written, "show how one discourse about television was founded on features that proved to be transient peculiarities of a technology still in its infancy. Television was 'cool' because of the low definition of its image and its small size: its image quality effectively blurred intellectual and perceptual distinctions on the part of the viewer."[4] Though McLuhan's ideas about television were pegged to its earliest incarnations (we cannot consider *television* one homogeneous category), the idea that TV creates active agents rather than passive consumers opened up new thoughts and possibilities—and it sparked the interest of artists as well.

The popularity of McLuhan's ideas about television would have made it difficult for artists interested in the technology to avoid his thinking. He lectured at art schools and museums, and his writings appeared across a wide range of platforms, from arts journals like *Location* to the cover of *Newsweek*, which featured the thinker's portrait displayed across an array of floating screens.[5] Artists, too, took him into the classroom: Frank Gillette taught a course on his work at the Free University on Fourteenth Street in Manhattan in 1967. That said, when McLuhan mused about television's relationship to art, he typically searched for precedents, noting how the French artist Georges Rouault's stained-glass work anticipated the logic of TV. He thought Georges Seurat's Pointillism did something similar. "At night the urban landscape belongs to Seurat and Rouault," he wrote. "It is a world of light *through* rather than light *on*. It is a world of TV and reverse perspective in which the viewer is the vanishing point."[6] But, if modernist art anticipated a future technology, once television arrived artists had other ideas about what to do with it.

McLuhan and television were virtually synonymous at this moment; it was difficult to pry the medium and the messenger apart. "Ever since Marshall McLuhan has become a household name, people have become aware of the tremendous force, both actual and potential, that TV is having and will have on their lives," the gallerist Howard Wise wrote in the catalog for the landmark exhibition *TV as a Creative Medium*, which opened at his gallery in May 1969.[7] If artists at this moment wanted to explore media, in other words, McLuhan offered the way to get there.[8]

Interestingly, Wise does not emphasize McLuhan's ideas as much as

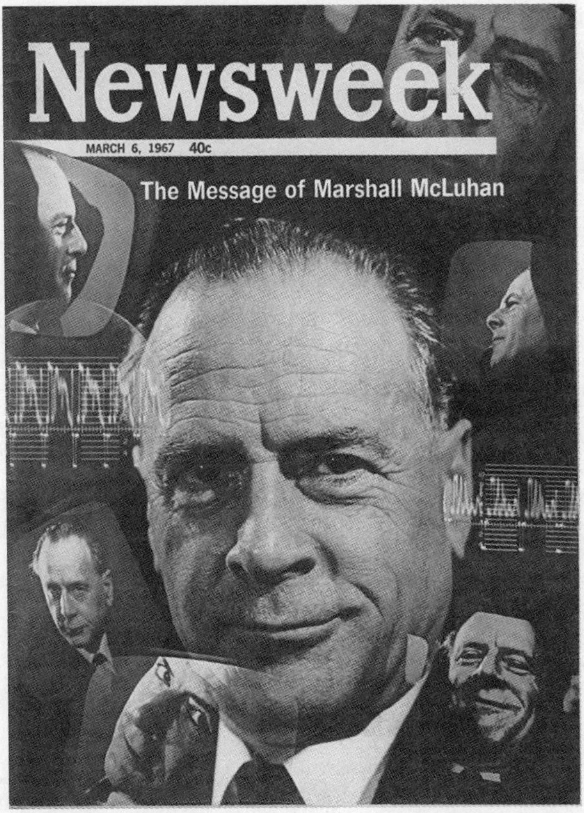


**4.2** Cover of *Newsweek*, March 6, 1967. Used with permission of Newsweek Copyright © 1967. All rights reserved.

he points to how McLuhan raised awareness about TV's importance; he goes so far as to suggest a likeness between him and his object of study. Just as the television set in the den had done, McLuhan, too, had become a household member, and other commentators at the time picked up on his ubiquity as well. "It has sometimes been said that Marshall McLuhan's most impressive achievement is his reputation," Jonathan Miller wrote in 1971. "The very growth of his own reputation seems to bear out his well-known thesis about the way in which modern knowledge is so widely shared in what he calls the global village."[9] It was not simply what McLuhan said but how he said it, in other words—his talent for communication and circulation—that grabbed people's interest (and sometimes their scorn). Reviewing NBC's 1967 television documentary *This Is Marshall McLuhan: The Medium Is the Massage* in the *New York Times*, Jack Gould noted that McLuhan's "brisk epigrams" have "much in common with the design of TV commercials."[10] This is a backhanded compliment to be sure, but Gould nevertheless acknowledges the currency of McLuhan's work and the way it mimicked contemporary forms of language. If McLuhan behaved like television, he must have had some understanding of its strengths and vulnerabilities. The anthropologist Edmund Carpenter, who worked closely with McLuhan in the 1950s and 1960s, made him an example of the media's effects in his 1972 *Oh, What a Blow That Phantom Gave Me!* "The moment Marshall McLuhan shifted from private media analyst to public media participant," he wrote, "he was converted into an image the media manipulated & exploited."[11] McLuhan did not simply comment on media images, in other words; he transformed into an image himself. Publicity and participation come at a cost: vulnerability to manipulation and exploitation alike.

## Paik

If many artists took an interest in McLuhan at this time, Nam June Paik paid him special attention. Born in Seoul in 1932, Paik moved to Germany in 1956 to study music. There, he met the composers Karlheinz Stockhausen and John Cage and began to translate his musical ideas into other forms. He found his place, in the early 1960s, in the context of Fluxus—a radical band of artists, musicians, and writers who often worked between media, transposing the protocols of one discipline onto another. Led by the Lithuanian-born provocateur George Maciunas, Fluxus had an international scope, staging events across Germany, Japan, and the United States. In many ways, music served as an apt and economic metaphor for Fluxus activities: scores lent themselves to easy distribution and often spurred the creation of new work. Paik's *Zen for Head* (1962), for example, which consisted of the artist dipping his head in a bucket of inky tomato juice and pulling it across a roll of paper, offered an interpretation of a 1960 La Monte Young score:

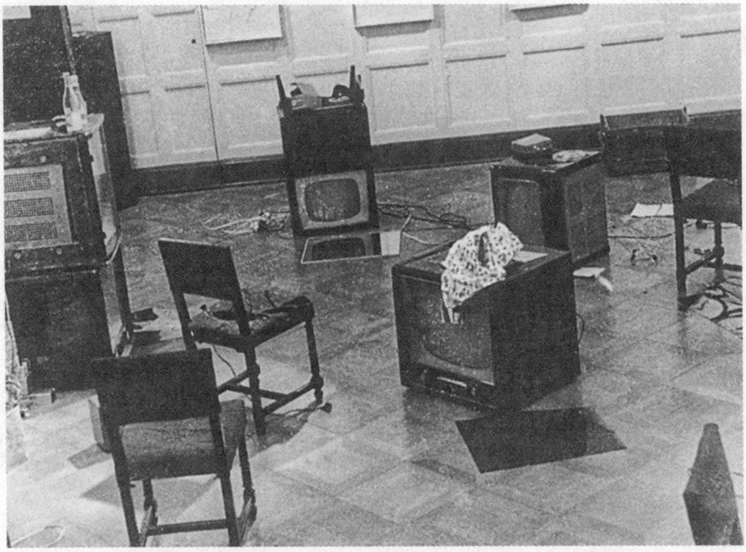

**4.3** Nam June Paik, installation view of *Exposition of Electronic Music–Electronic Television* at Galerie Parnass, 1963. © Nam June Paik Estate.

"Draw a straight line and follow it."[12] Though not evident in this work, Paik was also the Fluxus artist most preoccupied with technology; his historical conception of media—"as collage technic replaced oil paint, so cathode-ray tube will replace canvass [*sic*]"—also owed a debt to McLuhan's theories.[13] Focused on the presentation and manipulation of information, he was one of the first artists to bring television into the gallery, where he treated it not as an object for passive consumption but as a conduit for active manipulation. Like McLuhan, he too saw TV in terms of "convulsive sensuous participation," and he set about realizing its potential by subjecting the medium to flux, contingency, and chance.

Paik's 1963 *Exposition of Electronic Music–Electronic Television* at Galerie Parnass in Wuppertal was the artist's first foray into this terrain, and it bridged the gap between electronic music and televisual media.[14] Originally planned as a concert, the exhibition ran for a brief nine days—from March 11 to March 20—and primarily consisted of works made of musical material, such as magnetic tape, prepared pianos, and vinyl records. An installation of television sets, chairs, and other items appeared in a separate room, with detritus scattered across the gallery floor in a seemingly haphazard fashion. While Paik's use of television can be seen as an extension of advanced music's electronic turn, the billing given to TV in the show's title marked it as a distinct area of inquiry.

The casual configuration of elements—a rag was clumped on top of one of the television sets, wires snaked through the room, and relief works by the Surrealist Raoul Ubac were left in place from a previous installation—made the exhibition look more like an environment, an ersatz *Gesamtkunstwerk,* than a set of artworks displayed for aesthetic contemplation. ("My experimental TV is not always interesting but not always uninteresting like nature, which is beautiful, not because it changes beautifully, but simply because it changes," Paik wrote a year later, inviting the reader to consider the exhibition as a form of environment.)[15] Paik tuned all eleven sets to the same channel but altered the internal circuitry so that their radio signals were disrupted and no two sets transmitted the same image. Information and its presentation (its medium, in other words) were two different things, at times mediated by a third, participation: some works included microphones, which allowed visitors to manipulate the television image with their voices. Not all changes were intentional, however: two television sets had been damaged in transport, but the artist turned this to his advantage. Paik turned one over so that its screen faced the floor, while the other, which now cast only a single white line, was propped vertically and christened *Zen for TV*. The sensuous materiality of the medium was on full display.

Given that Paik first experimented with television in the early 1960s, McLuhan's thinking was not the source of his interest in the medium. As with Hamilton, the relationship between the two is closer to that of fellow travelers than master and apprentice. However, by the time of Paik's first show in the United States (*Electronic Art,* at New York's Galeria Bonino in 1965), McLuhan had become an object of the artist's attention, if not the father figure in an agonistic Oedipal drama. ("Don't confuse 'electronic' with 'electric,' as McLuhan often does," Paik warned a few years later.)[16]

At Paik's behest, John Cage contributed a short text to the exhibition catalog. ("Your writing will be as attractive as,,,,,,,,,,say,,,,,,,'Jack-

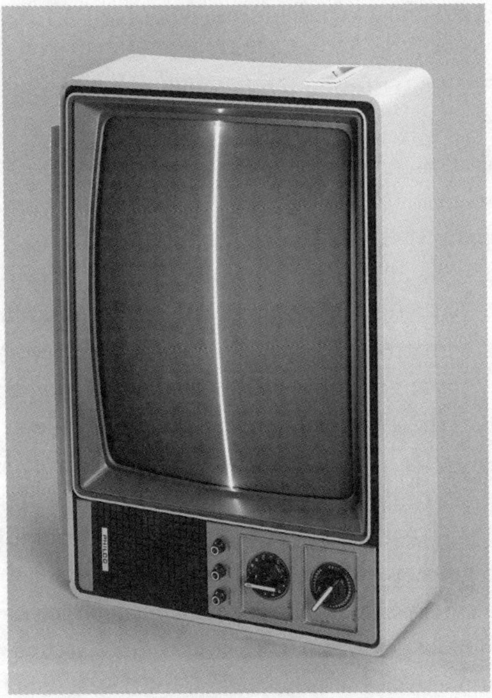

**4.4** Nam June Paik, *Zen for TV* (1963, executed 1981). © Nam June Paik Estate. Gilbert and Lila Silverman Fluxus Collection Gift, The Museum of Modern Art, New York. Digital Image © The Museum of Modern Art/Licensed by SCALA/Art Resource, NY.

line [*sic*] Kennedy's endorsement to Mayor Lindsay," Paik promised Cage.)[17] Laced with McLuhanesque turns of phrase, the text demonstrates how much the thinker's ideas about the hyperconnected field of contemporary media had permeated neo-avant-garde discourse.[18] "What is this thing called Art? TV?" Cage asks. "(Everything at once, no matter when/where we are?)" Cage continues questioning: "Five year guaranty on you Paik TV? Is that what you want? And since it's art, which art is it? Change your mind or change your receiver (your receiver is your mind). Enjoy the commercials, that is to say, while you still have them. Global village: they're not here to stay."[19] The meaning here is elusive—subject-verb agreement is tenuous, and related clauses seem far apart—but clearly Cage saw borders blurring between art, technology, and life. A television receiver functions akin to the way the human mind does: both technologies tune in and out. But why would commercials disappear in this new world order? Would the coming global village function differently? And, if so, was TV, on the verge of liberation, ready to be put to new uses? Cage's text does not answer these questions, but it implies that life is on the verge of a major change. "Art and TV are no longer two different things," Cage continues. "They're equally tedious. The geometry of the one devitalized the other. . . . TV's vibrating field's shaken our arts to pieces. No use to pick them up. Get with it: *Someday artists will work with capacitors, resistors & semi-conductors as they work today with brushes, violins and junk.*"[20] According to Cage, TV's dancing electrons destabilize art's structure. Television, he implies, created a hybrid, tactile environment that was neither TV nor art but a cybernetic union of the two. For Cage, like McLuhan, TV's real effects appeared, not in the realm of the image, but in a new concept of space.

Elsewhere in the catalog one finds a complicated equation involving both Cage and McLuhan. No longer an outsider, Cage the critic is now a variable in the "problem." As with Cage's own writing, it is difficult to unravel this equation, which includes the square root of "McLuhann [*sic*]" raised to the power of 3.5, subtracted from Cage and hovering over Norbert Wiener, the inventor of cybernetics, the postwar science that focused on the relationship between man and machine. With a sum total of "sorry," the equation suggests that simply talking about media, cybernetics, and systems theory is not enough. Sorry, Paik seems to say, but hands-on experimentation needs to be done.

That said, Paik invoked the work of these thinkers in order to build on it, and he frequently positioned McLuhan and Wiener in relation to one another, theorizing his practice in terms borrowed from their thought.[21] A year later, in his 1966 manifesto, he turned again to the relationship between McLuhan and Wiener: "Cybernetics, the science of pure relations, or relationship itself, has its origin in karma. Marshall McLuhan's famous phrase 'Medium is message' was formulated by Norbert Wiener in 1948 as 'The signal, where the message is sent, plays equally important role as the signal, where message is not sent.'"[22] Later that same year, he reiterated Wiener's importance,

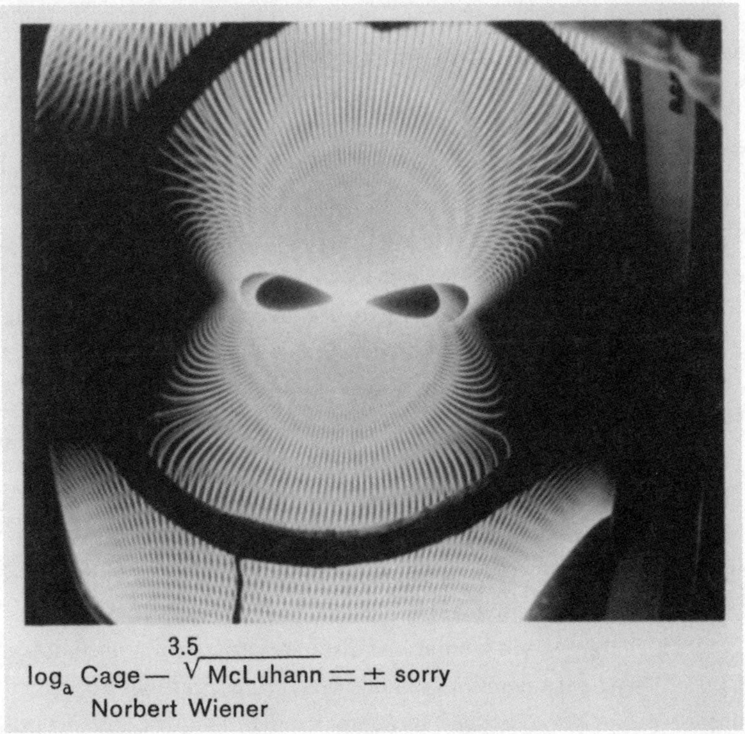


**4.5** Equation from *Nam June Paik: Electronic Art* (1966). © Nam June Paik Estate.

claiming his work as a precedent not only for McLuhan but also for contemporary art: "Twenty years ago Norbert Wiener, whose hobby was to read the Encyclopedia Britannica from A to Z, anticipated the Intermedia. . . . [He] brought forth an interscience called cybernetics, and the latter pushed the electric age (engineering with the technique of strong current) into the electronic age (control and communication using the weak current), which exploded as the escalated 'Mix Media' in Marshall McLuhan's 'global village.'"[23] Wiener's cybernetics, which theorized a system of "control and communication in the animal and machine," offered an early glimpse of the thinking that animated the intermedia environments of the 1960s: both envisioned technological feedback systems in which humans and machines would interact. Now that machines had sense organs, Wiener thought, people would interact with them in new ways. These closed systems offered capsule versions of McLuhan's global village, which, Paik implies, was more or less an expanded work of art.

Wiener saw the universe headed toward entropy, and, as a result, his interest in cybernetics was palliative, not corrective. "In a very real sense we are shipwrecked passengers on a doomed planet," he proclaimed in his 1950 *The Human Use of Human Beings*. "Yet even in a shipwreck, human decencies and human values do not necessarily vanish, and we must make the most of them. We shall go down but let it be in a manner to which we may look forward as worthy of our dignity."[24] Though he believed that humans were doomed, he also believed that they could still behave humanely (as Fred Turner has written, "Wiener's cybernetic self was collaborative and cooperative").[25] The prefix *cyber-*, after all, comes from the Greek word for *helmsman*, and Wiener's science held out the possibility that one might navigate an increasingly entropic world.[26] If communication could withstand noise, humankind would be able to retain its capacities for the time being.[27]

Paik characterized Wiener as a "square professor" mired in the "CIO-Riesman like pessimism of this age," tying him to the acclaimed author of *The Lonely Crowd*.[28] By comparison, he found McLuhan optimistic, calling him a "hippie Joycian" and an "elegantly cool essayist." "McLuhan, a convinced catholic, is glaring with Fuller-Cagean optimism," he wrote. (McLuhan, like the inventor Buckminster Fuller, thought technology could transform rather than simply maintain human relations.) Paik sought to occupy a third position between the suit and the hippie, between Wiener's practical pessimism and McLuhan's effusive optimism. He problematized the terms of the argument by engaging media directly.

## *McLuhan Caged*

In his 1968 exhibition at Galeria Bonino, *Electronic Art II*, Paik presented *McLuhan Caged*, a small jury-rigged device that presented the thinker "caged" in a TV set.[29] *Caged*, of course, meant various things in this context. McLuhan was trapped in the monitor, his head abutting its borders, but he was also caged in the sense that he was subjected to John Cage's ideas of indeterminacy and chance.[30] "Paik videotaped one of McLuhan's programs and 'massaged' it electronically to produce variable distortions," the artist Otto Piene wrote in 1968. "The results, Paik says, were 'Gabo-pop images, with a lot of John Cagean indeterminacy and humor.'"[31] To create the work Paik played footage from NBC's McLuhan documentary (more on this in chapter 5, "Massage, ca. 1966," below) on a small TV monitor wrapped in his Demagnitizer, a coiled device that he had introduced in 1965. Although the work was placed on a pedestal, visitors could still interact with it. A foot switch at the bottom of the pedestal turned the magnet on and off, while a small electrical transformer controlled the electricity flowing to the monitor. Paik appeared on an episode of the BBC technology program *Tomorrow's World* operating the Demagnitizer: like a DJ, he mixed prerecorded material, manipulating it in time, and even mainstream media understood this as a critical act. "Whereas TV sets torture most intellectuals," the *New York Times* critic John Canaday wrote, "Mr. Paik is an intellectual who tortures TV sets."[32] Though photographs document some of the paces Paik put McLuhan through (a tiny reproduction appeared in a profile of Paik in *TV Guide*),[33] few recordings exist.[34] One is left to consider strategies and techniques: the way the work opens outward toward the viewer's body and invites her to participate. Here, one could literally touch television and convulse its images. The work's sound component, however, followed a different set of rules. Since the magnets did not alter McLuhan's voice, one could listen to his ideas unchanged.

*McLuhan Caged* marks a shift in Paik's practice from a largely abstract vocabulary, which emphasizes the physical properties of television, to work dealing more directly with the manipulation of content (though one might also say it abstracts representation).[35] Either way, it implicitly challenges McLuhan's claim that the medium is the message—that form is total. Paik makes clear that media can be used to different ends depending on how they are used. Television, for example, is not a monolithic, one-way force but one capable of feedback. In the 1966 "Utopian Laser TV Station," Paik, like Warhol, criticized McLuhan for writing books while making predictions about television.

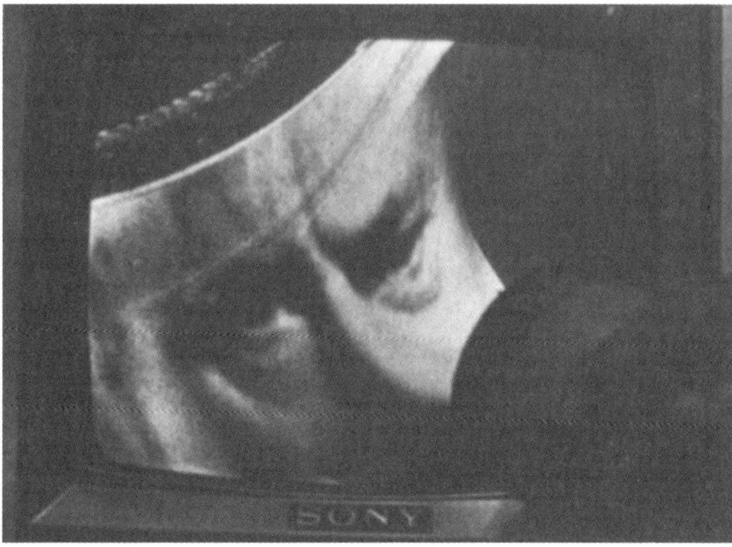

**4.6** Nam June Paik, *McLuhan Caged* (1968). © Nam June Paik Estate. Photo: Peter Moore.

"McLuhan is surely great," he wrote, "but his biggest inconsistency is that he still writes books. He became well-known through books, he doesn't care about the situation, and is excluded from the media for which he evangelizes."[36] If McLuhan wanted to investigate television, Paik suggests, he had to meet it on its own terms. While McLuhan often appeared on TV—in later years he became a TV staple, debating Norman Mailer on the CBC talk show *The Summer Way* in 1968, appearing on Dick Cavett's show in 1970, and discussing Jimmy Carter and Gerald Ford's debate with Tom Brokaw on the *Today Show* in 1976—he grappled with the technology only intellectually.[37] By plunging McLuhan into circuitry, Paik was claiming that the terms of the argument necessarily change when one engages directly with the technology and that McLuhan's message, too, is affected by the medium.

In his catalog essay for Paik's 1968 show, the artist Allan Kaprow, best known as the inventor of happenings, claimed Paik's importance lay in the way his work used simple means to generate profound effects: "Achieved by the flick of a dial, or the manipulation of an electromagnet. Simply and without complication. We can all do it. The movies could never so directly, or so cheaply, or so potentially democratically, engage in the visual fare of everyday life."[38] Laying out a media genealogy, Kaprow claimed that TV has more potential than film because its reception and distribution are easier to affect. Television's final product—the signal that it sends out over the airwaves—is not set in celluloid but remains open to manipulation, allowing one to feed back into the system. Describing TV, in McLuhanesque fashion, as a "medium that seems cool and detached," Kaprow insists that it would be truly participatory only if one could wrest it away from network control. Paik, too, viewed TV as a potentially utopian creative force, if it could be reorganized. Dedicated to thinking about TV in terms of education, he often spoke of an instant global university broadcast across the airwaves.[39] Indeed, his vision of participatory TV serves as a countermodel to network television's hegemonic structure, and many artists after him would seek to make good on such an idea.[40]

In the stills of *McLuhan Caged* in the catalog, McLuhan looks smudged and deformed. Captioned "McLuhan's face in electronic variations," the image is, as Kaprow describes another work from the exhibition, "stretched like Silly Putty, rolling flaccidly into a vortex." Below the stills, Paik appended three pithy statements:

> Marshall McSnob said, "Wind is moving the flag."
>
> Marshall McButterfly said, "Flag is moving the wind."
>
> Marshall McLuhan said, "Your mind is moving."

It is hard to know how to interpret Paik's pet names, though McSnob speaks for itself: McLuhan was too haughty and too removed from his object of study. McButterfly, on the other hand, sounds like 1960s jive, recalling the names of Grateful Dead–adjacent figures such as Pig Pen and Mountain Girl, a sign of McLuhan's hippie tendencies. The first two statements offer something like a theory of media. The formulation "'Wind is moving the flag' . . . 'Flag is moving the wind'" suggests that any analysis of an event depends on one's point of view, implying that either the medium or the message receives priority depending on how you look at it. But the third statement—"Your mind is moving"—cancels the first two. It does not matter whether you see things from the perspective of the wind or that of the flag: what is important is what happens to *you*.

## Process/Politics

Though McLuhan privileged medium over content, he realized that one might appear *in* a medium in ways that were more or less conducive to its form; one could, in other words, go with or against the flow. In "The Timid Giant," the section of *Understanding Media* devoted to television, he addressed the political uses of the TV image by stressing the power of playing it cool (*cool* was a key word in McLuhan's jargon, signifying the possibility of participation). He noted that, in 1960, Richard Nixon's popularity had declined after his debate with John F. Kennedy—the first televised presidential debate—but claimed that his problems had more to do with his image than with his policies. Speaking of Nixon's later appearance on the Jack Paar show (in 1963), he pointed out: "Instead of the slick, glib, legal Nixon, we saw the doggedly creative and modest performer. A few timely touches like this would have quite altered the result of the Kennedy-Nixon campaign."[41] (Nixon's colleagues caught wind of McLuhan's advice and channeled it toward his successful 1968 presidential run. When asked in the March 1969 *Playboy* interview, "Did Nixon take any lessons from you the last time around?" McLuhan responded: "He certainly took lessons from somebody."[42] As Rick Bernstein writes: "The Nixon team deployed McLuhan to sell Nixon—to break the back of the public's conviction, as Roger Ailes put it, that 'he's a bore, a pain in the ass.'")[43] Unlike film, "TV is a medium that rejects the sharp personality," McLuhan concluded. "It favors the presentation of processes rather than products."[44]

*Processes over products.* The phrase alone describes one of the most important shifts in the art of the 1960s—think of the move from Pop art to Postminimalism and Process art—and Paik's *Electronic Opera #1* (1969) takes the idea to an extreme by processing all sorts of televisual material. While Paik frequently described his work in musical terms—he used them as shorthand to describe working *in time*—he almost certainly lifted this particular title from Harold Rosenberg's

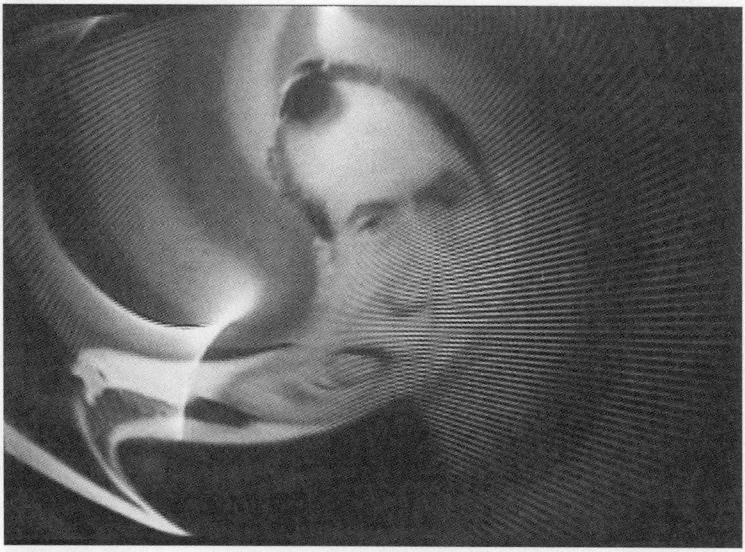

**4.7** Nam June Paik, *Electronic Opera #1* (1969). Courtesy Electronic Arts Intermix (EAI), New York.

review of *Understanding Media*, which claims that McLuhan's "conception of pop culture is no more conventional than an electronic opera."[45] Just as McLuhan inverted standard notions of popular culture, Paik would play television so that its qualities stood out by brushing it against the grain.

*Electronic Opera #1* first aired on Boston's WGBH in 1969 as part of the video art special *The Medium Is the Medium*, which also featured segments by Kaprow, James Seawright, and Aldo Tambellini, among others. The title of the program turns McLuhan's adage into a tautology: message drops out; medium is everything. Paik's segment begins with an announcer introducing the work: "His tools: magnets and junk television sets. His images: three hippies, a dancing model, and national political figures." (The soundtrack is Beethoven's *Moonlight* Sonata.) The video combines tools and images to create distortions, perhaps suggesting what a viewer might do to TV. If McLuhan thought that one had to follow television's flow, Paik demonstrated that one could change its direction, and it is telling that Nixon, who had been inaugurated the thirty-seventh president of the United States that year, serves as Paik's case in point. When a newscaster extols the president's "ability to manage people," Nixon's face enters a vortex, suggesting that TV too is a tool of management. The president's face bends into a torqued shape, much as McLuhan's face had when Paik had "caged" him three years before. One wonders whether Paik knew of McLuhan's influence on Nixon. Is it simply coincidence that he treated the two figures with such similar techniques?

But Nixon is only part of the *Electronic Opera* mix. The work also contains footage of a man and a woman massaging each other, which points to McLuhan's ideas about the tactility of the screen (a topic discussed in chapter 5 below). With Nixon's face in mind, however, bodily activity also looks like a metaphor for political management. Like McLuhan, Paik understood that television addressed the whole body, except that he believed that audiences might genuinely get involved. ("This is Participation TV," the announcer's voice states.) At the same time, he seemed ambivalent about what participation would look like. Should everyone stick magnets to their TV monitors and manipulate information? Or was it easier to refrain from watching television altogether? At the end of the segment, the announcer tells the viewer to "turn off your TV." Perhaps feedback was a fool's errand after all.

Nevertheless Paik's mantra, "Participation TV," served as a riposte to network television's one-way structure. He used the phrase again as the title of his contribution to Wise's 1969 exhibition *TV as a Creative Medium*. Devised from "3 or 4 color TV sets which show multi-color echoes, or fog, or clouds which are electronically produced," *Participation TV* combined footage from network television with a live feed from a closed-circuit camera. By inserting the viewer into the screen, Paik literalized McLuhan's claim that TV was tactile and involving. (Paik's *TV Bra for Living Sculpture* [1969], which Charlotte Moorman wore for a five-hour performance at the opening, made a similar, albeit less subtle, point.) At the same time, the work's emphasis on natural states—air, clouds, fog, and water—suggests that the new electronic world possessed elemental qualities that, in effect, formed a second nature. In many ways, Paik wanted both to tame TV and to acclimate the viewer to a new environment. His project, as he put it in the exhibition catalog, was to "humanize technology and the electronic medium, which is progressing rapidly—too rapidly."[46] Clearly, he found television to be more than a new tool for artists—it was too closely bound to institutional and social structures to be simply that—yet he simultaneously believed artists might affect mass-cultural structures and forms.

Though Paik produced single-channel videos—such as *Global Groove* (1973), a song-and-dance extravaganza, and *Good Morning, Mr. Orwell* (1984)—he did not take the "guerrilla" route of collectives such as TVTV (Top Value Television) and Paper Tiger Television, which turned their cameras on the media to dissonant ends. Nor did he assume the evangelical fervor of other video practitioners, such as Paul Ryan, who saw the technology as a tool of redemption.[47] He largely refused to illuminate the media's conflicts or contradictions by offering independent points of view. Nevertheless, he understood that television was an inherently political force and that it matters who controls it.[48] The properties of the medium varied depending on whose hands it was in. As Raymond Williams stated in an essay on McLuhan: "If the effect of the medium is the same, whoever controls or uses it, and whatever apparent content he may try to insert, then we can forget ordinary political and cultural argument and let the technology run itself."[49] For Paik, control ultimately boiled down to a question of form, not content. Certainly, he did not think technology should run itself—or, if it did, he wanted to bend it. He did not introduce alternative content as much as he reworked and reformulated what was already on the air. McLuhan's work opened the door to such thought. His statements brought awareness of the medium's power—and what might be done with it—but it took artists such as Paik to reveal the implications of those ideas. In the meantime, McLuhan moved beyond television toward an even more encompassing theory of media. He tried to figure out what it did to the body—both the individual and the political body. The code word for this was *massage*.

5

# Massage, ca. 1966

**The poet, the artist, the sleuth—whoever sharpens our perception tends to be antisocial; rarely "well-adjusted," he cannot go along with currents and trends.**
Marshall McLuhan, *The Medium Is the Massage: An Inventory of Effects* (1967)

*Massage* typically refers to a type of therapy performed on the body. Fingers push deep into tired muscles; fists pound on the back. Derived from the French word *masser*, the word appeared in English in the 1860s; the first example cited in the *Oxford English Dictionary* is taken from Donald Maguire's *The Art of Massage: Being a Short Essay on Its Powerful Therapeutic Agency*, published in 1866. But, if massage was originally a therapeutic art performed on a single body, a hundred years later McLuhan described it as a method of mass manipulation. In a lecture delivered on May 7, 1966, at the Ninety-Second Street Y in New York, he announced that his main theme would be "that the medium is the massage, not the message; that it really works us over, it really takes hold and massages the population in a savage way."[1] A couple of months later, in an article published in *Vogue*, McLuhan made a similar point about the power of media. "I have found sometimes that it helps to say 'The medium is the massage,'" he wrote, "because the medium is a complex set of events that roughly handles and works over entire populations. It changes their postures and their outlook."[2] McLuhan codified this idea in his 1967 *The Medium Is the Massage*. Riffing on his widely known dictum "the medium is the message," which entered public consciousness with *Understanding Media* (1964), the book's title extended the stakes of McLuhan's argument by bringing media into direct confrontation with the body—the book's cover pictures a stretched, if smiling, feminine-looking face—as well as the body politic. The media had to be understood through their effects on people, not in terms of their intrinsic traits. If media have physiological effects on solitary bodies, they also mold populations. The age of massage is a mass age.

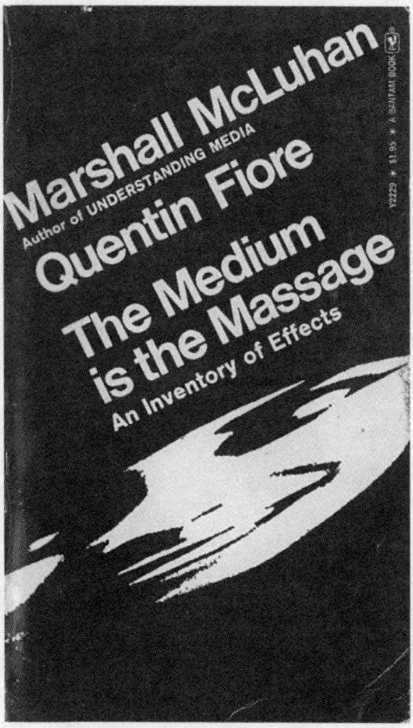


**5.1** Cover of Marshall McLuhan and Quentin Fiore, *The Medium Is the Massage: An Inventory of Effects* (1967).

McLuhan's thesis was novel, but so was its method of presentation. Where his earlier works, such as *The Gutenberg Galaxy* and *Understanding Media*, declared a shift from the mechanical mind-set of typographic man to the interactive reality of an electric community (the so-called global village), they did so as type-centric books, precisely the object whose decline McLuhan forecasted. *Massage* remedied this situation by finding an adequate form for McLuhan's thought. (The graphic designer Quentin Fiore receives equal billing on the book's cover.) Patched together from edited versions of previous writings along with new notes, the book challenges established reading habits by expanding the traditional structure of the book medium for a postliterate youth culture. Bantam published it in a mass-market paperback format small enough to slip into a back pocket.[3] The reader cracks the spine to find novel combinations of word and image, with many full-bleed spreads. Some flash Pop art–style exclamations (a Lichtenstein-like *Bang!* runs alongside a reminder that "the ear favors no particular 'point of view'"), while others indulge in alternate forms of shock value: a picture of a corporate logo printed on an egg yolk or a microchip resting on the tip of a finger. A surfer in a suit and tie makes an appearance, offering "a possible stratagem for understanding our predicament, our electrically-configured whirl." At one point, pictures of thumbs appear to hold open the pages just as the reader's do, drawing attention to the manual form of the book, while another spread delivers text backward: reading it requires the use of a mirror. Strange combinations of picture and caption also appear: A woman's manicured hand is accompanied by the fact that "30 million toy trucks were bought in the U.S. in 1966," while an apothegm from Montaigne—"The thing of it is, we must live with the living"—rests above an image of the avant-garde

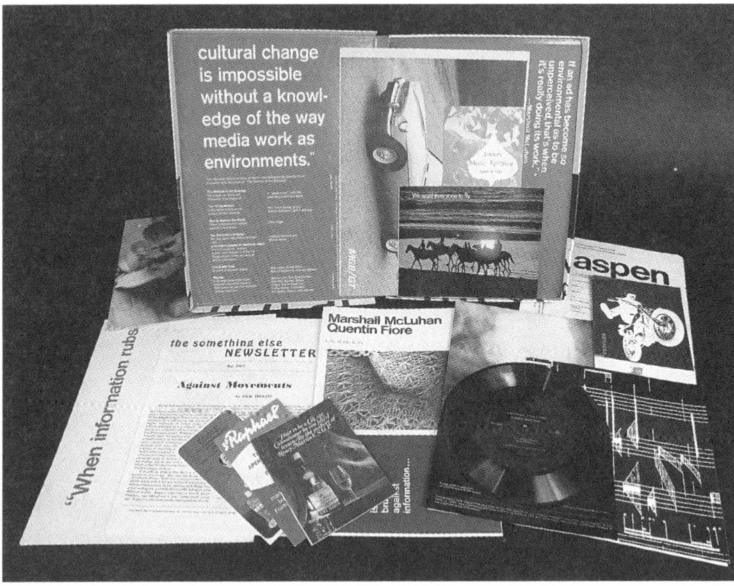


**5.2** Marshall McLuhan and Quentin Fiore, *Aspen*, vol. 4 (1967).

cellist Charlotte Moorman wrapped in plastic. Elsewhere, the book mimics a flip-book. A cinematic spread of photographs—ten pages of nubby toes transforming into a Plymouth car tire—illustrates McLuhan's thesis that the wheel extends from the foot. Image frequently overwhelms text: when text does appear, it sounds more like advertising than academic prose. All in all, the book has a cacophonous feeling—it lurches across a wide variety of cultural production and signifying systems—yet its force remains squarely aimed at the body.

*Massage*, however, was more than a book. Echoing other modern operations, McLuhan and Fiore disseminated their thesis through a variety of media; indeed, this diversity of forms was part and parcel of their message. Early prophets of cross-promotion, they refashioned their book into the fourth issue of *Aspen* magazine, which offered, among other curios, a Gordon Mumma flexirecord, a John Cage poster, page proofs from the *Massage* book, and an ad for Gordon's Gin, all in a neatly designed box.[4] The project later transformed into the documen-

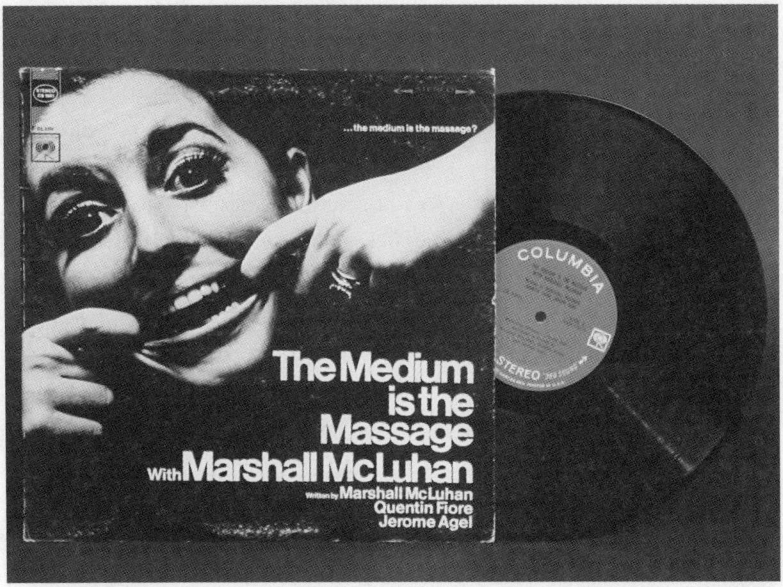


**5.3** Album cover for *The Medium Is the Massage* record (1967).

tary *This Is Marshall McLuhan*, which aired on March 19, 1967, as part of NBC's commercial-free series *Experiment in Television*, a short-lived attempt to stimulate viewers after Sunday football. Directed by Ernest Pintoff, and narrated by the actor Edward Binns, the program incorporated rapid-fire montages, sound effects, Mondrian and Picasso paintings, and a performance by Charlotte Moorman, who plays the cello in a water-filled drum while Nam June Paik looks on. (It is not altogether different in format from the experimental *Picnic in Space* made the same year.) Opening with an image of a flickering light bulb, the program features talking heads drawn exclusively from the art world, including the artists Allan Kaprow and Malcolm Morley, the MoMA curator Ines Garson, and the dealer Ivan Karp. McLuhan presides over it all, and he appears again in *Massage*'s final spin-off, an LP issued by Columbia Records that featured him reading his prose over a sonic landscape of discordant clangs and bangs, backward guitars, and commercial jingles.[5] The album channels an enveloping sense of allatonceness through its use of cut-up sound collage. (It also underscored the importance of auditory space to McLuhan's thought: characterized by disconnection and spontaneity, it eclipsed the continuous linear space of the visual. "We are *enveloped* by sound," McLuhan wrote in *Massage*. "It forms a seamless web around us.")[6] "The record is designed for young people," Jerome Agel, who produced the album, wrote to McLuhan. "It is designed to be a 40-minute interface—it is designed to be heard again and again and again and again and again, like a pop record."[7]

The *Massage* project's full-frontal media blitz, its literal massing of media, is significant given McLuhan's tendency to categorize media as hot or cold. "Hot" visual media, which included print and film, forged identity, while "cold" media, such as TV, encouraged tactility and interactivity. The former, he believed, had given rise to nationalism, while the latter would help bring about the global village.[8] With *Massage*, however, such distinctions were not always so clear: An icy-hot chorus of media buffeted the reader-viewer-listener from all directions. Loaded with similar content, TV, film, books, magazines, and records, all piled on top of one another, formed a kind of mediascape.[9] If different media have distinct qualities and play to divergent parts of the human sensorium, a continuum also exists between them that privileges sensation above all else. Yet McLuhan did not necessarily capitulate to this "post-medium" condition.[10] Instead, *Massage* emphasized the distinctions between media. The book strove for cinematic effects (remember the foot dissolving into the tire); the issue of *Aspen* turned the magazine's sequential order into a random box of things; the NBC documentary, circulated for educational use as a sixteen-millimeter print, hovered somewhere between television and film. The effect was not to deny the differences between media but to underscore them, to draw attention to the particularities of each so as to mark the constructed nature of the media environment. "The moment of the meeting of media is a moment of freedom and release from the ordinary trance and numbness imposed by them on our senses," he wrote in *Understanding Media*.[11] If one could not free oneself from the media's massage, one might at least rub its parts together to see how it came together and, perhaps momentarily, break its powerful trance.

McLuhan always claimed that media extend from "man" and that they could be traced back to human origins: Electric circuitry is an extension of the central nervous system, just as the wheel is an extension of the foot. For McLuhan, the idea of human origin placed people in control, yet, without overtly contradicting this position, *Massage* challenged it with various examples of technologies brutally reconfiguring human beings: The book's opening spread features a US Navy test subject in a wind tunnel, his skin blown back from his eyes and mouth.[12] Perhaps even more disturbing is Peter Moore's double-exposure photograph of a man's face with his ear grafted over his eye. (Importantly, Moore actively photographed happenings and performance art at this moment, which, as we shall see, provided another important realm for sensory testing.)[13] Based on a photograph from László Moholy-Nagy's *Vision in Motion* (1947), the photo suggests a reordered body, a proto-cyborg, with auditory faculties eclipsing visual capacities.[14] If media originally extended from the body, they now turned back on it, reconfiguring it in new ways. "All media work us over completely," McLuhan declares at the book's most programmatic moment. "They are so pervasive in their personal, political, economic, aesthetic, psychological, moral, ethical and social consequences that they leave no part of us untouched, unaffected, unaltered. The medium is the massage. Any understanding of social and cultural change is impossible without a knowledge of the way media work as environments."[15]

Having assumed environmental proportions, media now composed the very world in which one lived. But, instead of viewing the situation fatalistically, McLuhan believed that proper attention might place media back under human control. "There is absolutely no inevitability as long as there is a willingness to contemplate what is happening," he wrote. Through a process of reflection, humans could regain control over media by recognizing their powers in them. That said, McLuhan understood that he was living at a moment of great change and that the status of the human—let alone the human community—was undergoing a seemingly inevitable transformation: "Media, by altering our environment, evoke in us unique ratios of sense perceptions. The extension of any one sense alters the way we think and act—the way we perceive the world. When these ratios change, men change."[16] To his credit, McLuhan sought not so much to preserve past ratios as to calibrate them in a harmonious fashion. His humanism was evolutionary, not essentialist. Humans might be changing, in other words, but would not necessarily go extinct.[17]

## Artists and Antienvironments

"Electric circuitry does not create a Public," McLuhan wrote in *The Medium Is the Massage*. "It creates the mass."[18] Prying the word from its Marxist meaning of "working-class and revolutionary solidarity,"[19] McLuhan sees the mass take shape when electricity joins nervous systems together in a global network. Like Jürgen Habermas, McLuhan equated the public sphere with print, rational detachment, self-reflection, and differing points of view.[20] The mass, on the other hand, an absorbed and involved community prone to nervous reactions, thrives on simultaneity, and contemporary artworks, McLuhan believed, conveyed something of this new social form. "Anti-environments, or countersituations made by artists," he wrote in *Massage*, "provide means of direct attention and enable us to see and understand more clearly."[21] But, as artistic antienvironments visualized the present, he argued, they could also expand to merge with life and dictate its shape. As a result, art would no longer mirror life but manipulate it. It would leave the level of representation to engage the real, or as McLuhan put it: "We approach a time when the total human situation must be considered as a work of art."[22] Capable of shaping life to new ends, the artist "leaves the Ivory Tower for the Control Tower . . . in order to program the environment itself as a work of art."[23] This idea—a renovated version of the avant-gardist mandate to merge art and life—made its way through much futurist thinking at the time. "The future of art seems no longer to lie with the creation of enduring masterworks but with defining alternative cultural strategies," John McHale wrote at the end of his 1967 "The Plastic Parthenon." "The artist defines art less through any intrinsic value of art object than by furnishing new conceptualities of life style and orientation. . . . Life is defined as art."[24] A year later, in his "Systems Esthetics," the writer Jack Burnham concurred, insisting: "[The] emerging art paradigm . . . is fundamentally concerned with

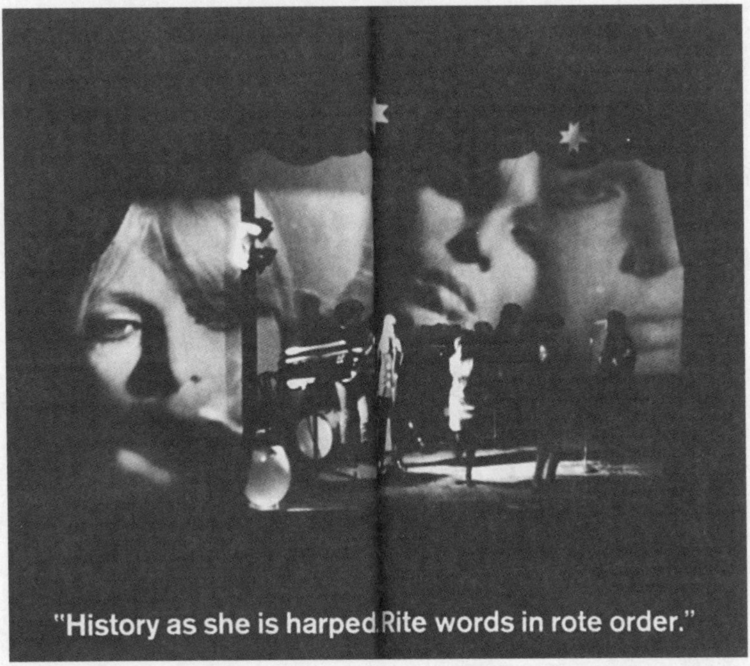


**5.4** Andy Warhol, *Exploding Plastic Inevitable* (1966), in *The Medium Is the Massage*. © 2021 The Andy Warhol Foundation for the Visual Arts, Inc./Licensed by Artists Rights Society (ARS), New York.

the implementation of the art impulse in advanced technological society."[25] Impulses, not objects, would lead the way, and, as art sought to control life, environments would be its new province. "'Art' may soon become a meaningless word," Allan Kaprow declared in 1966. "In its place, 'communications programming' would be a more imaginative label, attesting to our new jargon, our technological and managerial fantasies, and to our pervasive electronic contact with one another."[26]

*Massage* contains a number of projects that point to art's new shape, including Andy Warhol's *Exploding Plastic Inevitable* (*EPI*). Staged with the Velvet Underground in 1966 and 1967, *EPI* incorporated a variety of media technologies, including slide and film projectors, strobe lights, and speakers, creating environments in which people might blend together as a mass under the force of electric lights and amplified sound.[27] In *Massage*, a documentary photograph

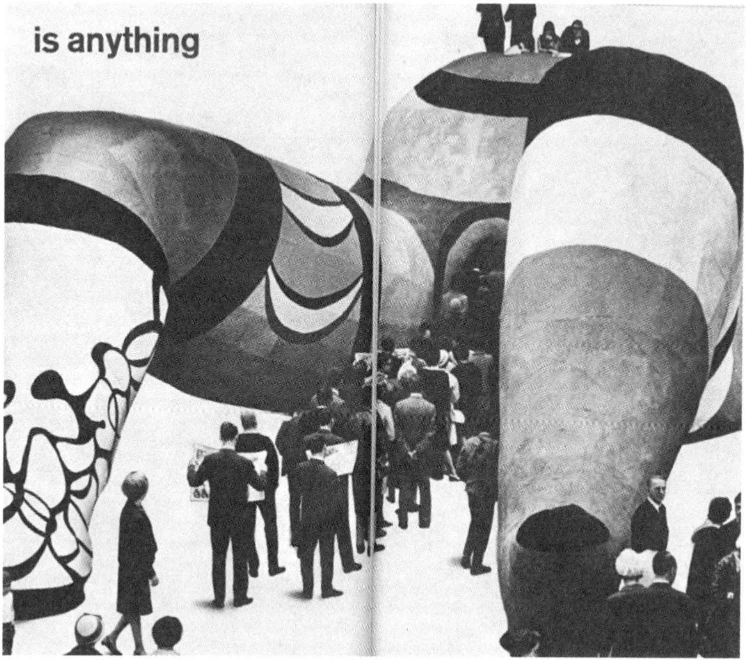


**5.5** Niki de Saint Phalle, *Hon: A Cathedral* (1966), in *The Medium Is the Massage*. 

shows multiple images of the Velvet Underground singer Nico projected on top of the band, suggesting the emergence of a corporate body. (The image's caption—"History as she is harped. Rite words in rote order"—which was borrowed from Joyce, emphasizes the ritual function of these occasions.) For McLuhan, the art historian Branden Joseph writes, "the EPI represented the 'auditory space' of electric media, which . . . was multidirectional, synaesthetic, and interactive."[28] But McLuhan did not endorse such projects without reservation. In the 1968 *Through the Vanishing Point: Space in Poetry and Painting*, written with the artist Harley Parker, he suggests that a "redesign of the so-called 'light shows' so that they cease to be merely bombardment and become probes in the environment would be most beneficial in an educational sense."[29] In other words, new work should not intensify the environment but modify its possibilities. Media already bombard people. The artist has to transfer trauma into rhythm, reprogram shock to salubrious ends.

Another artwork featured in *Massage—Hon: A Cathedral*, the enormous sculpture Niki de Saint Phalle, Jean Tinguely, and Per-Olof Ultvedt created at Stockholm's Moderna Museet in the summer of 1966—came closer to communicating McLuhan's hope. It also continued the tradition of reading technological transformation through a gendered body: *hon* is the Swedish pronoun for *she*. Patched together from wood, tar, paint, fabric, and lots of glue, the sculpture took the form of a tremendous prone woman, featuring a cinema and a milk bar, as well as an automat and a bottle crusher. (A gallery of fakes—ersatz paintings by modern masters—implicitly suggested that *real* art took on new dimensions.) Measuring eighty-two feet in length, and painted in bright bands of color like Saint Phalle's *Nana* sculptures, *Hon* lay in the gallery like a female version of Jonathan Swift's Gulliver. A technological labyrinth, it offers a gendered counterpoint to Hobbes's Leviathan, which creates its population through scepter and sword, in the body of the king. Plump and seemingly pregnant, *Hon* looked like an updated fertility goddess: While visitors entered and exited through the sculpture's vagina, a special spot for lovers, bugged by microphones, stressed an interest in reproduction of all kinds.[30] By calling the work *a cathedral*, however, the artists sanctified such activity. They also evoked a building type that necessarily incorporates various sorts of art making—mosaics here give way to movies—while summoning communal rites: *Hon* was a place for connectivity, communion, and perhaps worship, but it was also a folly, dedicated to pleasure.[31] People showed up en masse to experience this wonder of togetherness: over seventy thousand visitors navigated the work from June 4 to September 4, 1966.[32]

While visitors flocked to the sculpture, its images spread through the press—*Time* ran an article on *Hon* in its June 17, 1966, issue—but most pictured it from outside, leaving its core, where media was most apparent, invisible. (Its dark, grotto-like spaces did not lend themselves to image making in the same way.) Narrative description, however, filled in the gaps. "Entering the animated interior through the more than obvious portal," one review explained, "the visitor passes a goldfish pond with turning mill wheel to encounter a man sitting watching t.v. work by Ultvedt. . . . One may go into the left leg where there is a switchback and exhibit of fake pictures or to a showing of Garbo's first 1922 movie or seek privacy in the 'Banc des Amoreux.' Radio Stockholm supplies the 'sound' environ intermingled with amplified feedback of visitors' comments from various areas."[33] The sculpture was less essentialist icon than jury-rigged cyborg, less mechanical bride than electric lady.[34] Containing TV, film, radio, and telephone, it offered a multisensory environment literally made of media; indeed, it embodied it, made it incarnate. (Ultvedt's sculpture *Man in a Chair* [1966], which depicted said man watching television while receiving a massage, made the point literally.)[35] For McLuhan, *Hon* proved that the electronic age created a new, potentially utopian social body and that art could play a role in its creation. "Art is anything you can get away with," the book's text reads across three pages depicting *Hon*, pointing to an expanded field of possibilities. Unlike mechanization, which fastened Taylorized bodies to a factory line, *Hon*'s electric technologies favored an open score that invited the viewer to participate. "Electric technology has transformed the nature of the audience," McLuhan wrote in 1966. "The audience becomes eligible for custom-made servicing instead of uniform packaging. . . . The audience itself becomes an actor in the show."[36]

But, if McLuhan found something empowering in this new body—and Saint Phalle, too, suggested that, appearing amid feminism's first wave, *Hon* served the movement's ends—others found cause for concern despite the admonition painted on the sculpture's leg: *Honi soit qui mal y pense* (May he be shamed who thinks badly of it). Writing for the left-wing magazine *Ramparts*, the critics Arthur Secunda and Jan Thunholm portrayed *Hon* as a symbol of degradation: "*She* is double for we, flat on our backs in primeval position, victimized, helplessly mauled over, laughed at, exploited and used, painted as we paint ourselves, objectified as we find ourselves objects, and in a sense laughing on the outside while we are dying on the inside."[37] Less a site of pleasure than a zone of control and entanglement, *Hon* represented proof of manipulation, if not torture. The media's massage had transformed the social body into a sedate subject, not an empowered audience. *Hon* seemed to put a rosy face on a dire condition.

## *Massage*

**I am also anatomizing the work of art.** Claes Oldenburg, *Raw Notes* (1973)

Despite his hopes that the artist in the control tower (less a panopticon than a media thermostat) might shape art as life for the greater good, many artists read McLuhan against the grain, pointing to the dangers of the media environment. Claes Oldenburg's happening *Massage*, staged at the Moderna Museet on October 3, 4, 6, and 7, 1966, as part of the artist's solo exhibition, is one such example.[38] Significantly, the work took place immediately after Saint Phalle's *Hon* came down; in fact, Oldenburg arrived in Stockholm during *Hon*'s last days and briefly worked in its shadow. "I saw the citizens go in and come out," Oldenburg wrote, evoking the language of the body politic. "That seemed to me to move things forward a little. More Body-Art always helps." But, for Oldenburg, *Hon*'s most significant part was not its interactivity but its destruction. "I wish that those who saw and enjoyed *Hon* whole could have watched her being taken apart," he wrote. "Three months: Birth/Life/Death."[39] (In the *Hon* catalog, Oldenburg is pictured wandering around the wreckage.)

Death was central to Oldenburg's performance. The artist arrived in the city with only a vague idea for a happening and subsequently gathered inspiration from newspapers and current events. At the time of his arrival in Stockholm, the newspaper *Aftonbladet* ran an article about the late nineteenth-century Swedish murderer John Filip Nordlund, who had killed four people on a ferry. Oldenburg originally planned to stage *Massage* aboard a boat in Stockholm's harbor—his early notes describe the work as a piece of "physical theater for passengers on board a ship"—but, owing to logistic reasons, he moved his production to the museum's exhibition hall. His plan to present the work on a ship, however, suggests a desire to contain a social body and subject it to murderous forces—an antipode, perhaps, to *Hon*'s dreams of free movement.[40] (Tellingly, in an article published in 1967, he referred to *Hon* as a "colossal doll" that was as "big as a ship.")[41] He went so far as to imagine himself as a Nordlund-like figure. "Reading about the

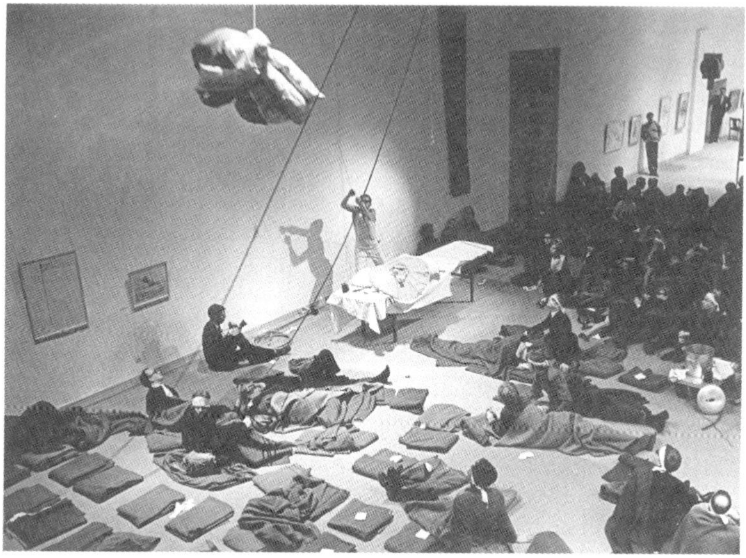

**5.6** Claes Oldenburg, *Massage* (1966). Moderna Museet, Stockholm.

murderer Nordlund," he wrote in his notes. "How he researched the ship where he intended to commit this berserk [*sic*] I realized I must do this too."[42]

Just as Oldenburg figured the artist as menace, *Massage* antagonistically broke down the boundary between performance and audience. Since the early 1960s, Oldenburg had been engaged in what he called "sensuous theater," in which the viewer figured as a kind of prop. "It is a theater of physical effects," he told Richard Kostelanetz in a 1968 interview. "There is a lot of ripping and tearing and squeezing and crushing and, also, falling 'bodies' which exhibit a sculptor's attraction for the effect of gravity. It is also a way to make objects of the players."[43] In his notes for the Stockholm performance, the artist continued to imagine audience members as "objects" by stripping them of subjective qualities. "There is no question of the spectators creating the piece (there never has been)," he wrote in his notebook,[44] refusing ideas of interactivity and participation in an implicit riposte to McLuhan's claim that "the audience becomes actor" in the electronic age.[45] "They are however at the center of the piece, a part of the scenery. This comes from a

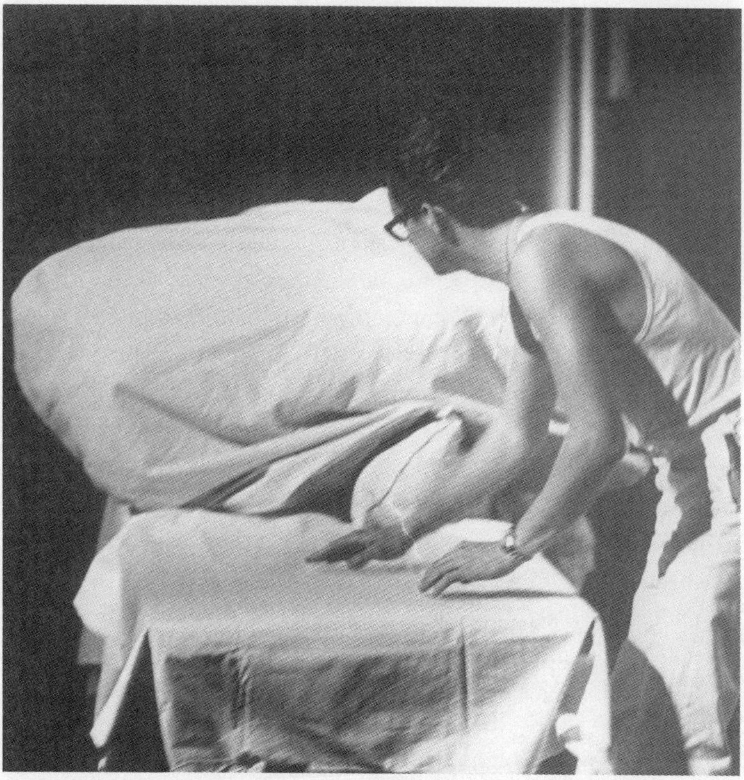

**5.7** Claes Oldenburg, *Massage* (1966). Moderna Museet, Stockholm.

recognition that they are as much 'objects' as the chairs they sit in. Their thoughts and their feelings may also be considered 'objects.'"[46] Viewers did not sit safely outside the action, in other words, nor could they offer a helping hand. Rather, they served as material for the artist to control. In the Stockholm performance, after filing into the gallery, each participant received a blindfold and a hot dog and were pointed toward a blanket on the floor, which Oldenburg compared to "fresh 'graves'" in a "cemetery."[47] Though difficult to reconstruct from notes and photographs, the forty-five-minute performance involved the hoisting of Oldenburg's soft sculptures and various actions carried out by a cast of characters that included a masseuse, a mailman, a nurse, and a bear. (In one image, the masseuse can be seen spreading out a fresh white sheet on a table.) But the happening's most notable aspect was also its least visible: the amplified sound of pounding typewriter keys grew steadily louder—a tape recording of Oldenburg composing his notes for the catalog.[48] "Typewriter is a way of speaking by sound," the artist wrote somewhat paradoxically in his notes for the work, as if speaking were a silent activity.[49] But, by recording and amplifying the typewriter, Oldenburg pushed a technology typically associated with the visual and the mechanical into the field of the aural and the electronic so as to create a spatialized and inescapable concrete poetry.[50] ("The magnified sound of a typewriter made it seem like a battlefield," the artist later explained to the critic Suzi Gablik.)[51] Clearly, he wanted to push senses to their limit, to shove one over into the other. The volume was turned up to intolerable levels. It was clearly an assault. In a strange synchronicity with the Nordlund affair, Oldenburg mentions that at the time of the happening "a sensational murder occurred in the city in which a man was beaten to death with a typewriter."[52]

Oldenburg ostensibly chose the title for his happening because of Sweden's association with massage, but a connection with McLuhan is inescapable. In his performance notes, Oldenburg asked a number of McLuhanesque questions ("Is electronics different from mechanism?"), jotted down McLuhanesque terms ("body electric"), and, like McLuhan, riffed on the word *massage*, transforming it into *massacre* and, in a number of instances, separating the letters to spell out "MASS AGE."[53] A year before the performance, Oldenburg had recorded a similarly McLuhanesque experiment in his journal: "Summer 1965. Drowning myself in media. Thirty dollars of magazines a week, all kinds, and leaving TV and radio (three) on all day also living a life of conversation in the midst. At dinner, eating and talking while reading four different magazines and watching TV and listening to the radio . . . all senses employed."[54] Note the evocative combination of body and media here: "all senses employed." Oldenburg's experiment is, in fact, quite similar to McLuhan's multimedia *Massage* project, yet it is worth noting that the artist pushes McLuhan's thought into other registers. "Though this term [*massage*] was just then associated with McLuhan," Oldenburg later wrote, "I felt my response personal enough to accept it as the title."[55] Indeed, in his play on the word, he takes it to a darker space, in one example manipulating it until he spells "Masoch," an allusion to the nineteenth-century writer Leopold von Sacher-Masoch, who gave masochism its name.[56] According to his notes, an alternate title for the performance had been "*MASSAGE (DRIVEIN BATTLEFIELD) MASSACRE*," but he changed it in the end, perhaps not wanting to spell things out too clearly. Yet the idea, Oldenburg felt, came out all the same. "At times the battlefield metaphor (which was not as consciously intended as it appeared to be) became embarrassingly direct, unambiguous," he says at the end of his notes.[57] That was his final thought on the performance: He was embarrassed by its fatalistic tone. In the end, massage *was* a massacre. If McLuhan believed that human awareness might spare one from the worst of the media's effects, Oldenburg figured the media's massage as triumphant, marking less a transition in the status of the human than its demise.

Yet Oldenburg also understood massage as a therapeutic activity, a form of shock treatment for the population at large. He, too, wanted to shake people out of their stupor. "People say that I'm against the audience, but that's not true at all," he said in a 1964 interview. "I wish to lead the audience into a special way of looking at things."[58] In 1968, he clarified his position when Kostelanetz asked whether his work demonstrated "a tendency to brutalize the audience—to make it feel uncomfortable." "It's really not to hurt them but to make them feel their bodies more," he responded.[59] This emphasis on bodily feeling cut across a wide range of cultural practices at the time. In her 1965 "One Culture and the New Sensibility," Susan Sontag describes "a new non-literary culture" to which Oldenburg certainly belonged: "Western man may be said to have been undergoing a massive sensory anesthesia (a concomitant of the process that Max Weber calls 'bureaucratic rationalization') at least since the Industrial Revolution, with modern art functioning as a kind of shock therapy for both confounding and unclosing our senses."[60] Such shock would not necessarily be pleasurable, Sontag made clear ("Having one's sensorium challenged or stretched hurts"), but it would ultimately prove palliative.[61] If McLuhan imagined that the media's massage extended the human into new forms (i.e., the electric body emblematized by *Hon*), Oldenburg and Sontag understood artistic practice as an antidote—the art of massage might return us to our senses. It was a kind of alarm clock or wake-up call. (Oldenburg explained his Stockholm exhibition in terms of sleep and awakening. "There was this obsession with sleep," he told Suzi Gablik, "as if the whole exhibition had sleep as the dominant metaphor. First the *Bedroom*, and then the *Light Switches* you could turn on and off.")[62] Massage functioned at this moment as a code word for human transformation, regardless of how one read its effects. With roots in therapy, it spoke of anxiety. As we will see in the following chapter, McLuhan and others sought to get a handle on this media environment by seeing it in terms of information.

6

# Information Environment

**It is not tangible.** Robert Barry (1970)

*McLuhan Caged* resurfaced a few months after Paik's Bonino show in *The Machine as Seen at the End of the Mechanical Age*, which opened at New York's Museum of Modern Art (MoMA) in November 1968.[1] Curated by Pontus Hultén, the exhibition offered an encyclopedic survey of the machine, reformatting in spatial form McLuhan's ideas about the passage from the mechanical to the electronic age.[2] Beginning with iconic works by Duchamp, including both the *Nude* and the *Bride*, and moving up through Rauschenberg's *Oracle* (1965), an orchestra of radio-controlled contraptions made in collaboration with the engineer Billy Klüver, it surveyed a wide swath of American and European art from the first half of the twentieth century, including Constructivist, Dadaist, Futurist, and Vorticist works. Nonart objects also appeared, ranging from eighteenth-century automatons, such as Jacques Vaucanson's duck (1733–34) and Pierre Jaquet-Droz's young writer (ca. 1770) to recent racecars.[3] The exhibition's coda consisted of collaborative works by members of Experiments in Art and Technology (EAT). The artist Robin Parkinson and the engineer Eric Martin contributed a hairy *Toy-Pet Plexi-Ball* (1968) stuffed with electronics (it rolled away from you when clapped your hands), while another artist-engineer team supplied a Duchampian computer graphic of a reclining female nude. Jean Dupuy and Ralph Martel's *Heart Beats Dust* offered a stethoscope connected to a prone speaker. Encased in a red-lit vitrine, the mechanism kept time with the viewer's pulse, releasing bilious clouds of colored powder in sync with heartbeats.[4] EAT members contributed so many works, in fact, that a second exhibition, *Some More Beginnings*, was held at the Brooklyn Museum.[5]

In his review of the *Machine* exhibition, the critic Max Kozloff

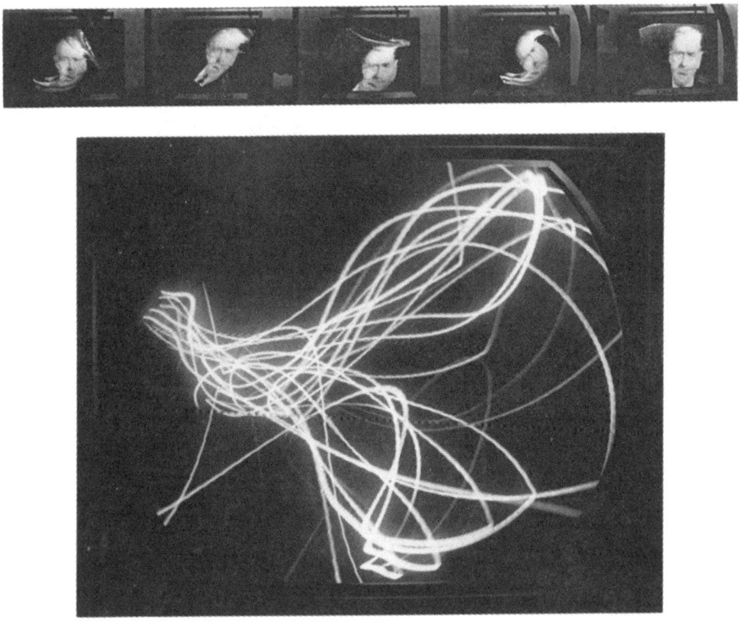

**Nam June Paik.** Korean, born 1932
*McLuhan Caged.* 1967
Video tape recorder, 27×16″
Shadow-mask color television screen, stereo tape recorder and amplifier, 35×25″
+ √ *Rondo Electronique.* 1966—1968
Bonino Gallery, New York, and Howard Wise Gallery, New York

Paik's manipulation of the TV set has the subtle brutality of judo, which turns someone's own force against himself. It is a direct frontal attack on the principal modern machine for manipulating men's minds for commercial or ideological reasons. Paik's counter-terrorism is, of course, based on ridicule.

Born in Seoul, Paik graduated in aesthetics from the University of Tokyo; studied music, art history, and philosophy in Germany; and since 1958 has been doing experimental work in electronic music in Germany and the United States. In 1965, he participated in John Cage's "Variation No. 5 with Electronic Television" at Philharmonic Hall, New York.

Only someone who had been deeply involved with the possibilities of the television medium could handle it with such precision. Paik has, in fact, a great faith in TV:

*Someday artists will work with capacitors, resistors & semi-conductors as they work today with brushes, violins and junk.*[161]

*I have treated cathode ray tube (TV screen) as a canvas, and proved that it can be a superior canvas. From now on, I will treat the cathode ray as a paper and pen .... If Joyce lived today, surely he would have written "Finnegan's Wake" on videotape, because of the vast possibility of manipulation in magnetic information storage.*[162]

197

**6.1** Nam June Paik, *McLuhan Caged*, in *The Machine as Seen at the End of the Mechanical Age*. © Nam June Paik Estate.

saw the EAT projects as part of "a very business-like generation of machined art, or rather, arty machines" that made little concession to either "Dada irony" or "messianic Constructivism."[6] The relationship between art and technology was taking a new shape, and Kozloff thought it looked a lot like business. In this context, Paik's work was something of an outlier, appearing in a darkened room that emphasized the eerie light of the "shadow mask" screen. Hultén, too, found Paik's work more critical than other contributions to the show. "Paik's manipulation of the TV set has the subtle brutality of judo, which turns someone's own force against himself," the catalog stated. "It is a direct frontal attack on the principal modern machine for manipulating men's minds for commercial or ideological reasons. Paik's counter-terrorism is, of course, based on ridicule."[7]

If Paik's work ridiculed television, much of the exhibition offered an elegy for the machine. "This exhibition is dedicated to the mechanical machine, the great creator and destroyer, at a difficult moment in its life when, for the first time, its reign is threatened by other tools," Hultén wrote in the catalog.[8] The exhibition served a retrospective function, in other words, placing the machine squarely in the past. "The Museum of Modern Art exhibition appealed to the sentiment of yesterday," Harold Rosenberg wrote in his *New Yorker* review, "Past Machines, Future Art." "It also endeavored, however, to link itself to the future—to what must, I suppose, be called the post-mechanical era of technology. Dr. Hultén seemed disappointed in the machine but hopeful about its electronic successor (this again seems to carry a tinge of the McLuhan state of mind)."[9] If the machine, safely in the past, now appeared alternately whimsical and brutal, the electronic future seemed to hold brighter possibilities.

## Information

As Rosenberg suggested, McLuhan made a big impression at MoMA during this period, and two years later, in 1970, the exhibition *Information* opened, offering a sequel to *The Machine*, and also owing a debt to McLuhan's thought.[10] Seventeen issues of *The McLuhan* DEW-LINE newsletter, a mailer for corporate types, appear in the *Information* files, while the catalog's bibliography lists four books by McLuhan, making him the most cited thinker after Claude Lévi-Strauss, the French anthropologist.[11] His influence, however, manifested in other ways, too: certainly, the design of the exhibition, which encouraged interactivity and participation, owed something to McLuhan's work with his colleague Harley Parker. While McLuhan did not originate information theory—the Bell Labs engineer Claude Shannon introduced the topic in 1948—it had long been a cornerstone of his thought. In *Understanding Media*, he insisted that new media ushered in an age of information: "When IBM discovered that it was not in the business of making office equipment or business machines, but that it was in the business of processing information, then it began to navigate with clear vision."[12] Some two years later, in 1966, he claimed that it is "the environment itself that is made of information," attributing a new identity to nature.[13] More and more, the world was knit together by a system of interconnected computers, and, while this infrastructure was crucial, it was the circulation of information between these stations that made machines important. Such theories quickly made their way through the art world, dovetailing with advances in conceptual art. The artist Dan Graham, for example, included a gloss on McLuhan's work in his 1967 text "Information" alongside descriptions of the Symbolist poet Stéphane Mallarmé and the Pop artist Roy Lichtenstein, and these ideas informed many of his key early works, which tabulated information in different ways. In *Information*, Graham was represented by a text work, *March 31, 1966*, which measured the artist's distance from eleven different sites, from the "edge of known universe" to "retinal wall."[14]

Curated by Kynaston McShine, *Information* surveyed new tendencies in conceptual art on an international scale. For McShine, the kernel of conceptualism lay in global communications. "Those represented are part of a culture that has been considerably altered by communications systems such as television and film, and by increased mobility," he explained. "Therefore, photographs, documents, films, and ideas, which are rapidly transmitted, have become an important part of this new work." Though certain works in the exhibition directly engaged political questions—Hans Haacke's *MoMA Visitor's Poll* asked visitors whether Governor Nelson Rockefeller's position on Vietnam would affect whether they voted for him in the next election, with each vote counted by a photoelectric sensor—the use of communications media was often portrayed as political in and of itself owing to its negation of the artwork's traditional object status.[15] Vito Acconci had his mail delivered directly to the museum, while Walter De Maria enlarged a

1969 *Time* magazine article about himself ("High Priest of Danger") and hung it on a gallery wall so as to make clear that secondary information was of primary importance. To make her *Context #7*, Adrian Piper simply provided blank sheets of paper for visitors to record their impressions. Beanbags were scattered around the floor. Despite the low-key nature of these gestures, McShine insisted that such work properly expressed current political anxieties. "If you are an artist in Brazil, you know of at least one friend who is being tortured; if you are one in Argentina, you probably have had a neighbor who has been in jail for having long hair, or for not being 'dressed' properly; and if you are living in the United States, you may fear that you will be shot at, either in the universities, in your bed, or more formally in Indochina," he wrote. "It may seem too inappropriate, if not absurd, to get up in the morning, walk into a room, and apply dabs of paint from a little tube to a square of canvas. What can you as a young artist do that seems relevant and meaningful?"[16] Working with information, McShine suggested, was more appropriate than moving paint around on canvas, tied as that process was to contemporary notions of power. This, too, paid a debt to McLuhan, who, in 1954, claimed that information refashioned politics, serving as a new tool for capitalism and imperialism. "Formerly we invaded foreign markets with goods," he reasoned. "Today we invade whole cultures with packaged information, entertainment, and ideas."[17] Perhaps, McShine implied, if artists took hold of information, they could launch a counterinvasion and bring people together in different ways. Certainly, the catalog's endpapers, filled with photographs from the 1963 March on Washington, connect the politics of information to the dream of a radical audience.

The catalog accompanying *Information* proved central to the exhibition, just as the catalog accompanying *Machine* two years prior had done for that show; their respective designs mirrored chapters of McLuhan's thought.[18] Where *Machine*'s embossed tin cover produced by a Swedish beer-can manufacturer depicts Philip Johnson's steely 1964 East Wing extension to MoMA with a taxicab sitting in front, *Information* sports a paperback jacket outfitted with Ben Day–dotted images of communications media: phone, typewriter, television, computer, and car.[19] (At 8.5 × 11 inches, its pages match the dimensions of

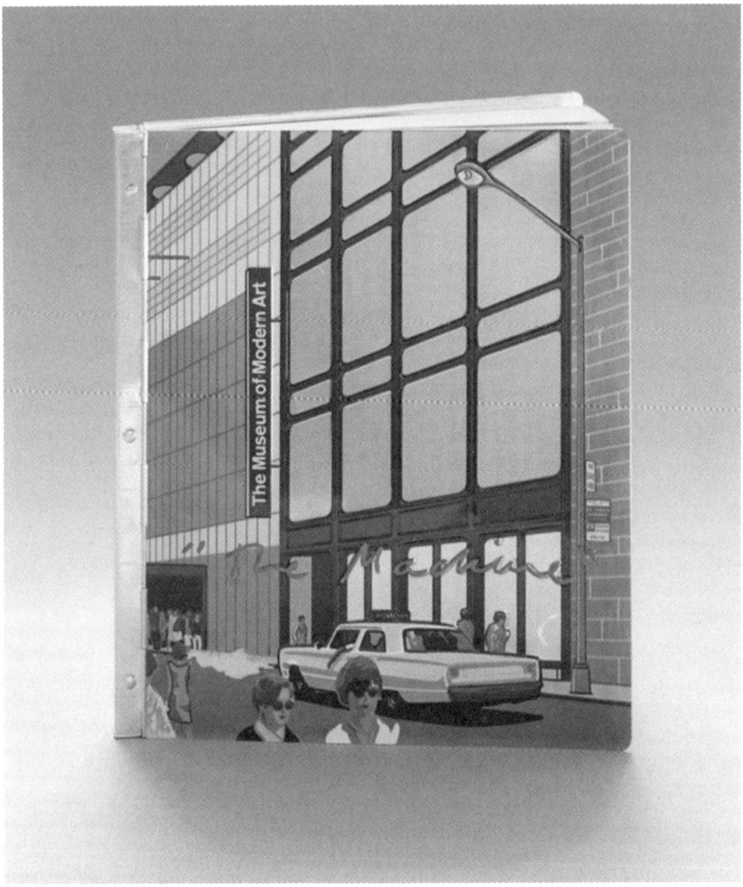


**6.2** Cover of *The Machine as Seen at the End of the Mechanical Age* (1968). Stamped on aluminum, printed in color, 9.75 × 8.5 inches (MS85). The Museum of Modern Art, New York. Digital Image © The Museum of Modern Art/Licensed by SCALA/Art Resource, NY.

a standard sheet of office paper.) Interestingly, the *Information* catalog also pushed back at McLuhan. "Contrary to the McLuhan thesis," McShine wrote, "books are still a major communications system, and perhaps becoming even more important, given 'the global village' that the world has become. After all *Time* magazine is available almost everywhere on Wednesday mornings."[20] Certainly, McLuhan knew the importance of *Time*, and, contrary to popular opinion, he did not

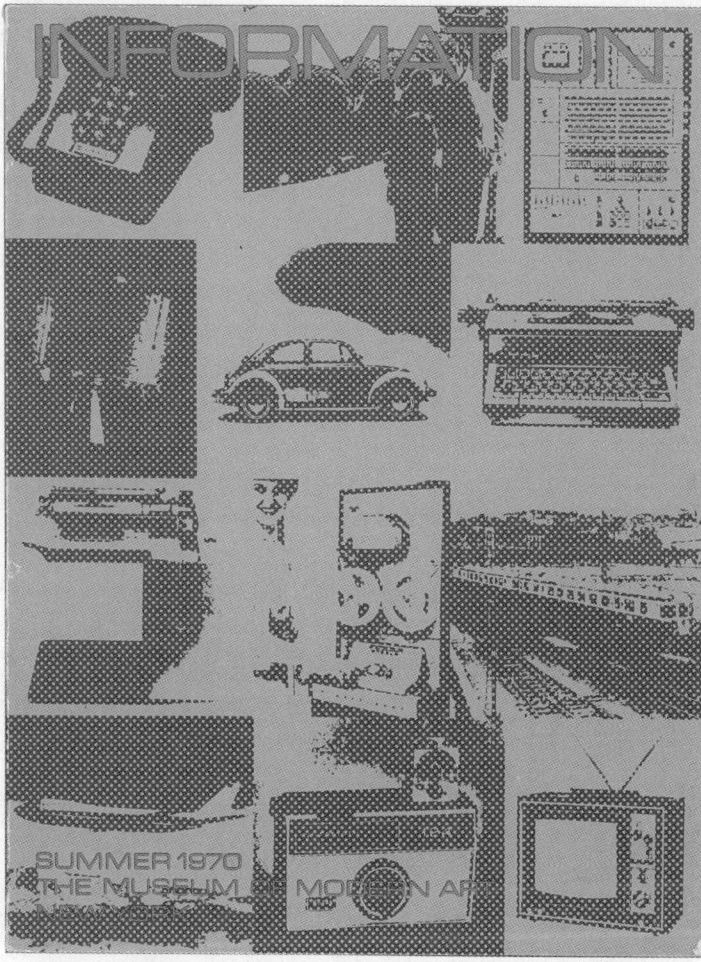


**6.3** Cover of *Information* (1970). Offset, printed in color, 10.75 × 8.25 inches. The Museum of Modern Art Library, New York. Digital Image © The Museum of Modern Art/Licensed by SCALA/Art Resource, NY.

dismiss the importance of books. (Indeed, he wrote a great number of them.) His theory of new media did not depend on the extinction of old ones. Rather, he saw that new media frequently carried older ones into the future, transforming them in the process. He examined how the book changed under the latest regime of technological reproducibility. He even planned a publication (which never materialized) on "the future of the book" with the publisher William Jovanovich to survey the impact of Xerography, which he believed would decentralize publishing and allow for a "tailor-made or custom-built service for the individual."[21] "Xerography makes the reader both author and publisher in tendency," McLuhan wrote. "The highly centralized activity of publishing naturally breaks down into extreme decentralism when anybody can, by means of xerography, assemble printed, or written, or photographic materials which can be supplied with soundtracks."[22]

Conceptual art used copying devices in similar ways. Seth Siegelaub's *The Xerox Book*, produced in 1968, seamlessly melds work and its reproduction—there is no original, one might say.[23] Featuring contributions by seven artists, including Carl Andre, Robert Barry, and Lawrence Weiner, the project served simultaneously as both exhibition and catalog, bound and ready to travel. While some artists employed the photocopier to replicate identical pages—Robert Morris contributed twenty-five images of a foggy earth—Andre's copies grow sequentially across the edition: the first page of his section features a single square, the last page twenty-five. Others, such as Joseph Kosuth, who offered a list of the project's technological components, insisted on the importance of ostensibly secondary considerations—all the work that goes on behind the scenes. McLuhan's ideas influenced many corners of art publishing at this moment, helping artists understand the book as a viable form of art. Ian Burn, a member of the British conceptual collective Art and Language, later wrote that "the 1960s were a time when Marshall McLuhan was widely read," which "led many artists into publishing their own books and journals, and to adopt that form as the primary outlet for their ideas and art."[24] A book, after all, transmits information more effectively than does painting or sculpture. As the art historian Anne Wagner writes: "Printed art travels fast."[25]

## *Counterblast* II

In 1969, a year before *Information*, McLuhan returned to *Counterblast* (1954), republishing it with Harcourt, Brace and World. After all these years, he was still blasting back at Lewis. At the height of his fame at this moment, he needed to produce material to meet demand, but *Counterblast* also made more sense some fifteen years later. Its claims about technological art resonated in a new way. For the updated edition, McLuhan's colleague the artist Harley Parker reorganized the original copy according to a new graphic regime. Gone are the blocky letters of Lewis's draft, mimicked by McLuhan in his earlier version. Now the fonts have a gee-whiz quality about them—words twist in spirals, and sentences turn into squiggly lines—with everything in a rush to announce its own hilarity. The large format of the first *Counterblast* was reduced to a size that could be easily held in the hand—it is clearly a book meant to be read on the go.

While most of the text is faithful to the original, the changes suggest important shifts in McLuhan's thought, especially in regards to the computer—a technology he first contemplated in the early 1960s.[26] In 1954 McLuhan had written: "The city is obsolete. Ask the military."[27] He now told the reader: "Ask the computer."[28] (Of course, the military was crucial to the computer's development, but now he addressed the root of the matter.) The city had always been under siege in his thought—it was antiquated even in 1954—but now the reasons for its demise lay elsewhere. For McLuhan, the computer represented something fundamentally new. "Perhaps our survival (certainly our comfort and happiness) depends upon our recognizing the nature of our new environment," he declared. "It is sometimes blamed on the computer, which we have the habit of calling a 'machine.'"[29] The computer was dangerous, in other words, only because it was not properly understood. One had to use language correctly in order to grasp it: the computer is not a mechanical device but an information-processing system. Ultimately, it would be at the center of the control room that the artist had to enter, leading the path to environmental management.

Writing some ten years later, in 1978, Jean-François Lyotard tied the computer to the advent of what he called "the postmodern condition." "The miniaturization and commercialization of machines is already changing the way in which learning is acquired, classified, made available, and exploited," he wrote. "The nature of knowledge cannot survive unchanged within this context of general transformation. It can

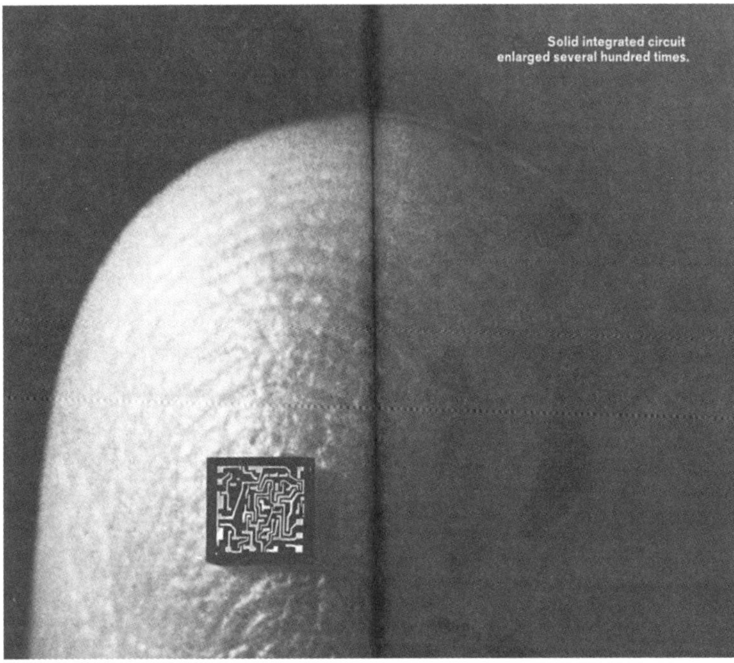


**6.4** Spread from Marshall McLuhan and Quentin Fiore, *The Medium Is the Massage*.

fit into new channels, and become operational, only if learning is translated into qualities of information."[30] Though Lyotard focuses on the structure of knowledge and education, his views resemble McLuhan's thoughts on urbanism and the environment: the arrival of a system of free-flowing information fundamentally restructures the organization of life. Such new utilities had already rendered the city irrelevant: one no longer had to sit in a building next to another building to hear the latest news. McLuhan suggested as much in the first *Counterblast* when he blessed "the TELEVISION TOWER on Jarvis St. elegant scoffer at Toronto's architecture," but the computer took things to the next level—a fact made clear when the Jarvis Street tower, constructed in 1952, was demolished some fifty years later. (It was upstaged by the massive CN Tower in 1976.) The scale of McLuhan's thought had always surpassed architecture; the computer simply made the point emphatic. "I think the computer is admirably suited to the artistic programming of such an environment, of taking over the task of programming the environment itself as a work of art," he wrote in the 1967 issue of *Perspecta*, the Yale architectural journal.[31] In his view, the computer kills architecture, replacing buildings with a managed media environment. One of McLuhan's gifts was his ability to think big and small at the same time, to limn the connection between the macro and the micro. The microchip sitting on the tip of a human finger in *The Medium Is the Massage* promises a key to a new world.

## Software

Unsurprisingly, people thinking about the computer and art at this moment thought about McLuhan too, and perhaps no one did so more than Jack Burnham, an *Artforum* critic who mounted the exhibition *Software: Information Technology: Its New Meaning for Art* at New York's Jewish Museum in 1970.[32] (In many ways, the exhibition served as a companion to MoMA's *Information*.) While Burnham had laced his writing with McLuhanesque ideas for some time, *Software* crystallized his thinking. "For McLuhan, reality is more than the immediate environment," he wrote in his 1970 "Alice's Head: Reflections on Conceptual Art." "It is extended by 'field space' or all the electronic devices that provide global awareness."[33] The concept of software surpassed vision and provided a model for how one might program the environment as a work of art. In thinking about the computer's implications for art, one had to gauge the computer's effects in a novel way. Building something that looked like a computer (as Edward Kienholz did for his contribution to *Machine* exhibition, *The Friendly Grey Computer—Star Gauge Model 54* [1965]) did not say much about the computer's potential repercussions. For Burnham, a computer's hardware was less important than its software—programming was key—and art was now to function like software: an invisible component that programmed larger systems. Like McLuhan, Burnham, too, had fantasies of merging art and life. "Once esthetics is removed from the tidy confines of the Art World," he wrote in his 1967 "Systems Esthetics," "it becomes infused with ethical, political, and biological implications that are overwhelming but nevertheless critical." The goal was to get "esthetics into budgets," not "finished products."[34] As such, art would step outside its traditional realms. This is one version of what the end of art looked like in the late 1960s: aesthetics breaking out of the museum and fusing with administered life.

Burnham insisted that this new paradigm made little distinction between art and nonart, and his closest collaborators in the *Software* exhibition came from the fields of architecture and science. Nicholas Negroponte, along with his Architecture Machine Group at the Massachusetts Institute of Technology, created a gerbil habitat consisting of silvered cardboard blocks that were moved by animal and machine alike (a computer-managed arm occasionally descended on the scene, rearranging the blocks as if the device were an arcade game).[35] The Smith-Kettlewell Institute for Visual Sciences supplied the Vision Substitution System, a kitted-out wheelchair equipped with devices intended to give the blind a way to see, allowing the visitor to grasp, according to the critic Grace Glueck, "visual patterns by means of vibrations produced on his back."[36] A group of "whiz kids" from Princeton, New Jersey, calling themselves RESISTORS (Radically Emphatic Students Interested in Science, Technology and Other Research Studies) helped artists realize various projects, yet technical difficulties plagued the show. (The plan to take the exhibition to the Smithsonian Institution in Washington, DC, was scrapped, perhaps ironically, owing to malfunctioning hardware.) Other artists made rather low-tech or do-it-yourself contributions: for his *Variable Piece No. 4* Douglas Huebler collected secrets from museumgoers, while the poet David Antin's *Conversation Room* prompted visitors to tell stories that were then recorded and played back. (While many entries in Huebler's project were confessional in nature—"I am a megalomaniac," "I have masturbated," "I love Mark"—others engaged directly with the theme of the exhibition. "The paper is software," one visitor wrote. "Software is the medium. The medium is the message. All messages are garbage. Garbage is waste but meaningful.")[37] Allan Kaprow videotaped professional painters repainting one of the museum's hallways over and over again and played the footage at local cinemas, including an art house, a porn palace, and a middlebrow theater. John Giorno ran a guerrilla radio station for poetry and

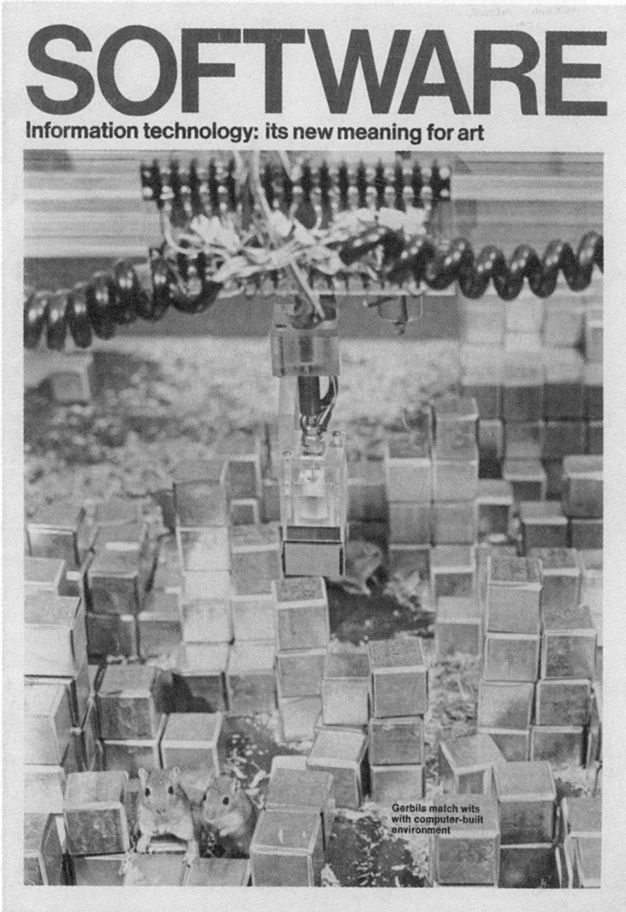


**6.5** Cover of *Software: Information Technology: Its New Meaning for Art* (1970). © Harry Shunk and John Kender. The Jewish Museum, New York. Photo: The Jewish Museum, New York/Art Resource, NY.

instructed others how to set up their own. Deeply dependent on language, and made of tape, video, and radio, the art was not wholly in the galleries; its spirit seeped out into networks and narratives.

Perhaps not surprisingly *Software*, like *Information*, paid special attention to its catalog. The curators originally hoped to create a vinyl-covered loose-leaf binder in which the viewer could gather "personalized computer print-outs" for a "self-organizing experience."[38] "As

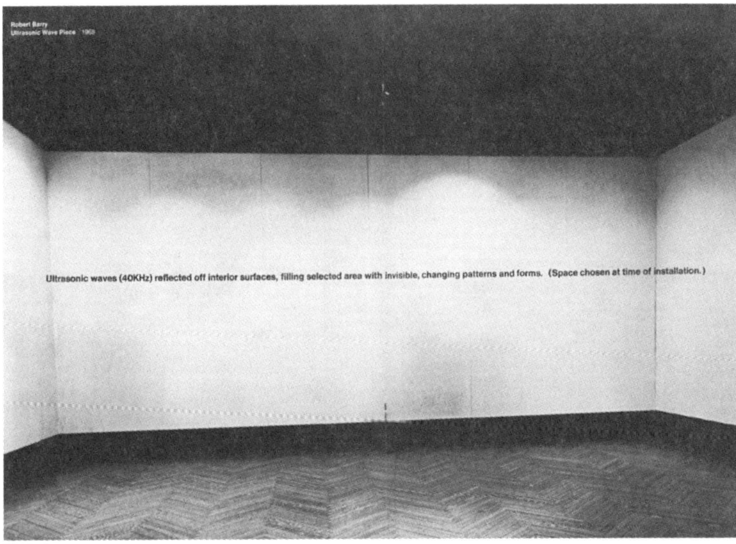


**6.6** Robert Barry, *Ultrasonic Wave Piece* (1968), in *Software*.

a visitor walks through the exhibition and picks up his personalized computer print-outs of the various pieces, he can clip them into his catalog," a planning note reads, but the idea was scrapped owing to cost. Instead, the organizers created a tall, stapled publication, designed by Robert Jakob, that offered a modernist take on a glossy magazine, complete with headlines and double-page spreads. Negroponte's dystopian-looking gerbil maze graces the cover. Though the catalog includes texts by Burnham and the computer guru Ted Nelson, the mastermind behind *hypertext*, photographs make up its bulk.[39] Images of the inaugural festivities ("an electric night to remember") highlight the social systems that supported the exhibition. One society-style photograph shows Burnham chatting with Roy Chapin Jr., the chairman of the American Motors Corporation and the lead sponsor of the exhibition, in an attempt to show budgets at work.

Art and business veered close to one another at this moment as museums and corporations started to figure out how each could benefit the other, but other fields borrowed from each other, too.[40] As Chapin saw it: "*Software* is an exhibition which utilizes sophisticated communi-

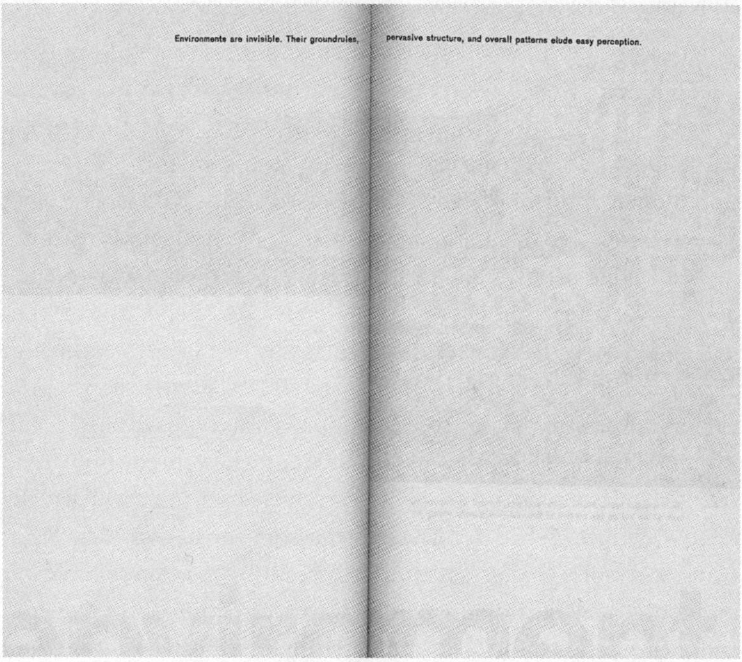


**6.7** Spread from Marshall McLuhan and Quentin Fiore, *The Medium Is the Massage*.

cations technology, but concentrates on the interaction between people and their electronic and electromechanical surroundings. This is the same exploration, in human factors, which we use in the engineering of our automobiles as a human environment."[41] The automotive industry began to see itself less as a manufacturer of commodities and more as an engineer of interfaces, cyberneticians regulating relationships between man and machine. Cars, the consummate hardware, were going soft.[42]

After the party pictures, the catalog assumes its traditional function of documenting the work in the show, but even here one notes a difference: the catalog is comprised primarily of installation shots, suggesting that the work could not be extricated from its context. There is a photograph of Vito Acconci trailing visitors around the halls of the museum in a version of his *Following Piece* (1969), while Hans Haacke's *News* (1969), a bank of five Teletype machines, fills another gallery with the day's news reports.[43] A double-page spread featuring a work by Robert Barry in one of the museum's otherwise empty townhouse galleries, however, remains invisible: all we see is spotlit walls and parquet flooring. (In 1970, Barry told Burnham: "I can't think of any way to use photographs or anything visual in relation to some of the recent work. It doesn't have a place, or the place is unknown.")[44] A description running across the center of the page explains: "Ultrasonic waves (40KHz) reflected off interior surfaces, filling selected area with invisible, changing patterns and forms." The graphic design was not incidental. The spread mimics two completely blank pages from McLuhan and Fiore's *Massage* book save for a tiny text printed at the top: "Environments are invisible. Their groundrules, pervasive structure, and overall patterns elude easy perception."[45] An emphasis on invisibility underlines both projects: art and environment were equally hard to see. "What I was trying to do, really, was create something which really existed, and which had its own characteristics and its own nature, but which we couldn't really perceive," Barry said in a 1969 interview about his work, which in addition to radio waves also made use of radiation and inert gases.[46] Information and invisibility were inextricable from one another: the world was now ruled by forces that fell beneath the level of visibility but that nevertheless had massive and often visible effects.[47] Or so *Software* saw it. Art's task, however, was no longer to make the invisible visible as much as it was to harness invisible forces and push them in new directions. (As we have seen, art now had the responsibility of reshaping the environment.) In many ways, *Software* represented a last gasp of such utopian thinking, for at the same time many artists began to insist on art's limits, injecting a dose of skepticism into excited thought. And they often did so by turning to the earth itself.

## Environment or Antienvironment

At first glance, few things appear more distant from information art than earth art, yet the two movements emerged at roughly the same time and shared many of the same concerns.[48] Both circled around questions of environment. When McLuhan spoke of *information*, he emphasized the ways in which it created a new environment. "Man in the electronic age has no possible environment except the globe and no possible occupation except information-gathering," he wrote in 1963, emphasizing that information had become a new world resource, no matter how uneven in distribution.[49] He used the term again and again in his writings, and in many ways it was synonymous with art itself: Environment had become art's field of play.

McLuhan was not the first to understand this. Many of the postwar period's most important artistic experiments, such as György Kepes's *The New Landscape* exhibition in 1951 and *Parallel of Life and Art*, an exhibition organized by Independent Group members Alison Smithson, Peter Smithson, Nigel Henderson, and Eduardo Paolozzi in London in 1953, explored the effects of photographic technology on what was just then beginning to be called *environment*.[50] Later, in the 1960s, countercultural projects such as the *Whole Earth Catalog* increasingly connected imaging technology to the idea of the earth as a complete system (the *Catalog*'s catchphrase: "Why haven't we seen a photograph of the whole Earth yet?"). McLuhan himself pegged the emergence of an information environment to the launch of the Sputnik satellite in 1957, inaugurating "the sudden awareness that nature itself has dropped out."[51]

Art history has become increasingly attentive to this imbrication of earth art and media in recent years. "It would not be wrong to state that some Land art works were produced for the media and by the media simultaneously," Philip Kaiser and Miwon Kwon have written, "raising the more difficult question as to whether Land art can exist without the media."[52] What is perhaps even more important, however, is not just that land art was a mediated practice but that the turn to the land was itself an effect of media. "As the planet becomes the content of a new information environment," McLuhan wrote in 1964, "it also tends to become a work of art."[53] The emergence of a new data environment, created by satellites and cables, brought attention to the preceding environment (the earth itself), and artists made it their task to mine the connections between the two. (We might think of land art as the art form of the global village.) "If the planet itself has thus become the content of a new space created by satellites, and its electronic extensions," McLuhan continued a few years later, "then we can confidently expect to see the next few decades devoted to turning the planet into an art form. We will caress and shape and pattern every facet, every contour of this planet as if it were a work of art."[54] As we know from the work of artists such as Robert Smithson and Michael Heizer, who carved shapes deep into the earth's surface, this is precisely what happened.

Looking back, it is striking how many works in *Information* take up questions of environment and landscape. Where Heizer contributed eight photographs of a desert explosion to the catalog, Barry Le Va conjured "sand blown off a mesa top into a valley or canyon," and Richard Long offered photographs of various earth depressions. Yoko Ono sent in a short text called *Cloud Piece*: "Imagine the clouds dripping. Dig a hole in your garden to put them in." Siah Armajani exhibited designs for a tower tall enough to cast a shadow across North Dakota. For its part, the Canadian N.E. Thing Co. LTD. made a "territorial claim" by marking landscapes with urine, while the Austrian architect Hans Hollein sent in four photographs of a bucolic landscape: "Various locations have been selected, photographed, and declared as sites for non-buildings, subterranean buildings, or slight modifications to the surface." Dennis Oppenheim presented a slideshow of himself doing push-ups atop a bed of mud. "Energy in the form of ground pressure expended for its own sake," he wrote in a caption accompanying the work. Rafael Ferrer placed eight tons of ice in the MoMA sculpture garden. Smithson's contribution, *Asphalt Rundown* (1969), a dump truck of asphalt let loose in a Roman quarry, twists the connection between information and environment to increasingly entropic ends.[55]

Best known for his earthwork *Spiral Jetty* (1970), a twisting coil of rubble sited in the Great Salt Lake, Smithson frequently invoked McLuhan's name in his writings, though he typically did so in order to counter McLuhan's position.[56] Indeed, McLuhan functioned as a foil for Smithson, providing something for him to push against. (If, in one example, McLuhan wanted both to animate the museum and to release art from its shackles, Smithson argued that, in fact, museums should be celebrated for their mausoleum-like qualities.)[57] His work does not so much "caress" the earth as assault it: in addition to *Asphalt Rundown*, he also imagined dumping glass in a pristine environment off the west coast of Canada.[58] Smithson was also one of the land artists most engaged with questions of media, as can be seen from his dark, haunt-

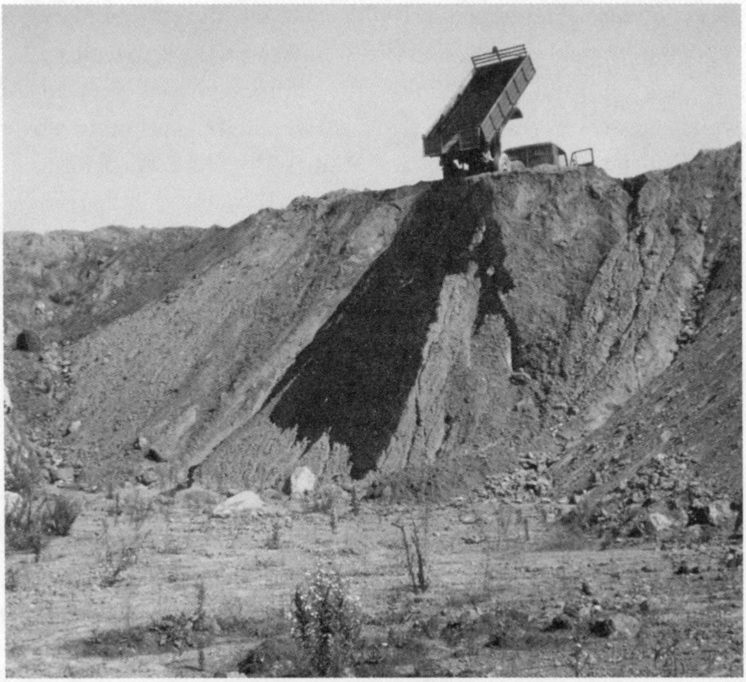

**6.8** Robert Smithson, *Asphalt Rundown* (1969). © 2021 Holt/Smithson Foundation/licensed by VAGA at Artists Rights Society (ARS), NY.

ing film *Spiral Jetty* (1970), which offers documentation of the work's making—tractors and backhoes scrape the land—cut with images of maps and natural history museums.[59] (*Spiral Jetty*'s placement near the Golden Spike, which marks the completion of the first transcontinental railroad, serves as another riposte to narratives of technological progress.[60] Not insignificantly, the spiral also echoes the vortex celebrated by Lewis [see chapter 2 above].)[61] In Smithson's hands, media figure less as "extensions of man" than as entropic and antihuman forces—he was early to acknowledge that the Anthropocene, the age of man, is simply one episode in the earth's larger history. For him, the close connections between media and environment had made the latter virtually uninhabitable. In his 1967 "A Tour of the Monuments of Passaic, New Jersey," Smithson describes how the "noon-day sun cinema-ized the site" and "turned the bridge and the river into an over-exposed *picture*."

He continues: "Photographing it with my Instamatic 400 was like photographing a photograph. . . . When I walked on the bridge, it was as though I was walking on an enormous photograph that was made of wood and steel, and underneath the river existed an enormous movie film that showed nothing but a continuous blank."[62] For Smithson, like McLuhan, the world had become like a work of art—a "*picture*"—through its encounter with media, but, for him, it had become autonomous, uninhabitable, and impossible to enter, whereas, for McLuhan, its artlike status rendered it a creative site.

In Smithson's view, these "world photographs and films" did not brim with content as much as they offered "continuous blanks." In a certain way, this is a very McLuhanesque idea of media—the medium is the message, not the content it displays—but Smithson's critique of McLuhan functions on another level. His suggestion that the dominance of media led to deathliness points to a conclusion that the theorist refused to imagine: at a certain point, media could not be controlled and turned to emancipatory ends. A year after his tour of Passaic, in "A Museum of Language in the Vicinity of Art," Smithson wrote that "cinematic 'appearance' took over completely sometime in the late 50s," pegging the rise of cinema to the moment that television successfully installed itself in American life. "'Nature' falls into an infinite series of movie 'stills'—we get what Marshall McLuhan calls 'The Reel World.'"[63] ("The Reel World" is the title of a chapter in *Understanding Media*.) If, for McLuhan, the world of cinema, with its high-definition images and nation-states, was fading by the mid-1950s in favor of the contracted, tribal world of TV, Smithson saw a posthistoric, fossilized time taking its place. As he wrote in "A Sedimentation of the Mind: Earth Projects": "The manifestations of technology are at times less 'extensions' of man (Marshall McLuhan's anthropomorphism), than they are aggregates of elements."[64] It was this material density, this inhumanity of media, that Smithson contemplated in his work. He aimed to counter McLuhan's control tower with uncontrollable forces. But, if he welcomed this entropic, antihuman ending, other artists *détourned* McLuhan's message to less nihilistic, more subversive ends. They dreamed less of a hardened world than a more elastic one.

7

# Culture Was His Business

**Poets and artists live on frontiers. They have no feedback, only feedforward. They have no identities. They are probes.** Marshall McLuhan, *Culture Is Our Business* (1970)

As the art world embraced his ideas about information and environments in the 1960s, McLuhan returned to some of his earliest explorations. The advertising image still possessed him after all these years, and in 1970 he published *Culture Is Our Business*, a sequel to *The Mechanical Bride*. In the 1967 *Newsweek* profile, he referred to the book as *Daughter of the Bride*, and, while the new volume resembles its precursor in key respects, it also demonstrates how the advertising image had transformed in the twenty or so years separating the two books.[1] Where *Bride* concerned itself with the instrumentalization of the body and the regulation of the mind and understood these forces as threats to culture, by 1970 McLuhan saw a new cultural formation taking shape. Instead of dismissing high culture, businessmen now made it central to their work. Far from being marginalized, culture was now incorporated into business. A merger between culture and

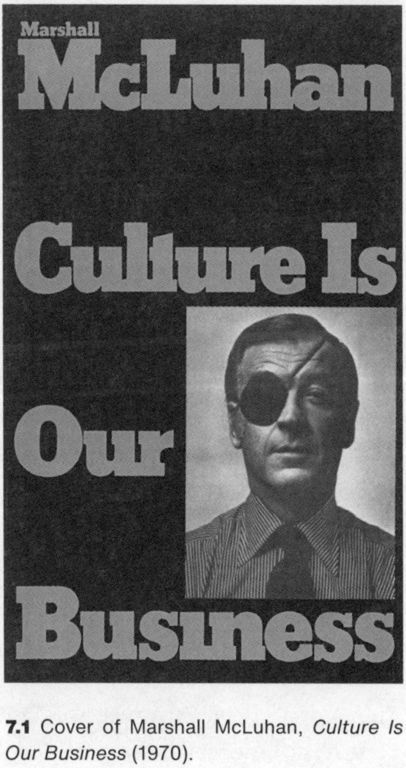


**7.1** Cover of Marshall McLuhan, *Culture Is Our Business* (1970).

the corporate world was well on its way, and McLuhan made it his work to size up the situation.

The aphoristic nature of the book's title—*Culture Is Our Business*—strikes the reader as both affirmative and ironic at once. While the title echoes Theodor Adorno and Max Horkheimer's concept of the culture industry, which insists that popular culture, from film to radio to magazines, is characterized by standardization and sameness, McLuhan's phrase also evokes something along the lines of the creative industries, the collapse of graphic design, marketing, public relations, music, and art into one mélange, marking his very different relationship to culture as well.[2] The title's use of the first-person plural possessive—*our*—is to the point. Where Adorno and Horkheimer assumed a position of critical distance, McLuhan proclaims that this is *our* culture; it is not something we can look on from outside.

If the title laments a new top-down management of culture, it also betrays a quixotic glee. "Art used to be the province of Ma, but now it is big business, the domain of Pop—Pop art," McLuhan announced in his film *The Medium Is the Massage*, with Warhols in the background. Pop art marked a new relationship between art and business, doing away with traditional ideas about the timelessness of culture, and as a result it was regendered as well, masculinized and publicized. Where art used to stay home or keep quiet in a museum, it now moved outside in a world of speculation and commerce. (Visiting Toronto in 1969, John Lennon and Yoko Ono called on McLuhan to discuss environments, moods, rhythm, and software. "One thing this age is about is no museums," Lennon quips, explaining why he had just quit the Beatles.)[3] Certainly, McLuhan had always advocated that the artist take a more active role in society, but now artistic work was being be done under commercial cover. In *Culture Is Our Business*, he followed up on this thread, seeking to understand this new relationship by parsing the increasing proximity between art and business. "Commercially, new art is kooky and worthless," he wrote before noting: "The gap between the kooky and the commercially valuable is closing fast."[4] While he had once insisted that media were too important to be left in the hands of "Peter Pan executives" and that artists should harness their powers, he now saw the two melded into one, artists imagining themselves in the executive's image, and vice versa. What was to be done?

The title *Culture Is Our Business* forms a chiasmus. It was not only that art had annexed the resources of business but also that business had assimilated the lessons of art, stocking its offices with creative spirits. As the futurist Alvin Toffler noted: "Today a rapprochement is under way between business and art in America, and it threatens to undo the cherished alienation of the artists as it changes the position of art in the American context."[5] As the structure of advanced capitalist economies shifted from mechanical manufacturing to information processing, so began an interest in creativity that exploded the bland, bureaucratic world of the "organization man."[6] McLuhan, in fact, facilitated such a merger through his work with the San Francisco adman Howard Luck Gossage in the mid-1960s, and he kept close contact with businessmen throughout his career, at one point even establishing his own consulting firm.[7] Corporate honchos were eager to trot him out as an oracle spouting enigmatic phrases that left the business world starry-eyed.[8] He participated in a *TV Guide*–funded workshop, *The Meaning of Commercial Television*, and drafted a report for ABC.[9] From 1968 to 1970, he and Eugene Schwartz, president of the Human Development Corporation, published a monthly fact sheet for corporate clients. Dubbed *The McLuhan* DEW-LINE, it took its name from the Distant Early Warning Line radar stations set up by the US military in the Canadian Arctic to protect against Soviet incursion. (An ad for the newsletter running in the August 3, 1968, edition of the *New York Times* asked: "[Which] danger signals have you already interpreted falsely?" "[Which] technological breakthroughs are completely hidden from your view?") Topics ranged from the university and the city to politics in Russia, and issues incorporated novel designs: while one collated loose leaves and encouraged the reader to "try shuffling the pages," another cut out a column of text from every other page, promoting a double take.[10] The newsletter promised businesses the ability its namesake had—to spot change on the horizon—a task McLuhan had long ascribed to artists.[11] (A deck of playing cards printed with McLuhan's adages was released in 1969: "In addition to the conventional card games, the Dew Line deck performs as THE MANAGEMENT GAMES," the instructions read.) Indeed, what one notices at this moment is McLuhan's appeal to artists and corporations alike. Both craved the next new thing.

"The title of this book [*Culture Is Our Business*] . . . points to a flip in American society from hardware to software," McLuhan wrote in the introduction. "In shifting from hardware to software, and from products to processes, and from goals to roles since TV, America has entered a phase of culture in which the old mechanical specialisms, whether of industry or the organization chart, have yielded to new forms of images." These new images spoke of a wired subject—not a mechanical bride—but women somehow still remained a barometer for cultural change: whereas *Bride* captured machinic bodies, *Business* trades in images of female intelligence. "This Monroe calculator has a memory like a woman's," one ad avows. "It can recall information even *you've* forgotten."[12] Changes in technology certainly did not lead to liberation, and the misogyny of such ads, now standing in the face of feminist consciousness, goes unchallenged.

But McLuhan did employ new methods to handle such ads; these artifacts could not be dismissed with the same mixture of irony and critical vision that kept the old mechanical world at bay. Where *Bride* sparred with its objects in essay form, *Business* pairs ads with a combination of quotes from Joyce and Lewis, an excerpt from *Life*, and McLuhan's own bons mots—perverse, ambiguous little quips—related only tangentially to the themes presented in the image. Obscurity seems part of the trick. Poems built out of found parts, these pairings are truncated, jumpy, jury-rigged things, a sign, perhaps, of how quixotic advertising had become and how difficult it was to respond. Truth be told, much of the book is difficult to grasp—at least analytically. It is suggestive, it points in different directions, but it is rarely clear in its aims. The section "Psychological Interrogation," for example, pairs an ad for Warner's lingerie with a statement proclaiming: "All preliterate societies are communist, just as they are tribal." What motivates this couplet is unclear: its disconnection might be part of the point. Perhaps one could respond to the moment only with opacity and obscurantism. Or maybe McLuhan's analytic tools were simply not as efficacious as they had once been.

As we have seen, McLuhan expressed ambivalence about the merging of art and business. In 1954, and again in 1963, he insisted: "The new media . . . are not toys; they should not be in the hands of Mother Goose and Peter Pan executives. They can be entrusted only to new artists."[13] That said, he also understood that capitalist markets deeply affected art, and, as his work evolved, he imagined a hybrid relationship between executives and artists. "The mass market tyrannized over the artist" of the nineteenth century, he wrote in *The Gutenberg Galaxy*, and, as a result, "the artist in isolation achieved new clairvoyance concerning the crucial role of design and of art as a means to human order and fulfillment." Threatened by the market, artists learned its powers and saw how it imposed its own "human order"—they might do something similar, too. Concluding on a utopian note, he wrote: "Retrospectively, it may well prove necessary to concede to the period of mass marketing the creation of the means of a world order in beauty as much as in commodities."[14] Just as Marx believed that capitalism paved the way for communism, McLuhan imagined that the market prepared the ground for art by creating new models of connection. The traditional disciplines of painting and sculpture were no longer capable of connecting art to the world.[15] Corporate forms were needed. Many considered such a model the innovation of the day: while the Los Angeles County Museum of Art's Art and Technology Program placed artists in corporate headquarters across southern California, others imagined that artists and corporations might work together on advertising projects.[16] "The artist might help the corporation in establishing its corporate image while the corporation might help the artist in freeing some of the limitations in relation to the reader and socio-economic frameworks," the artist Dan Graham wrote in 1970.[17] A couple of years earlier, Nam June Paik declared: "I urge that the top 500 businesses create an 'artist in residence' position to advise in marketing, advertisement, and the research of new products on the top level, so that their unorthodox, fresh sense can vitalize a big corporation hierarchy."[18] While some artists approached this relationship with their tongues firmly in their cheeks—consider the media activist Raindance Corporation whose name riffed on the military-minded RAND Corporation—others could not have been more sincere.[19] For many, even Paik's plea was not enough. "This business of being artist-in-residence at some corporation is only part of the story," the artist

Stan VanDerBeek declared in 1970. "What we really want to be is artist-in-residence of the world, but we don't know where to apply."[20]

If McLuhan imagined the artist as a forecaster, an antenna catching signs in the ether and broadcasting warnings back home, he recognized that this role also had the possibility for dissent. "One of the functions of the artist that is understood in recent decades is that it is, above all, to prevent us from becoming adjusted to our environments," he wrote in the 1973 "Art as Survival in the Electric Age." "The job of the artist is dislocation of sensibility to prevent us from becoming adjusted to total environments, and to becoming the servant and robots of those environments."[21] Here, the artist is antagonist once again, insisting that one pay attention to nefarious forces, and stopping people from adjusting too much to the powers that be. For McLuhan, survival was at stake. But many saw such admonitions as too little, too late. In an increasingly politicized (art) world, McLuhan's "probing" struck many as tepid, and he was frequently criticized for what was perceived as his corporate collusion. "A hedonistic age had its own appropriate prophet—Marshall McLuhan," the sociologist Daniel Bell wrote in 1976. "A hedonistic age is a marketing age, defined by the fact that knowledge becomes coded in messages organized as formulas, slogans, and binary distinctions. . . . All in all, Marshall McLuhan was an advertising man's dream, in more ways than one."[22] (For his part, Bell argued that only religious revival offered a path out of hedonism.)

But, if he dealt with the business community, McLuhan was also interested in the corporate in some larger sense. For him, *corporate* evoked more than bottom lines; it spoke of groups of people and the forms into which they assembled. It had a collective, utopian echo. In 1960, he wrote that print gave rise to "a new kind of corporate life in the school."[23] In *Understanding Media*, he uses *corporate* in a range of contexts, from "medieval corporate guilds and monasteries" to "emotional and corporate family feeling."[24] And, in *Massage*, he writes: "It was the funeral of President Kennedy that most strongly proved the power of television to invest an occasion with the character of corporate participation."[25] A corporate image, then, suggested more than a company's logo: it offered a sign in which people could witness themselves coming together. Realizing that business was now crucial to art, artists at this moment also embraced corporate forms, though some did so more incisively—and unexpectedly—than others.[26]

## General Idea

The members of General Idea—AA Bronson, Felix Partz, and Jorge Zontal—came together in late 1960s Toronto, in a maelstrom of mail art and media frenzy, and, in many ways, they portrayed themselves as McLuhan's children—analyzing, critiquing, and mimicking the media, though not seeking to overthrow it.[27] When they first got together, they went by their given names—Michael Tims, Ron Gabe, and Jorge Saia (and Saia, an immigrant many times over, had had still other names before)—but in time the three assumed new identities and took on other guises: while they started off as longhaired hippies, they soon went clean, sliding into different personae. One might think of their self-appellations as stage names, and, in fact, "all the world's a stage" is not a terrible way of getting one's head around what General Idea was up to. They were fascinated by the potentials of performance, the role of the audience, and the "borderline" space linking the two. One of General Idea's founding documents, from 1969, is a self-portrait of the three men hanging out on a couch, holding up the cover of the new Velvet Underground album, which shows the rock group sprawled out in a similar situation. There's always a question about how to refer to General Idea, and, perhaps not surprisingly, they returned to the group portrait throughout their careers, imaging themselves as babies, doctors, and night-school students. They operated like a collective but considered themselves more like a band. They were artists but not quite. They undertook theatrical productions. Under the guise of architecture, they constructed pavilions. They were independent media producers who cut tape and edited a magazine. In short, they were a quasi-corporate entity—in more ways than one.

General Idea's first collective home at 78 Gerrard Street West—strangely, the same address where Wyndham Lewis lived during his exile in Toronto—fell somewhere between corporate headquarters and hippie commune. Its members made a "fake storefront in their store-

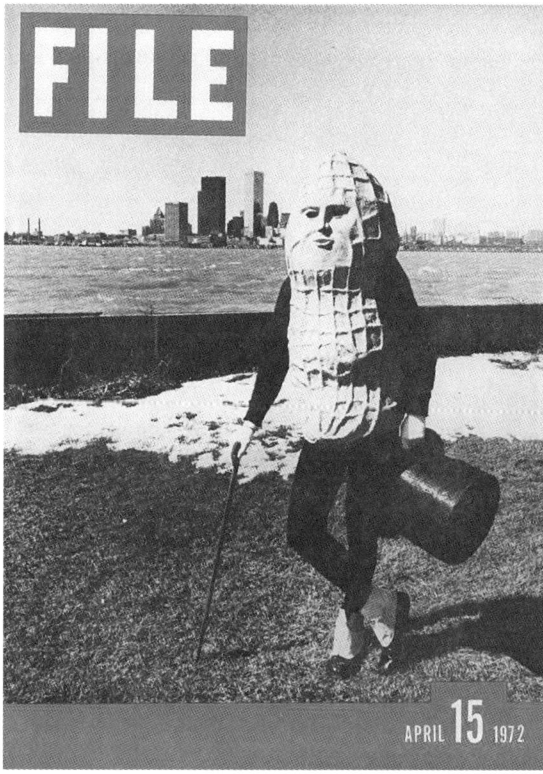


**7.2** General Idea, FILE *Megazine* 1, no. 1 (April 1972), *The Mr. Peanut Issue*. Web offset periodical, 32 pp. plus cover. © The Estate of General Idea. Courtesy of the Estate and Mitchell-Innes & Nash, New York.

front residence," gathering vintage dresses, and giving them new lives. Soon after, the group moved to an old loft building on Yonge Street, where, beginning in 1972, it edited and published the "megazine" FILE, the logo of which plays on the *Life* logo much in the way that McLuhan had punned on it years before.[28] ("FILE is LIFE out of hand," the group wrote in an editorial, "a handy map of scenic networks tracing the globe for you.")[29] *Life*, in fact, had ceased publication in 1972—it went on to publish special issues before reappearing as a weekly in 1978—and the timing of General Idea's appropriation seems significant: that *Life* belonged to an earlier age allowed General Idea to rejigger the past. The visual rhyme of white letters in a red box hit so close to its target, however, that Time Life threatened to sue, calling for the destruction of original artwork and all back issues, and in 1977 General Idea began to render the magazine's name in other ways.[30] While serving as an artist publication, the magazine doubled as an alternative newspaper, maintaining a circulation of three thousand copies sent to an international group of participants. With ads for "deluxe food" restaurants, galleries, and other periodicals, *FILE* exceeded the boundaries of the typical art magazine by linking art with ecology, fashion, politics, gossip, nightlife, and urban renewal. In its early years, the quarterly magazine also offered an annual artists' directory. It had a section devoted to "books, zines and records" and party coverage, such as the opening of General Idea's Colour Bar Lounge, which may or may not have actually taken place (the media were good for crafting fictions). Perhaps more than anything, *FILE* generated myths and spread them through social networks. For example, it wrote of an opening in which "the crowd was arriving and collecting in the gallery and gossip was collecting and trends were developing."[31] This describes General Idea's project in a nutshell: the creation of an overarching narrative that linked together disparate activities. In 1973, Willoughby Sharp interviewed the group for *Avalanche* magazine, the New York–based publication dedicated to post-Minimal and Conceptual art. "You're propagating fake mysteries, aren't you?" Sharp asked, trying to get to the heart of the project. "All over the place," Jorge Zontal answered.[32]

At first, General Idea worked in a vein similar to that of other conceptual and performance artists. They typed texts on index cards, produced "orgasm energy charts," and shot grainy black-and-white video. In *Double Mirror Video: A Borderline Case* (1971), they star as a bunch of Canadian longhairs using the video-mirror language of the day—think Vito Acconci, Dan Graham, Joan Jonas, and especially Robert Smithson's *Yucatan Mirror Displacements* (1969)—to make a *mise-en-abyme à la plage*. Having placed two large mirrors across from one another, they rotate them so that their video cameras and hard stares get caught up in an infinite regress. It quickly becomes difficult to tell which image is real and which reflection. Standing on the shores of Lake Ontario, they look across the watery border at the United States, simultaneously probing subjective states and nation-states alike. While this mir-

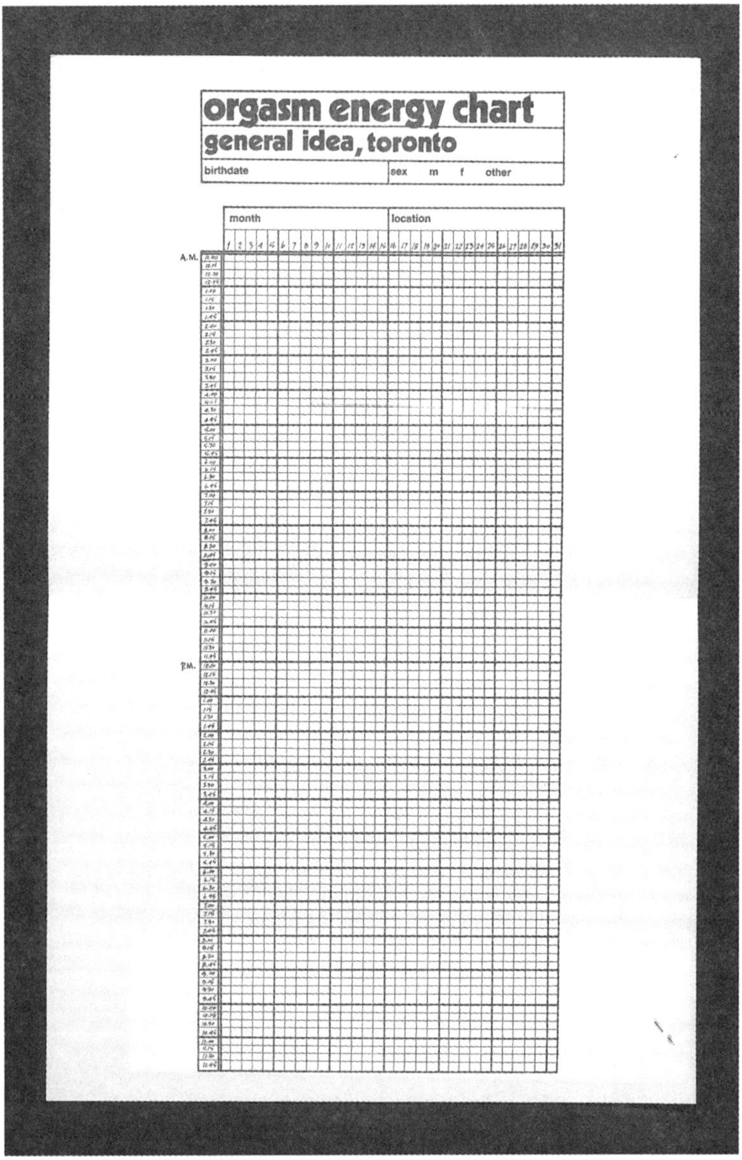


**7.3** General Idea, *Orgasm Energy Chart* (1970). Offset on bond paper, 16.5 × 11 inches, 42 × 27.8 centimeters. © The Estate of General Idea. Courtesy of the Estate and Mitchell-Innes & Nash, New York.

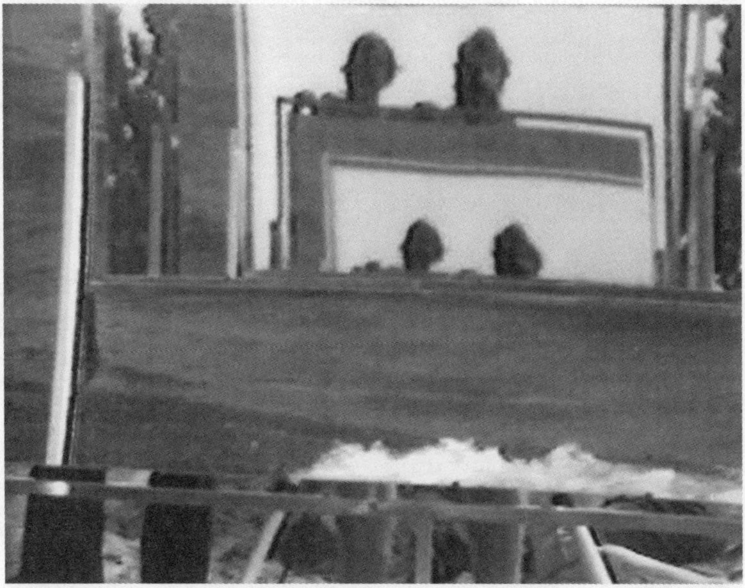

**7.4** General Idea, *Double Mirror Video* (1971). Courtesy Electronic Arts Intermix (EAI), New York.

ror play was recorded on video, it was more of a psychic experiment than a mode for completing works of art. An advertisement for the video notes that the work "is currently being re/performed in a variety of locations: including inside/outside situations and in addition to the original earth/water location."[33]

Research into the borderline was central to General Idea's work at this time. A year later, in 1972, in FILE's first issue, readers were asked to sketch in the US-Canadian border on a map of North America and send it back to headquarters as part of their *Borderline Research Project*.[34] A composite of the submitted drawings was featured in the inside front cover of the next issue, while the front cover—a blurry photograph of a woman named Ahsram Rrac, her arms bent around her head—was the result of a mail-art project, *Manipulating the Self: A Borderline Case*, begun in 1971, for which General Idea asked people in their network to send in photos of themselves with their arms wrapped around their heads.[35] Shortly thereafter, they designed a facade for the 1984 Miss General Idea Pavilion, *Luxon V.B.*, made of mirrored venetian blinds "so that the reflections of inside and outside are collaged together."[36] While borderline personality disorder, which challenges the contours of a fixed identity, provides one reading for these explorations, McLuhan's work on Canada's borderline personality and its effect on artistic temperament also points to national concerns. In a 1967 lecture, "Canada, the Borderline Case," McLuhan declared that Canada has "a kind of world art role in making visible the vast, man-made American environment that is now becoming a world environment."[37] With most of its population living in close proximity to the US border, Canada occupied an ideal position from which to gauge America's imperial effects. "Until the last 10 years, there was no such thing as Canadian culture," Bronson said in 1979, when asked in an interview about McLuhan's influence. "There was only American culture, and it all came through the television, through the newspapers, through the magazines, to us. So we were constantly in the position of observers—observers of culture. . . . McLuhan was the most verbal synthesizer of a lot things that were happening in Canada at the time."[38] For McLuhan and Bronson, then, art had its genesis in observing what was happening just across the border, but it had to mime what it saw—to create a mirror image—to have an effect.

If their first forays into art making stuck close to the language of conceptual art, General Idea soon pollinated conceptual art with Pop economy to form a corporate aesthetic. While the interest in corporations connects with their fascination with the dream world of the 1950s, they also understood that, by the 1970s, the term *corporation* had a vexed status in North American culture. As Elke Town wrote of the group in 1982: "Ambiguity, paradox and irony have given them an image as impenetrable as that of a large mega-corporation."[39] Another critic claimed: "There is a corporate gloss to everything they make that is positively eerie in its perfection."[40] In other words, they became the "hip artificers" John McHale imagined in his *Understanding Media* review, discussed in chapter 3. While other artists flirted with the corporate world—think of Claes Oldenburg's Ray Gun Manufacturing Company or Warhol's Factory as well as his claim that "being good in business is the most fascinating kind of art"[41]—General Idea faced the fact head-on in their work and self-presentation.[42] Binding three artists together,

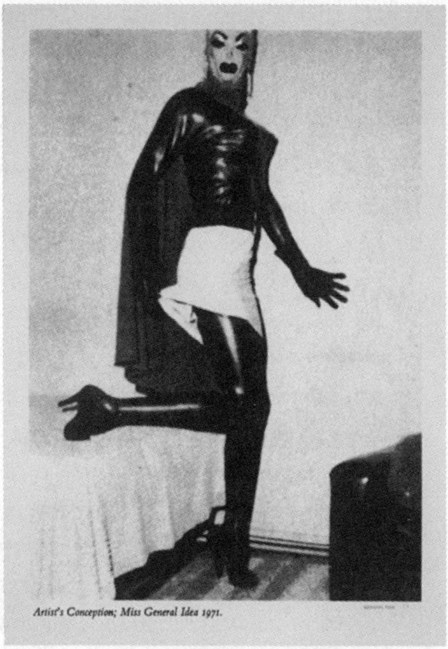


**7.5** General Idea, *Artist's Conception: Miss General Idea* (1971). Screen print on buff paper, 40 × 26 inches, 101.5 × 66 centimeters. © The Estate of General Idea. Courtesy of the Estate and Mitchell-Innes & Nash, New York.

the group's name riffed on corporate naming conventions, as in General Motors and General Electric, just updated for the information economy. (It might also suggest another fictional persona, that of a high-ranking military officer.) Beginning with the first Miss General Idea Pageant, held at the Art Gallery of Ontario on October 1, 1971, the group staged a number of interconnected projects, including a pavilion, a cocktail bar, and a boutique associated with the 1984 pageant. Theirs was a multiplatform, cross-promotional enterprise. Indeed, much of the group's work doubled as paraphernalia and souvenirs for ceremonial occasions. Following McLuhan, General Idea also saw femininity as a barometer of cultural change—the "mechanical bride" transformed into Miss General Idea, paralleling the shift from manufacturing to an information economy—and, while some slammed the group over the ostensible complacency of its beauty pageants, its projects also maintained a wry, camp sense of humor that challenged gender norms: an ingenue named Marcel Idea was crowned Miss General Idea in 1971.[43] *Miss*, of course, is also shorthand for misfit, and misinformation.

Ultimately, General Idea concerned itself less with singular works of art than the enterprises and lifestyles binding the group together. One might say they wanted to generate myth, a topic close to McLuhan's heart.[44] And General Idea wanted to do this effectively. "What do you mean by 'effective' art?" the group asked itself in a fall 1977 *FILE* editorial, echoing McLuhan on the centrality of effects. "Obviously art that has effect. Obviously art that affects an audience. Obviously being effective requires an audience. Obviously art that has effect is art that has an audience."[45] It could be said that audience constituted the object of General Idea's art, but the way the group sought to get at the audience is what set it apart from its countercultural forebears. "General Idea emerged in the aftermath of the Paris riots, from the detritus of hippie communes, underground newspapers, radical education, Happenings, love-ins, Marshall McLuhan, and the International Situationists," AA Bronson claimed in retrospect.[46] (He might also have noted William S. Burroughs's writing on viruses, which served as another cornerstone of General Idea's thought.) Mixing all these elements together, General Idea streamlined them into a new form. If General Idea stemmed from Situationism, student sit-ins, and riots, they refashioned these political sources to question the very idea of subversion, imagining it as a modulation in a system rather than a radical break. Certainly, this tactic owed a debt to systems theory, which always prefers equilibrium to revolution, but General Idea gave it a new spin.[47] Like McLuhan, they worked within, not against, power structures.

The group specialized in shape-shifting. A posthippie outfit, it shelved the iconography of the 1960s counterculture to infiltrate the media's conventions. Fashion and glamour offered two potential ways of operating. The artist Mike Kelley once asked Bronson about the changes in General Idea's appearance and "how that affected the notion of . . . cultural production": "And also the kind of shift in the look of the people from a hippie aesthetic into something where you put on a front of normalcy." "It's quite true," Bronson responded. "I like the idea of normalcy, because that's what it was in many ways I think. At the beginning we took on alter egos, false names and identities that allowed us to function in the world in many ways we felt we couldn't have. And then we got to a certain stage in our career, the so-called alter-egos had to appear as real beings, as real normal beings that had careers and ambitions and value systems and what have you."[48] Playing it straight and adhering to conventions allowed General Idea's work to circulate through media channels in ways that a countercultural position might have prevented, but it also allowed the group to reshape them. Rather than drop out, they went inside, infiltrating the system with generic-looking works—"infected" paintings, posters, stamps, and videos. (In

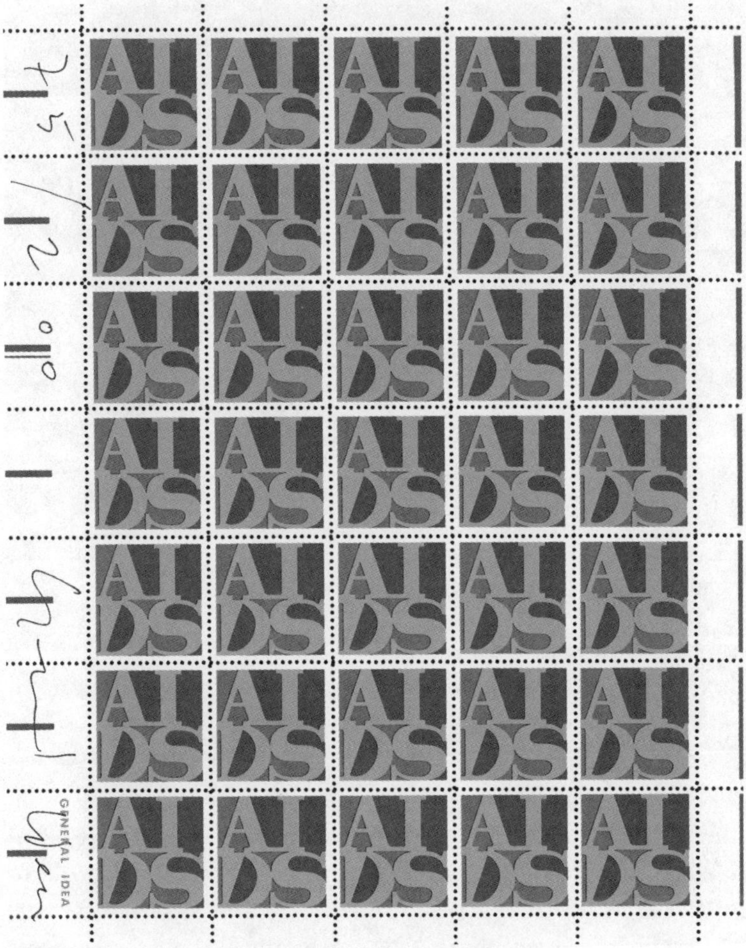

**7.6** General Idea, *AIDS Stamps* (1988). Offset on perforated paper, 4pp. Published by Parkett-Verlag AG, Zurich. © The Estate of General Idea. Courtesy of the Estate and Mitchell-Innes & Nash, New York.

their project *Imagevirus*, which ran from 1987 to 1994, they revised Robert Indiana's LOVE icon using the word *AIDS* and spread it across the world.)[49] In a 1975 profile of General Idea published in the magazine *Toronto Life*, the future McLuhan biographer Philip Marchand wrote: "Think of them as undiscovered pop stars who play the media instead of guitars."[50] "It's a waste of time telling the media to shut the fuck up,"

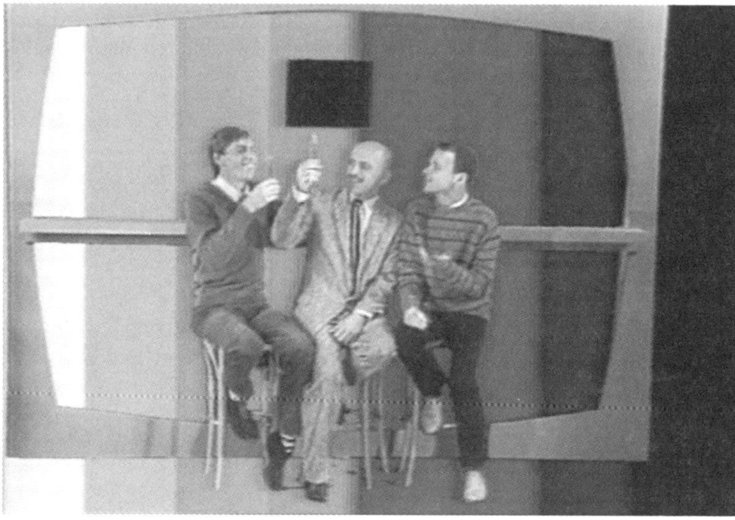

**7.7** General Idea, *Test Tube* (1979). Courtesy Electronic Arts Intermix (EAI), New York.

as General Idea put it in a 1984 video while still, of course, telling it to do so.[51] Understanding media as a fact of life, General Idea navigated it with irony and play. The group did not so much try to raise awareness as transfigure attention.

General Idea made its position clear in *Test Tube* (1979), a made-for-television-about-television video in which the group's three members hang out in the Colour Bar Lounge.[52] Here, both drinks and decor mimic the TV test pattern, vertical bars made out of yellow, green, blue, and red, making a metaphor between art and drink: both mix elements to produce intoxication. But this is also a test, an experiment; General Idea wants to figure out what artists can do with television. While commercials appear throughout the thirty-minute video, including a bizarre spot for Nazi Milk, the rest of the program provides an infomercial for the artists' ideas. "More and more artists are turning to popular media in an effort to examine the effectiveness of their work, not only in an attempt to reach a larger audience but to obtain access to the immediacy of newspapers, magazines, rock 'n' roll, and, of course, television itself," Bronson claims. "We think of television as our test tube . . . to test out new formulae for making art consumable." Zontal adds: "We don't want to destroy television as we know it. We want to add to it, stretch it until it starts to lose shape, stretch the social fabric. . . . Imagine all those new sensibilities taking up more and more room, those chaotic situations on the fringe of society flooding the mainstream." General Idea might have imagined themselves in a fringe position, but they wanted to enter the halls of power. Like McLuhan, they did not deconstruct as much as they combined: they sought to add, stretch, prepare, and distort media, not abolish them. They wanted to infuse the media with new sensibilities and alternative sexualities. As Partz put it in *Test Tube*, such tactics were best deployed not on the level of "content" but on that of "format." Rather than debunk media and advertising, General Idea wanted to create a new "global myth" that would inject the system with difference.[53]

## Folly

**Painting is a tangible sensual experience, an intense state of emotion engendered by the joys and tragedies of man and also an experience in space which, fed by the instinct, leads to a living form.** Karel Appel, *New Images of Man* (1959)

If General Idea represents the corporate arm of McLuhan's legacy, McLuhan himself moved in another direction, and in 1980—he passed away on December 31 of that year—he wrote a short essay on the Dutch painter Karel Appel, a crucial artist in the postwar CoBrA movement.[54] Its name an acronym for "Copenhagen, Brussels, and Amsterdam"—the three primary cities from which it drew members—the group critiqued high culture with paintings of colorful creatures rendered in a childlike hand. Appel worked in a similar vein throughout his career: his primitivism aimed to humble humanity as much as it communicated a desire to regrow culture in the face of destruction.

Appel's work is an odd final subject for someone who dedicated his life's work to understanding media, yet there are points where the two subjects meet. McLuhan wrote of the close connection between play and "the very nature of touch" in Appel's work, suggesting that the "world of play erases the border between child and adult," an idea he often explored in relation to the electronic age and acoustic space.[55]

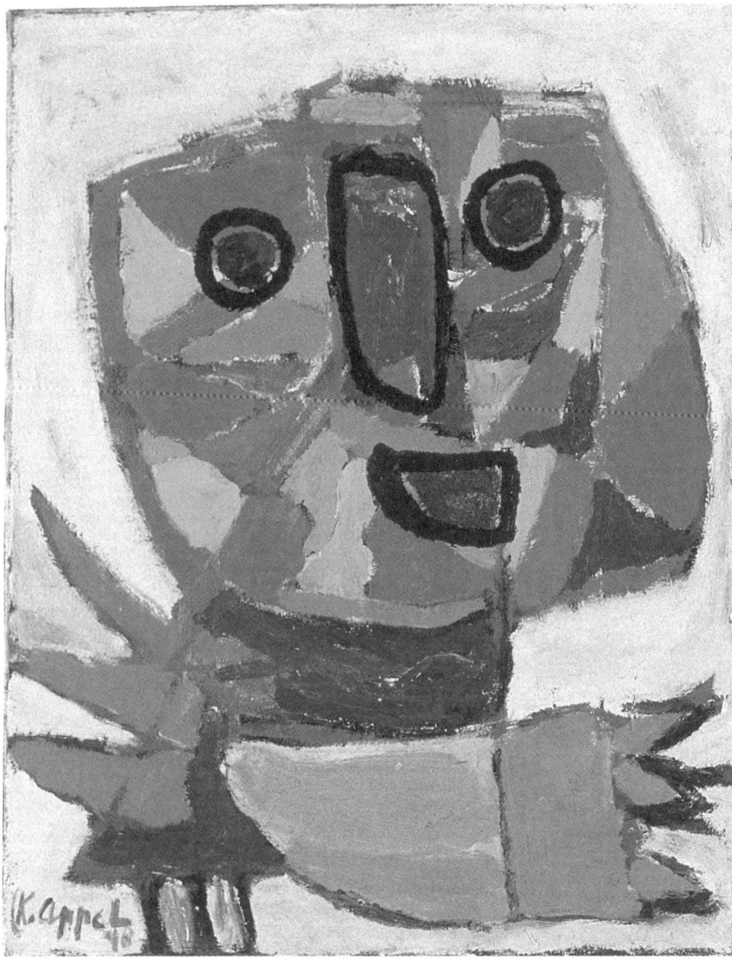


**7.8** Karel Appel, *Cry of Freedom* (1948). © 2021 Karel Appel Foundation/Artists Rights Society (ARS), New York/c/o Pictoright Amsterdam.

New technologies, he always stressed, potentially led back to an earlier age, and Appel's work resurrected the spirit of the folk carnival as a preliterate form of celebration. It evokes the retribalization of man, which McLuhan claimed as one of the primary effects of the electronic age: people's lives would become more integrated as specialization fell away. The result was a global village for a nonlinear society dominated by touch instead of type.

It is worth noting, however, that Appel's art is as tied to a postwar phenomenon as it is to a postprint one. His work tried to imagine viable images of man that might endure crises and, at the same time, be base enough to account for history's barbarity.[56] Appel studiously avoided any engagement with "new" media throughout his career, preferring thick pâtes of oil paint instead. It is both strange and fitting, then, that McLuhan would wind up here—in a world of touch, in a world of the folk festival, a world that tried to grow the world again—by taking a route that seemingly bypassed advanced technology. He had spoken of all these things, but for him they were inextricably tied to mediation. And, while art does not have to incorporate a television set in order to reflect on the media's effects, the fact that Appel served as McLuhan's last touchstone seems to reflect a final desire to exorcise the question of media. Was his dream of coming out the other side whole and human looking increasingly less likely? Was navigating such a complex world more difficult than he had thought? Could one endlessly sustain the awareness he championed? Were the media's transformative powers now out of reach to artists? Or was this idyllic world, in fact, what he had hoped for all along?

In his text, McLuhan connects Appel to Erasmus, the Catholic Renaissance thinker: "Like Erasmus, Appel puts on a series of fantastic masks, reminding us of the constantly shifting borderline between the hilarious and the serious."[57] Erasmus is famous for his praise of folly, and McLuhan claimed that Appel extolled a similar sense of inversion and satire. One might extend this idea to McLuhan as well; his work was a form of play. He tried to *play* the system—he was deeply interested in chance and its outcomes—but, as gamblers know, the house typically wins. It would remain for others to examine the questions of power and ideology McLuhan often omitted from his analyses and to respond to them in novel ways. McLuhan might have had too much faith in the power of art and believed too deeply in the power of media. That said, his probing was not in vain. "The world will pass its judgment on me," Erasmus wrote, "but unless my 'self-love' entirely deceives me, my praise of folly has not been altogether foolish."[58] One might say the same for McLuhan, too.

# Postscript
## McLuhan's Art Today

The divergent paths laid out in this book provide a glimpse of the fecundity of McLuhan's thought, its possibilities and pitfalls alike. Over a roughly thirty-year period, from the late 1940s to 1980, McLuhan imagined new possibilities for art practice, ideas that remain important today as new technologies continue to emerge and we—both artists and critics—try to figure out what to do with them as well as what they might do with us. (The different formats he imagined for writing and criticism remain potent as well.) Not only have his ideas influenced artists considering the informational medium of the Internet—indeed, a whole book could be written on this topic alone—but they also point to ways in which theory and practice need one another in order to sustain their goals. At the same time, McLuhan's capacious positions point to art's limits as much as they suggest its possibilities: his utopian ideas about programming environments feel far from us today, at least as a possibility for art practice—and, in this sense, his neo-avant-garde model is no longer operative.[1] While the first generation of Internet artists considered cyberspace a free frontier, others understood that the Web's military origins would lead to new methods of corporate domination, a fact only too clear today.[2] Turned off by the prospect of taking control, many artists court an idea of art closer to McLuhan's concept of antienvironment, whereby objects raise awareness of larger social and technological fields but do not intervene in them directly.

Late in the first decade of the twenty-first century, when I first began thinking about McLuhan (I was working on a dissertation about the Independent Group and considering what path I might take as a critic), I watched a number of storefronts in my Brooklyn neighborhood transform into massage parlors and makeshift spas.[3] Divided into narrow cubicles, these businesses offered customers just enough space to lie down.[4] The first time I entered one, I thought it looked like a call center, albeit one engineered for touch communication.[5] (The first iterations of the iPhone were just hitting the market.) Requiring little overhead, these businesses were as close to a pure service industry as one can imagine, their costs reduced to rent and wages for the masseuses (the exploitatively low wages paid to these often immigrant workers perhaps only proves the point). Artisanal in scale, they sold a craft product—human touch—made available by increasing discrepancies in the economic and social order. It dawned on me that McLuhan's mantra—"the medium is the massage"—had become literal; the constant massage of the media had brought forth a desire for actual touch, which was less an antidote to mediation than its end point.[6] The interconnected light shows of the 1960s—such as Warhol's *Exploding Plastic Inevitable*, which bound individuals into a mass—had transformed into individual "hot spots," and the promise of an electric global village gave way to the pressures of what I called *iSolation*—an effect even more pronounced now in our pandemic age.

The multiplication of these massage parlors coincided with a shift in the production of contemporary art, which some dubbed *post–Internet art*, a potentially misleading term given that we are still very much in the Internet's hold.[7] The *post–*, however, serves as a prefix to *Internet art*, a prominent force in the 1990s, which took the Internet as both subject and space of exhibition. "The digitalization of the image was initially thought of as a way to escape the museum or, generally, any exhibition space—to set the image free," Boris Groys writes.[8] Much of this art was activist or interventionist in nature; it turned its back on galleries and museums, which were imagined as irrelevant or elitist or both, in order to engage virtual space.[9] But, if the Internet is the realization of the information environment that McLuhan prophesied, it is not necessarily the place where artists today do their work, even if they inevitably get swept up in its sites. Post–Internet art returned to the gallery space in order to contemplate how webs of information are linked to the fate of the object and body alike in a time of unsurpassed communication and interactivity. Such practices, not incidentally, often betray a wariness about art's ability to insinuate itself into larger systems.

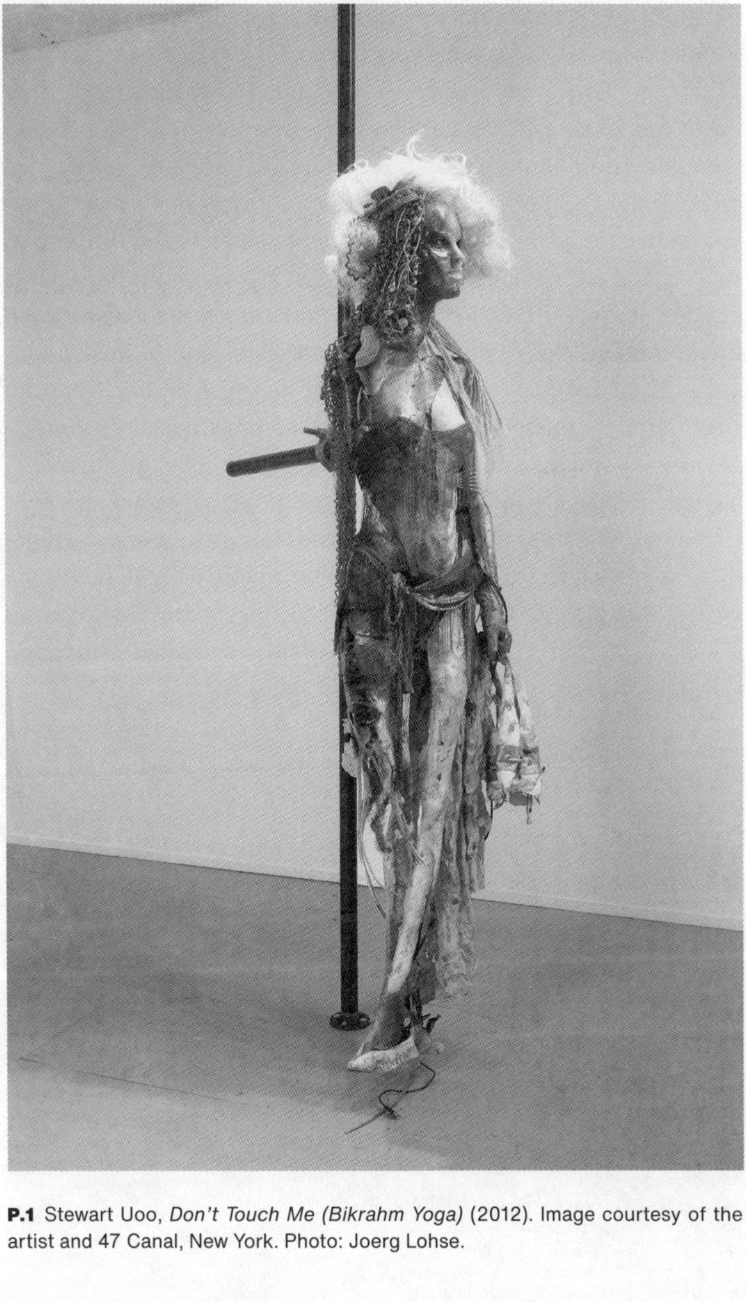

**P.1** Stewart Uoo, *Don't Touch Me (Bikrahm Yoga)* (2012). Image courtesy of the artist and 47 Canal, New York. Photo: Joerg Lohse.

That said, McLuhan's idea that artists forecast the future has become a self-appointed task for many now. Corporate-type entities, incubated in art schools yet comfortable with consultants, predict trends, seriously and/or subversively, all day long. But little hope is bound up with this vision. Optimization is all. More often than not, going out in style seems to be the best that can be done. As for post–Internet artists committed to the object, almost all their work serves up the body as relic: they study the remains of the human era, with the body figured as content processed by media. Look, for example, at Pamela Rosenkranz's bottled "flesh" or Stewart Uoo's scorched figures. Their visions are both hot and cold at once: the charred body and the liquid population. Certainly, this work is about the end of something more than art. Perhaps we will have to wait until we are, in fact, over the Internet to see what will happen next, yet another technological paradigm is hard to fathom. Will our current conditions simply grow more and more dire, or will we figure out something else we can do with the media we have? In the meantime, there are bleak days ahead. One wants to know whether we can do something to prepare and whether there are warnings we—artists and critics—might transmit.

# Acknowledgments

Books germinate in unexpected ways. There is typing on the computer and research in the library, but there is also the serendipitous find in a bookstore and a friend pointing you toward an exhibition or a text. I am happy to be able to thank many people for a variety of things. I am grateful for Hal Foster's critical conversation, and I am lucky to have Ed Halter as an interlocutor and friend. Domenick Ammirati, Eric Banks, Eli Diner, Josephine Graf, Tom Huhn, Claire Lehmann, Sam Lewitt, Annie Ochmanek, and Robert Slifkin all read my work closely and asked me probing questions. Two anonymous readers asked me tough ones, too. Sean Paul and Craig Buckley have been fellow travelers. Fern Bayer and Sarah Sharma, both in Toronto, and Philip Dombrowsky at the Library of the National Gallery of Canada, in Ottawa, helped me find hard-to-find things. The good people at the Library and Archives Canada (also in Ottawa) brought me box after box of crinkly paper covered with exciting ideas. The Museum of Modern Art Library and Archives delivered me crucial material in a charmed aerie. The Jewish Museum allowed me to flip through its *Software* files; and the Cornell University Library shared with me the papers of Wyndham Lewis. Ann Butler, Bronwen Bitetti, and Betsy Cawley helped me navigate the libraries at Bard, and Samantha Gregg gave me a sneak peek at the Getty Research Institute's Claes Oldenburg trove. Sheelagh Bevan and David Senior were fantastic when I had questions about printed matter, and Rebecca Cleman, of Electronic Arts Intermix, was remarkable when I had queries about electronic things. Gordon Hughes and Jeannine Tang offered live audiences for my work, and Lloyd Wise at *Artforum* ushered my first ideas (about General Idea) into print, as did the editors at *October*, who published chapter 5 in its beta form. Hannah Kay helped me gather images (eternally grateful!), and Chris Calhoun made sure this project found a home. Susan Bielstein and James Whitman

Toftness at the University of Chicago Press believed in it and saw it to completion. The Barr Ferree Publication Fund at Princeton University helped cover crucial costs. My colleagues and students at Bard College provided a wonderful place to teach and think. My family (Jill, Barry, Zak) set everything in motion.

# Notes

## Introduction

1 The portrait was commissioned for an article in *People* magazine. See Barbara Rowes, "If the Media Didn't Get Marshall McLuhan's Message in the '60s, Another Is on the Way," *People*, September 20, 1976, 82–84, 87, 88, 91.

2 The painting now hangs in the Canada Room dining hall at the University of St. Michael's College, University of Toronto.

3 Marshall McLuhan, "Notes on the Media as Art Forms," *Explorations*, no. 2 (April 1954): 8.

4 McLuhan alerted people to current realities and dissuaded them from looking in "the rear-view window." "The mere accumulation of past human experience in blood banks called art does not really contribute very much toward the perception of our current environment," McLuhan wrote in 1966. Instead of a transfusion, he wanted a new circulatory system. Marshall McLuhan, "The Medium Is the Massage," in *Understanding Me: Lectures and Interviews*, ed. Stephanie McLuhan and David Staines (Cambridge, MA: MIT Press, 2003), 82.

5 McLuhan wrote about art in the abstract—what it was and what it could be—and paid special attention to individual artists and works of art.

6 Marshall McLuhan, *The Mechanical Bride: Folklore of Industrial Man* (New York: Vanguard, 1951), vii.

7 For a recent, incisive account of the term *global village*, see Ginger Nolan, *The Neocolonialism of the Global Village* (Minneapolis: University of Minnesota Press, 2018).

8 Richard Gilman, "The Doors McLuhan Opens," in *The Confusion of Realms* (New York: Random House, 1969), 27. As a Catholic convert, McLuhan held political positions, including prolife views, that made him an odd bedfellow for many of the artists who followed his work.

9 Artists from Argentina to Amsterdam all gathered under McLuhan's banner. For more on the Argentinean context, see *Listen, Here, Now! Argentine Art of the 1960s: Writings of the Avant-Garde*, ed. Inés Katzenstein (New York: Museum of Modern Art, 2004), 165–66. For the Dutch context, see chapter 7 below.

10 Harold Rosenberg claimed McLuhan as "a kind of artist," arguing that "his quick leaps from datum to axiom . . . are often aesthetically pleasurable." "In his communications-constructed world," he continued, "the artist is the master figure—in fact, the only personage whom he differentiates from the media-absorbing mass." See Harold Rosenberg, review of Marshall McLuhan, *Understanding Media: The Extensions of Man*, *New Yorker*, February 27, 1965, reprinted as "Philosophy in a Pop Key," in *The Case of the Baffled Radical*, by Harold Rosenberg (Chicago: University of Chicago Press, 1985), 64. McLuhan and Rosenberg were introduced by Gerd Stern of the artist collective USCO. See Tina Rivers Ryan, "Toward a Stroboscopic History," in *Hippie Modernism: The Struggle for Utopia*, ed. Andrew Blauvelt (Minneapolis: Walker Art Center, 2015), 380.

11 McLuhan was inspired, in part, by the economic historian Harold Innis, who "presents his insights in a mosaic structure of seemingly unrelated and disproportioned sentences and aphorisms." He likens Innis to an artist: "For anyone acquainted with poetry since Baudelaire and with painting since Cézanne, the later world of Harold A. Innis is quite readily intelligible. He brought their kinds of contemporary awareness of the electric age to organize the data of the historian and the social scientist." Marshall McLuhan, introduction to *The Bias of Communication*, by Harold A. Innis (Toronto: University of Toronto Press, 1964), vii. Nam June Paik wrote: "In McLuhan sometimes the quotations are more 'collage' than logical demonstration." Nam June Paik, "Norbert Wiener and Marshall McLuhan," *Bulletin* (Institute of Contemporary Arts, London), nos. 172–73 (August–September 1967), reprinted in *Nam June Paik: Videa 'n' Videology, 1959–1973*, ed. Judson Rosebud (Syracuse, NY: Everson Museum of Art, 1974), n.p.

12 As John Cage wrote: "*The Gutenberg Galaxy* is made up of borrowings and collages: McLuhan applies what I call silence to all areas of knowledge, that is, he lets them speak. The death of the book is not the end of language: it continues. Just as in my case, silence has invaded everything, and there is still music. . . . Typographic changes, like the 'mosaic' form, are noises which erupt in the book! At one and the same time, the book is condemned to nonexistence and the book comes into being. It can welcome anything." John Cage, *For the Birds* (London: Marion Boyars, 1981), 117.

13 Marshall McLuhan, *Counterblast: 1954 Facsimile* (Berkeley, CA: Gingko, 2011).

14 Marshall McLuhan, *The Gutenberg Galaxy: The Making of Typographic Man* (Toronto: University of Toronto Press, 1962), and *Understanding*

*Media: The Extensions of Man* (New York: McGraw-Hill, 1964).

15 Marshall McLuhan and Quentin Fiore, *The Medium Is the Massage: An Inventory of Effects* (New York: Bantam, 1967).

16 McLuhan, *Understanding Media*, 14.

17 Marshall McLuhan, *Counterblast* (New York: Harcourt, Brace & World, 1969).

18 Marshall McLuhan, "Introduction to the Second Edition," in *Understanding Media*, 2nd ed. (New York: McGraw-Hill, 1966), ix.

19 Marshall McLuhan, "Encyclopaedic Unities," review of *Vision in Motion*, by László Moholy-Nagy, and *Mechanization Takes Command*, by Sigfried Giedion, *Hudson Review* 1, no. 4 (Winter 1949): 599–602. For more on McLuhan and Moholy-Nagy, especially in terms of technology and book design, see Tamara Trodd, *The Art of Mechanical Reproduction: Technology and Aesthetics from Duchamp to the Digital* (Chicago: University of Chicago Press, 2015), 144.

20 Tom Wolfe, "The New Life out There," in *McLuhan: Hot and Cool*, ed. Gerald Stearn (New York: Dial, 1967), 26.

21 McLuhan and Fiore, *The Medium Is the Massage*, 68.

22 Marshall McLuhan, *Culture Is Our Business* (New York: Ballantine, 1970).

23 Jean Baudrillard, "The Masses: The Implosion of the Social in the Media," in *Selected Writings*, ed. Mark Poster, trans. Jacques Mourrain (Stanford, CA: Stanford University Press, 1988), 208.

24 John Durham Peters, "Introduction: Friedrich Kittler's Light Shows," in Friedrich Kittler, *Optical Media*, trans. Anthony Enns (Cambridge: Polity, 2010), 6. Others critique McLuhan for viewing media as essentially opposed, if not deleterious, to human life. "For Kittler and McLuhan alike, media means hypomnesis," Alexander Galloway writes. "They define media via the externalization of man into objects. Hence a fundamentally conservative dimension is inaugurated . . . between the good and balanced human specimen and the dead junk of the hypomnemata. Contrast this with an alternate philosophical tradition that views techne as technique, art, habitus, ethos, or lived practice." Alexander Galloway, *The Interface Effect* (Cambridge: Polity, 2012), 16.

25 Some read McLuhan in purely humanistic terms. In 1967, the curator Germano Celant insisted that Italian artists were struggling against technological society. "The shift that has to be brought about is thus the return to limited and ancillary projects where the human being is the fulcrum and fire of research, in replacement of the medium and the instrument. The man is the message, to paraphrase MacLuhan [*sic*]." Germano Celant, "Arte

Povera: Notes for a Guerilla War," in *Flash Art: Two Decades of History*, ed. Giancarlo Politi and Helena Kontova (Cambridge, MA: MIT Press, 1990), 190.

26 See Marshall McLuhan and Quentin Fiore, *War and Peace in the Global Village* (New York: Bantam, 1968).

27 McLuhan's global village, e.g., owes much to Wyndham Lewis's idea of world government. See Wyndham Lewis, *America and Cosmic Man* (Garden City, NY: Doubleday, 1949). As we will see, he took from others, too, including the poet T. S. Eliot and the art historian E. H. Gombrich.

28 Others, too, experimented with style at this moment. In a 1973 conversation, the art historian George Kubler compared his method with McLuhan's: "We seem to share an impulse to communicate by the aphorism, by the epigram." See Robert Joseph Horvitz, "A Talk with George Kubler," *Artforum*, October 1973, 32. Pamela Lee, however, sees this type of writing in a darker light. She speaks of "the radical abridgement of language in postwar corporate culture, as witnessed in the proliferation of the acronym and the stunted syntax associated with the rhetoric of advertising." Pamela M. Lee, *Chronophobia: On Time in the Art of the 1960s* (Cambridge, MA: MIT Press, 2004), 30.

29 Richard Kostelanetz, *The Theatre of Mixed Means: An Introduction to Happenings, Kinetic Environments, and Other Mixed-Means Performances* (New York: Dial, 1968), 60.

30 "The instantaneous world of electric informational media involves all of us, all at once. No detachment of frame is possible." McLuhan and Fiore, *The Medium Is the Massage*, 53.

## Chapter One

1 Marshall McLuhan to Ezra Pound, June 30, 1948, in Matie Molinaro, Corinne McLuhan, and William Toye, eds., *Letters of Marshall McLuhan* (New York: Oxford University Press, 1987), 194.

2 Jonathan Miller, *Marshall McLuhan* (New York: Viking, 1971), 62.

3 McLuhan makes frequent mention of Margaret Mead's *And Keep Your Powder Dry* (New York: William Morrow, 1942), another important example of self-anthropology.

4 "Traditional folklore consists of the arts of song and dance of agricultural and nomadic peoples," McLuhan writes. "But an industrial world cannot produce the same folk forms as can a society in a state of harmonious equilibrium with the seasons. Yet much of the industrial world's entertainment

and public expression is just as unconsciously expressive of its inner life." *The Mechanical Bride*, 113.

5 "A Dialogue—Marshall McLuhan and Gerald Emanuel Stearn," in Stearn, ed., *McLuhan: Hot and Cool*, 268.

6 McLuhan, *The Mechanical Bride*, v.

7 McLuhan, *The Mechanical Bride*, 87, 45.

8 A review in the *New York Times* found the book too hard on advertising and chastised it for its lack of humor: "If [McLuhan] had toned down his words now and then, and had permitted himself a little humor—'amusement' to which he is given is not the same thing—his would have been a better book for a wider audience." David L. Cohn, "A Touch of Humor Wouldn't Hurt," *New York Times*, October 21, 1951, 26.

9 The art historian Moira Roth characterizes McLuhan's tone as "a language of neutrality developed during the McCarthy period," marking the arrival of a "new tone of indifference." Moira Roth, "The Aesthetic of Indifference," *Artforum*, November 1977, 47.

10 McLuhan, *The Mechanical Bride*, 26.

11 Greil Marcus, "Twentieth-Century Vox: Marshall McLuhan and the Mechanical Bride," *Artforum*, September 2012, 461.

12 Marshall McLuhan, "Sight, Sound and Fury," in *Mass Culture: The Popular Arts in America*, ed. Bernard Rosenberg and David Manning White (Glencoe, IL: Free Press, 1957), 490.

13 McLuhan, "Notes on the Media as Art Forms," 9.

14 McLuhan published frequently on changes in education. See, e.g., Marshall McLuhan, "Classroom without Walls," in *Explorations in Communication*, ed. Edmund Carpenter and Marshall McLuhan (Boston: Beacon, 1960), 1–3; and Marshall McLuhan and George B. Leonard, "The Future of Education: The Class of 1989," *Look*, February 21, 1967, 23–25. He also coauthored (with Kathryn Hutchon and Eric McLuhan) *City as Classroom: Understanding Language and Media* (Agincourt, ON: Book Society of Canada, 1977).

15 Marshall McLuhan, "The End of the Work Ethic," in *Media Research: Technology, Art, Communication*, ed. Michel A. Moos (Amsterdam: G+B Arts International, 1997), 108.

16 Philip Marchand, *Marshall McLuhan: The Medium and the Messenger* (New York: Ticknor & Fields, 1989), 43.

17 Edwin Diamond, "The Message of Marshall McLuhan," *Newsweek*, March 6, 1967, 54. In a dialogue with G. E. Stearn that year, McLuhan said: "In 1936, when I arrived at Wisconsin, I confronted classes of freshmen and I

suddenly realized I was incapable of understanding them. I felt an urgent need to study their popular culture: advertising, games, movies. It was pedagogy, part of my teaching program. To meet them on their grounds was my strategy in pedagogy: the world of pop culture." "A Dialogue—Marshall McLuhan and Gerald Emanuel Stearn," 268.

18 For more on this, see Marshall McLuhan, "Canada, the Borderline Case," in McLuhan and Staines, eds., *Understanding Me*, 105–23.

19 I. A. Richards, *Practical Criticism* (New York: Harcourt Brace, 1949), 6.

20 I. A. Richards, *Principles of Literary Criticism* (New York: Harcourt, Brace & World, 1925), 157.

21 Terry Eagleton, *The Function of Criticism* (London: Verso, 1984), 74, 77.

22 F. R. Leavis and Denys Thompson, *Culture and Environment: The Training of Critical Awareness* (London: Chatto & Windus, 1931), 6, 3, 18, 1.

23 Eagleton, *The Function of Criticism*, 81. According to Harold Rosenberg, Leavis imagined the literary man as a leader. "Insurrection," in *The Case of the Baffled Radical*, 22–40. For a blistering critique of Leavis's moral fervor and "disguised politics," see ibid., esp. 27–28 (quote 27).

24 In a March 2, 1966, letter to the downtown gadfly Richard Kostelanetz, McLuhan wrote: "If you study the writings of [Richards and Leavis], you will see how I began to study popular culture. Cf. especially *Culture and Environment* by Leavis and Thompson." Marshall McLuhan to Richard Kostelanetz, March 2, 1966, Marshall McLuhan Fonds, vol. 29, file 30, Library and Archives of Canada, Ottawa.

25 Leavis and Thompson, *Culture and Environment*, 1. McLuhan, by contrast, asks how a study of the great books "differs from any other merely verbal and mechanized education in our time?" *The Mechanical Bride*, 43.

26 Marshall McLuhan, "The Mechanical Bride" (n.d., typescript), Marshall McLuhan Fonds, vol. 64, files 1, 5.

27 Michel de Certeau, *The Practice of Everyday Life*, trans. Steven Rendall (Berkeley and Los Angeles: University of California Press, 1984), 173.

28 Leavis and Thompson, *Culture and Environment*, 1.

29 Later, McLuhan criticized himself for clinging too tightly to book culture. "When I wrote *The Mechanical Bride* some years ago I did not realize that I was attempting a defense of book-culture against the new media," he wrote in 1954. "I can now see that I was trying to bring some of the critical awareness fostered by literary training to bear on the new media of sight and sound. My strategy was wrong, because my obsession with literary values blinded me to much that was actually happening for good and ill. What we have to defend today is not the values developed in any particular culture

or by any one mode of communication . . . [but rather] all human values." "Sight, Sound and Fury," 495. In this gloss on his project, McLuhan dedicates himself to sketching out human values over and in distinction to literary ones.

30 Giedion and McLuhan began corresponding in the late 1940s and maintained a professional relationship for many years after. For more on that relationship, see Mark Wigley, "Network Fever," *Grey Room* 4 (Spring 2001): 82–122; and Reto Geiser, *Giedion in America: Repositioning the History of Modern Architecture* (Zurich: gta Verlag, 2018), 372–88.

31 Sigfried Giedion, *Mechanization Takes Command: A Contribution to Anonymous History* (New York: Oxford University Press, 1948), v, 2.

32 McLuhan, *The Mechanical Bride*, 15.

33 Giedion, *Mechanization Takes Command*, 192.

34 Giedion, *Mechanization Takes Command*, 714, 200. "The ruling artistic taste in the nineteenth century was formed by exploiting certain dormant wishes of the public," Giedion writes. "The public loves what is sweet, smooth, and outwardly appealing. These desires can be strengthened, weakened, or diverted into positive channels." Ibid., 200–201.

35 Giedion, *Mechanization Takes Command*, 196. Giedion's denunciations would become more emphatic with time. "Public taste today is formed mainly by publicity and the articles of daily use," he wrote in 1967. "Responsible are the art directors in industry and advertising firms . . . who act as censors and level down the designs of the artists to their own conception of the public's taste. They are supposed to feed the assembly line in the speediest way and as a safeguard they judge the public taste lower than it really is." Sigfried Giedion, "Art Means Reality," in *Language of Vision*, by György Kepes (Chicago: Paul Theobald, 1967), 7.

36 McLuhan, "Encyclopedic Unities," 599. Three years later McLuhan wrote: "The Swiss cultural historian Sigfried Giedion has had to invent the concept of 'anonymous history' in order to write an account of the new technological culture in Anglo-Saxondom." McLuhan, *Counterblast: 1954 Facsimile*, n.p.

37 McLuhan, "Notes on the Media as Art Forms," 8.

38 It is striking to compare this moment with our own today when the complete industrialization of food has led to a mania for unrefined flour and artisanal loaves.

39 McLuhan, *The Mechanical Bride*, 51.

40 Marshall McLuhan, "American Advertising," *Horizon* no. 93–94 (October 1947): 134, 133.

41 Marshall McLuhan, "The Psychopathology of Time & Life," *Neurotica* 5 (Autumn 1949): 9. The essay was reprinted in *The Scene Before You: A New Approach to American Culture*, ed. Chandler Brossard (New York: Rinehart, 1955), 147–160. Clement Greenberg and Harold Rosenberg also contributed essays to the volume.

42 McLuhan, *The Mechanical Bride*, 10.

43 McLuhan, *The Mechanical Bride*, v. For a return to the Poe story, see McLuhan, *Understanding Media*.

44 Richards, *Practical Criticism*, 11.

45 Futurism offers an important point of reference. In the section "The Drowned Man," McLuhan claims: "It is helpful in getting our bearings in these circumstances to notice the reaction of certain Europeans to the same flood of goods and sensations created by applied science." But he contrasts Marinetti's "Nietzschean brio" and embrace of the machine with his own tendency for "critical reflection." *The Mechanical Bride*, 90.

46 McLuhan, *The Mechanical Bride*, 50.

47 Giedion, *Mechanization Takes Command*, 44.

48 Pierre Cabanne, *Dialogues with Marcel Duchamp* (New York: Viking, 1971), 34.

49 Giedion, *Mechanization Takes Command*, 107.

50 McLuhan, *The Mechanical Bride*, 100.

51 Marshall McLuhan, "Duchamp" (n.d., typescript), Marshall McLuhan Fonds, vol. 128, file 34. The French art historian Michel Sanouillet commissioned McLuhan's essay "The Ghost of Mechanization" for the fifth number of *Cahiers Dada-Surréalisme*, which was to be dedicated to Marcel Duchamp, but the issue was never published. (A copy of the essay can be found in the Marshall McLuhan Fonds.) The fourth issue appeared in 1970.

52 McLuhan, "The Mechanical Bride," Marshall McLuhan Fonds, vol. 64, file 1.

53 McLuhan tore his copy from the March 10, 1947, issue of *Life*.

54 Giedion, *Mechanization Takes Command*, 99.

55 Giedion, *Mechanization Takes Command*, 98.

56 McLuhan, *The Mechanical Bride*, 93. The relationship between industry and sexuality was much discussed at this time. "It is worth drawing attention to the way in which industrialists (Ford in particular) have been concerned with the sexual affairs of their employees and with their family arrangements in general," Gramsci observes in the *Prison Notebooks*, written in the early 1930s. "One should not be misled, any more than in the case of prohibition, by the 'puritanical' appearance assumed by this con-

cern. The truth is that the new type of man demanded by the rationalization of production and work cannot be developed until the sexual instinct has been suitably regulated and until it too has been rationalized." Antonio Gramsci, *Selections from the Prison Notebooks*, trans. and ed. Quintin Hoare and Geoffrey Nowell Smith (New York: International, 1971), 296–97. But, again, this is about the disciplining of the worker. McLuhan is interested in the stimulation of the consumer.

57 Karl Marx, *Grundrisse*, trans. Martin Nicolaus (New York: Penguin, 1993), 693.

58 Siegfried Kracauer, "The Mass Ornament," in *The Mass Ornament: Weimar Essays*, trans. and ed. Thomas Y. Levin (Cambridge, MA: Harvard University Press, 1995), 75, 79, 78, 77.

59 McLuhan, *The Mechanical Bride*, 156, 94, 96. Kracauer, too, notes that the mass ornament calls forth a certain type of audience: "The regularity of their patterns is cheered by the masses, themselves arranged by the stands in tier upon ordered tier." "The Mass Ornament," 76.

60 McLuhan, *The Mechanical Bride*, 98.

61 For more on this, see Andreas Huyssen, "Mass Culture as Woman: Modernism's Other," in *After the Great Divide: Modernism, Mass Culture, Postmodernism* (Bloomington: Indiana University Press, 1986), 44–62.

62 McLuhan, *The Mechanical Bride*, 157.

63 For one example, see Judith Williamson, *Decoding Advertisements: Ideology and Meaning in Advertising* (London: Marion Boyars, 1978).

64 "Even to acknowledge the mass media in postwar Britain was a very radical move, and the constituency of the IG's idea was tiny," Martin Harrison notes. "I would guess, for example, that they represented the entire audience in the UK for Marshall McLuhan's 1951 *The Mechanical Bride*." Charlotte Cotton, "Round Table: Pop and the Traveling Image," in *International Pop*, ed. Darsie Alexander (New York: D.A.P., 2016), 195.

65 "The scrapbook quality of *Mechanization Takes Command* secured it an avid reception in the circle of the Independent Group in London during the very early days of British pop art," the architectural historian Stanislaus von Moos has written. Stanislaus von Moos, postscript to Giedion, *Mechanization Takes Command*, 763.

66 McLuhan visited the Institute of Contemporary Arts on June 27, 1963, giving a talk, cosponsored by the Royal College of Art, titled "Changing Modes of Perception since TV."

67 John McHale, "The Man from Mascom," *Progressive Architecture*, February 1967, 172.

68 Michael Craig-Martin, "Richard Hamilton in Conversation with Michael Craig-Martin," in *Richard Hamilton*, ed. Hal Foster with Alex Bacon (Cambridge, MA: MIT Press, 2010), 6. For more on McLuhan and the IG, see Nigel Whiteley, *Reyner Banham: Historian of the Immediate Future* (Cambridge, MA: MIT Press, 2002), 324–25.

69 David Robbins, "American Ads," in *The Independent Group: Postwar Britain and the Aesthetics of Plenty*, ed. David Robbins (Cambridge, MA: MIT Press, 1990), 59.

70 Herbert Marshall McLuhan, "TIME, LIFE, and FORTUNE," *View*, Spring 1947, 33–37. McLuhan's article played an interesting role in the context of the Surrealist *View*, which had dedicated issues to Max Ernst and Marcel Duchamp. The journal possessed a camp spirit and featured ads for cosmetics. Its hybrid character suggests that Surrealism now belonged to mass culture rather than the domestic interior, where it first flourished. Surrealism's dream world, in other words, had been pushed out of the individual unconscious into the newly managed collective mind. As McLuhan would write in 1954, the media had become a "cornucopia of daily SURREALISM." *Counterblast: 1954 Facsimile*, n.p. In many ways, McLuhan bridges a gap between changing conceptions of the avant-garde, connecting Surrealism to Pop. At this moment, the two were closer than we typically think.

71 McLuhan, "TIME, LIFE, and FORTUNE," 33. McLuhan's article was occasioned by the rumor that Henry Luce planned to start a "high-brow" culture magazine. For an expanded version of the essay, see Marshall McLuhan, "The Psychopathology of Time & Life," *Neurotica* 5 (Autumn 1949): 5–16.

72 McLuhan, "TIME, LIFE, and FORTUNE," 37.

73 Alison Smithson and Peter Smithson, "But Today We Collect Ads," in *Modern Dreams: The Rise and Fall and Rise of Pop* (Cambridge, MA: MIT Press, 1988), 53.

74 Lawrence Alloway, "Technology and Sex in Science Fiction: A Note on Cover Art," *Ark* 17 (Summer 1956): 19.

75 Reyner Banham, "Vehicles of Desire," in *Modern Dreams*, 69.

76 John McHale, "The Expendable Ikon," *Architectural Design*, February 1959, 82.

77 Banham, "Vehicles of Desire," 69. "The spectator dreams in the darkened theater," McLuhan writes. "He dreams the dreams that money can buy but which he can neither afford nor earn in the daylight world." *The Mechanical Bride*, 97. In Richter's film, Duchamp directed the dream sequence, which spliced together Rotoreliefs from his "Anemic Cinema" with a live-action nude descending a staircase.

78 Craig-Martin, "Richard Hamilton in Conversation with Michael Craig-Martin," 6.

79 See Richard Hamilton, "An Exposition of *$he*," in *Collected Words, 1953–1982* (London: Thames & Hudson, 1983), 35–39.

80 Hal Foster insists on a difference between the two bodies. "But the exchange between the two bodies is not equal," he writes. "The car appears almost animate, while the woman appears almost spectral, drained of life, her carnality all but given over in fetishistic transfer, to the Chrysler." Hal Foster, *The First Pop Age: Painting and Subjectivity in the Art of Hamilton, Lichtenstein, Warhol, Richter, and Ruscha* (Princeton, NJ: Princeton University Press, 2012), 27.

81 Richard Hamilton, "For the Finest Art Try—POP," in *Collected Words*, 43.

82 On occasion, Hamilton participated directly in popular culture. See, e.g., his design for the self-titled 1968 Beatles album commonly known as the *White Album*. For more on this, see Andrew Wilson, *Richard Hamilton: Swingeing London 67 (f)* (London: Afterall, 2011), 90–97.

## Chapter Two

1 Marshall McLuhan, *The Gutenberg Galaxy: The Making of Typographic Man* (Toronto: University of Toronto Press, 1962), 11.

2 McLuhan, *Understanding Media*, 27.

3 Marshall McLuhan and Harley Parker, *Through the Vanishing Point: Space in Poetry and Painting* (New York: Harper Colophon, 1968), 197.

4 Marshall McLuhan, *The Classical Trivium: The Place of Thomas Nashe in the Learning of His Time* (Berkeley, CA: Gingko, 2006). For more on McLuhan's medievalism, see Alexander Nagel, *Medieval Modern: Art Out of Time* (New York: Thames & Hudson, 2012), 155–68.

5 McLuhan, "Notes on the Media as Art Forms," 9. Elsewhere, McLuhan wrote: "To write his epic of the modern Ulysses [Joyce] studied all his life the ads, the comics, the pulps, and popular speech." *The Mechanical Bride*, 59.

6 Marshall McLuhan, "Pound's Critical Prose," in *The Interior Landscape: The Literary Criticism of Marshall McLuhan*, ed. Eugene McNamara (New York: McGraw-Hill, 1969), 77. As noted in chapter 1 above, McLuhan visited Pound at St. Elizabeth's Hospital in Washington, DC, in 1948.

7 Marshall McLuhan, "Culture and Technology," in *Astronauts of Inner-Space: An International Collection of Avant-Garde Activity*, ed. Jeff Berner (San Francisco: Stolen Paper Review Editions, 1966), 18.

8 "The printed book had encouraged artists to reduce all forms of expression as much as possible to the single descriptive and narrative plane of the printed word," McLuhan wrote. "The advent of electric media released art from this strait jacket at once, creating the world of Paul Klee, Picasso, Braque, Eisenstein, the Marx Brothers, and James Joyce." *Understanding Media*, 54.

9 Scholars have long argued about Cubism's meaning, with some insisting that Picasso's inclusion of articles about the Balkan Wars signals his opposition to militarism and imperialism. McLuhan, on the other hand, spied an interpretation of a wider media system. "What became cubism was implicit in the technological conditions of reportage and news presentation more than a hundred years earlier," he wrote in a précis on Paul Klee. Mass communications predated Cubism, but Cubism made mass communications visible. "Implicit in the juxtaposition of many different spaces (news items) is multiplicity of times, since different areas of the world represent widely varied stages of historic acculturation. In a word, the press landscape as art form is intimately linked to the technology of spatial communication and control, but it is also a revolutionary medium, artistically and politically." Marshall McLuhan, "Paul Klee," *Shenandoah* 4, no. 1 (Spring 1953): 78–79.

10 Borrowed from the field of chemistry, *interface* refers "to the interaction of substances in a kind of mutual irritation." McLuhan, introduction to *The Bias of Communication*, viii.

11 McLuhan, "Pound's Critical Prose," 77.

12 Jeffrey Meyers, *The Enemy: A Biography of Wyndham Lewis* (London: Routledge & Kegan Paul, 1980), 55.

13 For more on Omega, see *Beyond Bloomsbury: Designs of the Omega Workshops, 1913–19*, ed. Alexandra Gerstein (London: Courtauld Gallery, 2009). The workshops produced a mix of pottery, prints, publications, and fashion. For more on Lewis's break, see Virginia Woolf, *Roger Fry: A Biography* (London: Vintage Lives, 2003), 192.

14 "Popular art does not mean the art of poor people, as it is usually supposed to," Lewis wrote. "It means the art of individuals." Wyndham Lewis, *Blast* (Santa Rosa, CA: Black Sparrow, 1989), n.p. Popular art is the art of individuals because only individuals can impress ideas on the populace.

15 Lewis, *Blast*, 55.

16 Paul Edwards, "BLAST and the Revolutionary Mood of Wyndham Lewis's Vorticism," in *Vorticism: New Perspectives*, ed. Mark Antliff and Scott W. Klein (Oxford: Oxford University Press, 2013), 200.

17 Wyndham Lewis, *Time and Western Man* (London: Chatto & Windus, 1927), 39.

18 Hugh Kenner, *Wyndham Lewis* (New York: New Directions, 1954), 240.

19 Hugh Kenner, *The Pound Era* (Berkeley: University of California Press, 1971), 232.

20 Wyndham Lewis, introduction to *Wyndham Lewis and Vorticism*, ed. John Rothenstein (London: Tate Gallery, 1956), 3.

21 Wyndham Lewis, *Men without Art* (1934; Santa Rosa, CA: Black Sparrow, 1987), 99.

22 For Lewis, art delivers "us from the time mechanism of existence," McLuhan wrote in 1953. Against Henri Bergson's theory of time, McLuhan claimed Lewis on behalf of the static and the spatial. If Bergson posited memory as the link between the spirit and the material, Lewis tried to break the chain. Marshall McLuhan, "Wyndham Lewis: His Theory of Art and Communication," in McNamara, ed., *The Interior Landscape*, 84.

23 Kenner, *Wyndham Lewis*, 243.

24 John Rothenstein, "Wyndham Lewis and Vorticism," in Rothenstein, ed., *Wyndham Lewis and Vorticism*, 7.

25 Hal Foster, *Prosthetic Gods* (Cambridge, MA: MIT Press, 2004), 131.

26 For more on Hulme, Worringer, and what Hulme called "a new constructive geometric art," see T. E. Hulme, *Selected Writings*, ed. Patrick McGuinness (Manchester: Carcanet, 1998), 128.

27 McLuhan quoted this passage many years later. See McLuhan, *Culture Is Our Business*, 172.

28 Wilhelm Worringer, *Abstraction and Empathy*, trans. Michael Bullock (Chicago: Ivan R. Dee, 1997), 4, 16, 17. See also T. E. Hulme, *Speculations: Essays on Humanism and the Philosophy of Art* (New York: Harcourt, Brace, 1924).

29 McLuhan, "Wyndham Lewis," 77. Later, McLuhan made this point more explicitly: "An art of mimetic resonance, devoid of any contrapuntal stress, would be a betrayal of the art function of heightening awareness." Marshall McLuhan, "Art as Anti-Environment," *Art News Annual* 31 (1966): 56.

30 Marshall McLuhan, "The Emperor's Old Clothes," in *The Man-Made Object*, ed. György Kepes (New York: George Braziller, 1966), 91. McLuhan borrowed this formulation from E. H. Gombrich's *Art and Illusion* (New York: Pantheon, 1960).

31 Ezra Pound, "Selections from *The New Age*," in *Ezra Pound and the Visual Arts*, ed. Harriet Zinnes (New York: New Directions, 1980), 6.

32 Lewis, *Blast*, 142.

33 T. E. Hulme, "Modern Art II: A Preface Note and Neo-Realism" (1914), in McGuinness, ed., *Selected Writings*, 286. The idea that old ways were falling into ruin was a leitmotif of Vorticist thought. "I start with the conviction that the Renaissance attitude is breaking up," Hulme wrote, "and then illustrate it by the change in art, and not vice versa." Ibid.

34 Wyndham Lewis, *The Art of Being Ruled* (London: Chatto & Windus, 1926).

35 Wyndham Lewis, *Hitler* (London: Chatto & Windus, 1931), 4, 36.

36 Fredric Jameson, *Fables of Aggression: Wyndham Lewis, the Modernist as Fascist* (London: Verso, 1979), 184. "[Lewis]," Jameson argues, "means to convey the spirit, to the British public, of a phenomenon culturally alien to it; he intends to translate and to explain the Nazi movement as a matter of some historical significance, but not necessarily to endorse it." Ibid., 180.

37 In 1954, three years before his death, Lewis published the novel *Self-Condemned*, a retrospective look at his exile and a scathing indictment of Toronto. McLuhan, who is fictionalized as Professor McKenzie, reviewed the book alongside Lewis's recent jeremiad *The Demon of Progress in the Arts* (London: Methuen, 1954) on the CBC program "Critically Speaking" on August 21, 1955.

38 The same year Lewis also published *The Jews: Are They Human?*, which, in his typically sardonic manner, sought to "make out a case for their humanity." Wyndham Lewis, *The Jews: Are They Human?* (New York: Gordon, 1972), 8.

39 Wyndham Lewis, *The Hitler Cult* (1939; New York: Gordon, 1972), 5, 247.

40 About a rally at the Sportpalast, he writes: "In this gigantic assembly of twenty thousand people there was something like the physical pressure of one immense, indignant thought—it was impossible to be present and not to be amazed at the passion engendered in all these men and women, and the millions of others of whom these were only a fraction, by the message of these stormy platform voices, calling upon them to pursue relentlessly the path marked out, and to recapture their freedom at whatever cost." Lewis, *The Hitler Cult*, 10–11.

41 Kenner, *Wyndham Lewis*, 70, 72.

42 Eric Michaud, "Artist and Dictator," in *The Cult of Art in Nazi Germany*, trans. Janet Lloyd (Stanford, CA: Stanford University Press, 2004), 3–25. This line of thinking has a long history. In 1913, Guillaume Apollinaire wrote: "Poets and artists together determine the shape of their time and the future submissively falls into line." Guillaume Apollinaire, *The Cubist Painters*, trans. Peter Read (Berkeley and Los Angeles: University of Cali-

fornia Press, 2004), 19. Peter Cohen's documentary film *The Architecture of Doom* (1989) is also helpful on this topic.

43 Wyndham Lewis, *The Caliph's Design* (Santa Rosa, CA: Black Sparrow, 1986), 19–20.

44 "Of course politics and art have much in common," Lewis wrote. "Both are occupations that demand very little intelligence and no training to speak of; both are a refuge for people who could shine in no other walk of life—for human throw-outs in short." *The Hitler Cult*, 75.

45 Boris Groys, "The Hero's Body: Hitler's Art Theory," in *Art Power* (Cambridge, MA: MIT Press, 2013), 133.

46 Wyndham Lewis, *Blasting and Bombardiering* (Berkeley: University of California Press, 1967), 63.

47 McLuhan taught in St. Louis at the time. He returned to Canada in 1944, first to Assumption College in Windsor, then to the University of St. Michael's College at the University of Toronto, where he would remain for the rest of his career. He taught exclusively at Catholic schools.

48 McLuhan's "extracurricular" activities closely aligned with his academic work. In 1953, he joined the editorial board of *Explorations: Studies in Culture and Communication*, a journal started by his colleague the anthropologist Edmund Carpenter and funded by a grant from the Ford Foundation. *Explorations* published work on culture and technology by prominent intellectuals, including Sigfried Giedion and the sociologist David Riesman.

49 Marshall McLuhan to Wyndham Lewis, December 18, 1954, in Molinaro, McLuhan, and Toye, eds., *Letters of Marshall McLuhan*, 245.

50 Henry Luce, "The American Century," *Life*, February 17, 1941, 61–65.

51 The text was reprinted in *Explorations*, no. 4 (1955): 26–28.

52 Certainly, McLuhan had ample opportunity to do so. In a 1969 reminiscence, he spoke of his friendship with Lewis. He mentions a mutual friend who "had a very keen political mind and used to rib Lewis a good deal about his supposed fascism," but nothing more is said. Marshall McLuhan, "Wyndham Lewis," *The Atlantic*, December 1969, 93.

## Chapter Three

1 Donald Barthelme to Marshall McLuhan, March 10, 1962, Marshall McLuhan Fonds, vol. 18, file 78. In addition to Barthelme, the film critic Parker Tyler served as managing editor, while the art critics Thomas Hess and Harold Rosenberg edited the publication.

2 John Cage later made a number of computer-generated mesostic poems using this text. See his "Writing through 'The Agenbite of Outwit,'" *Tyuonyi* 1 (1985): 62–67.

3 F. R. Leavis once described his project as an attempt to save a culture that had lost "any sense of the difference between life and electricity." Geoffrey Hartmann, "Placing Leavis," *London Review of Books*, January 24, 1985, 10. McLuhan saw electric light as representing a similar rupture but, in contrast, he sought to understand its potential.

4 Marshall McLuhan, "The Agenbite of Outwit," *Location* 1 (Spring 1963): 41–44.

5 Robert Rauschenberg, "Random Order," *Location* 1 (Spring 1963): 27–31. Some of Rauschenberg's other notes also seem to speak to McLuhan's ideas about technology, language, and the human sensorium: "With sound scale and insistency trucks mobilize words, and broadside our culture by a combination of law and local motivation which produces an extremely complex random order that cannot be described by accident."

6 Kostelanetz, *The Theatre of Mixed Means*, 80.

7 McLuhan, "Notes on the Media as Art Forms," 6. McLuhan continues: "This assumption blinds people to the aspect of communication as participation in a common situation. And it leads to ignoring the form of communication as the basic art situation which is more significant than the information or idea 'transmitted.'" Ibid.

8 McLuhan, *Understanding Media*, 8. McLuhan's name was often mentioned in discussions of artists who worked with electric light. Kynaston McShine references him in relation to Dan Flavin's fluorescent light sculptures. See Kynaston McShine, introduction to *Primary Structures* (New York: Jewish Museum, 1966), n.p.

9 McLuhan, *Understanding Media*, 18. McLuhan's sentence owes a debt to T. S. Eliot: "The chief use of the 'meaning' of a poem, in the ordinary sense, may be . . . to satisfy one habit of the reader, to keep his mind diverted and quiet, while the poem does its work upon him: much as the imaginary burglar is always provided with a bit of nice meat for the housedog." T. S. Eliot, *The Use of Poetry and the Use of Criticism* (Cambridge, MA: Harvard University Press, 1933), 144.

10 McLuhan, *Understanding Media*, 9 (emphasis added).

11 Rosenberg, "Philosophy in a Pop Key," 198.

12 For more on *Picnic in Space*, see Richard Cavell, *McLuhan in Space: A Cultural Geography* (Toronto: University of Toronto Press, 2002).

13 See John M. Lee, "M'Luhan's Views Reshape Museum," *New York Times*,

February 26, 1967, 32; and Harley Parker, "New Hall of Fossil Invertebrates, Royal Ontario Museum," *Curator: The Museum Journal* 10, no. 4 (December 1967): 284–96.

14 "McLuhanism in the Museum," *Museum News* 46, no. 7 (March 1968): 16. "The slides-in-color showed Dutch scenes, including some of the New Amsterdam models in the permanent Dutch gallery and some views of Holland and of Seventeenth-Century Dutch paintings, along with views of New York as it looks today. The movie, in black and white, showed street scenes of New York and featured children playing together." Ibid. The exhibition was *New York—the Scene 67/17.*

15 Conversation between Marshall McLuhan, Harley Parker, and Jacques Barzun, in *Exploration of the Ways, Means, and Values of Museum Communication with the Viewing Public* (New York: Museum of the City of New York, 1969), 1. McLuhan proposed concrete ideas about how one might create a dynamic, participatory space in a museum. "Let's suppose that an object is shown on a video tape, closed circuit, in the act of being made, instead of as the end product—that you actually showed an Eskimo making and enjoying one of these things," he wrote. "This could be done for almost any item in a museum." Ibid., 26.

16 *Museum of the City of New York and Marine Museum of the City of New York Annual Report, 1967–1968* (New York, 1968), 11.

17 For more on Dorner, see Julian Rose, "Society of the Spectator," *Bookforum*, June–August 2019, 54.

18 Though Johns did not know McLuhan when he made the sculpture, he learned about him soon after. "[Johns] keeps himself informed about what's going on, particularly in the world of art," John Cage wrote in a 1964 essay on the artist. "This is done by reading magazines, visiting galleries and studios, answering the phone, conversing with friends. If a book is brought to his attention that he believes is interesting, he gets it and reads it (Wittgenstein, Nabokov, McLuhan)." John Cage, "Jasper Johns: Stories and Ideas," in Alan Solomon, ed., *Jasper Johns* (New York: Jewish Museum, 1964), 21.

19 Jasper Johns, "Marcel Duchamp (1887–1968)," in *Jasper Johns: Writings, Sketchbooks, Notes, Interviews*, ed. Kirk Varnedoe (New York: Museum of Modern Art, 2002), 22. The phrase is Duchamp's.

20 Johns's *Field Painting* (1963) also contains a neon light shaped like the letter *R*. It shares the variegated canvas, full of stenciled letters and swaths of paint, with a Savarin Coffee tin and a light switch.

21 Joshua Shannon, *The Disappearance of Objects: New York Art and the Rise*

*of the Postmodern City* (New Haven, CT: Yale University Press, 2009), 58.

22 Max Kozloff, *Jasper Johns* (New York: Harry N. Abrams, 1972), 24. In an earlier version of his essay, Kozloff writes at length about the similarities between Johns's and McLuhan's investigations. See Max Kozloff, *Jasper Johns* (New York: Harry N. Abrams, 1968).

23 Kozloff, *Jasper Johns* (1968), 38. Kozloff also mentions McLuhan's theories on electric light.

24 McLuhan, *Understanding Media*, 65.

25 Diamond, "The Message of Marshall McLuhan," 57.

26 Peter Bürger, *Theory of the Avant-Garde*, trans. Michael Shaw (Minneapolis: University of Minnesota Press, 1984), 57–58.

27 For more on EAT, see Bettina Funcke, *Pop or Populus: Art between High and Low* (Berlin: Sternberg, 2009), and *E.A.T. (Experiments in Art and Technology): Open-Ended*, ed. Deoksun Park (Seoul: National Museum of Modern and Contemporary Art, 2018).

28 On June 22, 1965, McLuhan was introduced on the short-lived CBC television show *Other Voices* as the "world's first Pop philosopher." On the program, he speaks of "the Andy Warhol effect of duplicating the same image over and over again": "That has a strange effect upon the image. If you take a picture of Liz Taylor or anybody at all and repeat it and repeat it the effect is to transform Liz Taylor into a corporate, mass image and not a private picture of any given individual at all." "Marshall McLuhan 1965: Other Voices: A Pop Philosopher," https://www.youtube.com/watch?v=XE-74Haej2o.

29 The panel ("Would You Believe Pop?") was held in conjunction with the exhibition *11 Pop Artists: The New Image*. Gene Swenson also participated. *The New Image* was a print portfolio and traveling exhibition sponsored by Philip Morris. Rosenquist contributed three prints, including *Circles of Confusion*, featuring multiple iterations of the General Electric logo over a field of Ben Day dots. See *11 Pop Artists: The New Image* (Munich: Galerie Friedrich + Dahlem, 1966). Rosenquist's original drawing is held in the collections of the National Gallery of Art, Washington, DC.

30 Rosenberg, "Philosophy in a Pop Key," 63.

31 For a précis of this idea, see McLuhan, "Art as Anti-Environment," 55–57. The essay is prefaced by Roy Lichtenstein's *Girl in Mirror* (1964) along with the caption: "New technological environments need new arts to make us aware of the change." Ibid., 54.

32 Marshall McLuhan, "Great Change-Overs for You," *Vogue*, July 1, 1966,

117. McLuhan reiterated this point in a 1969 interview: "Because we are benumbed by any new technology—which in turn creates a totally new environment—we tend to make the old environment more visible; we do so by turning it into an art form and by attaching ourselves to the objects and atmosphere that characterized it, just as we've done with jazz, and as we're now doing with the garbage of the mechanical environment via pop art." "Marshall McLuhan: A Candid Conversation with the High Priest of Popcult and Metaphysician of Media," *Playboy*, March 1969, 56.

33 McLuhan, "Great Change-Overs for You," 117.

34 Marshall McLuhan, "The Invisible Environment: The Future of an Erosion," *Perspecta* 11 (1967): 165. "The Invisible Environment" was first delivered at the Vision '65 conference in Carbondale, IL.

35 Andy Warhol and Pat Hackett, *POPism: The Warhol Sixties* (New York: Harcourt Brace Jovanovich, 1980), 3.

36 Warhol and Hackett, *POPism*, 215.

37 One commentator described McLuhan as a "combination Spengler, Picasso and Mort Sahl." John Clellon Holmes, *Nothing More to Declare* (New York: E. P. Dutton, 1967), 39.

38 Gregory Battcock, "The Warhol Generation," in *The New Art*, ed. Gregory Battcock (New York: Plume, 1973), 21.

39 Bob Colacello, *Holy Terror: Andy Warhol Close Up* (New York: Vintage, 2014), 194.

40 McLuhan, "The End of the Work Ethic," 96.

41 Dwight Macdonald compares McLuhan's tribal man to Rousseau's "Noble Savage." Dwight Macdonald, review of *Understanding Media*, in Stearn, ed., *McLuhan: Hot and Cool*, 205.

42 John McHale, review of *Understanding Media*, *Progressive Architecture*, February 1967, 170, 172, 176, 188, 199. See also my introduction to John McHale, *The Expendable Reader: Articles on Art, Architecture, Design, and Media, 1951–1979*, ed. Alex Kitnick (New York: GSAPP, 2011), 12–30.

## Chapter Four

1 McLuhan, *Understanding Media*, 233, 314.

2 With TV, "the viewer is the screen," McLuhan wrote. *Culture Is Our Business*, 110.

3 Conversation between Marshall McLuhan, Harley Parker, and Jacques Barzun, 2.

4 Jonathan Crary, "Eclipse of the Spectacle," in *Art After Modernism: Rethinking Representation*, ed. Brian Wallis (Boston: David R. Godine, 1984), 284.

5 McLuhan, "The Agenbite of Outwit" (*Location*); *Newsweek*, March 6, 1967. McLuhan also lectured at the Museum of Modern Art in New York on June 27, 1966, as part of a three-day workshop seminar entitled "Film and the Public Library."

6 McLuhan, "The Emperor's Old Clothes," 91. This idea is also discussed in Edmund Carpenter and Marshall McLuhan, introduction to Carpenter and McLuhan, eds., *Explorations in Communication*, x.

7 According to the artist Frank Gillette, McLuhan attended the opening. Frank Gillette, interview by the author, January 20, 2015.

8 This was the case with Paul Ryan, who worked as McLuhan's research associate during his time at Fordham. "McLuhan claimed artists could decode new media," Ryan said in a 2010 interview. "So I said: OK, besides my own experimentation, we have got to get video in the hands of serious artists. Somebody introduced me to Frank Gillette, a painter who had taught a course on McLuhan at the 14th Street Free University. I handed over two portable video cameras and editing equipment we had at Fordham. . . . Not long after, Frank founded Raindance, an alternate video group now widely known for publishing *Radical Software*." Ayreen Anastas and Rene Gabri, *Paul Ryan* (New York: D.A.P., 2011), 7. Ryan subsequently explored the educational potential of videotape, especially in regard to feedback. Paul Ryan, "Videotape—Thinking about a Medium," *Media and Methods*, December 1968, 36–41.

9 Miller, *Marshall McLuhan*, 1.

10 Jack Gould, "TV: Experiment McLuhanizes Marshall McLuhan," *New York Times*, March 20, 1967, 63.

11 Edmund Carpenter, *Oh, What a Blow That Phantom Gave Me!* (New York: Bantam, 1972), 166. As one reviewer pointed out, Carpenter "maintained his privacy, and can only have the slow influence that a book man will have." Maurice Farge, "Bruises Are Real," *Open Letter*, Summer 1974, 124.

12 Paik performed the work at the Fluxus International Festival for Very New Music at the Städtisches Museum in Wiesbaden in 1962.

13 Nam June Paik, *Nam June Paik: Electronic Art* (New York: Galeria Bonino, 1965), n.p.

14 The gallery was housed in a villa belonging to the architect Rolf Jahrling. For a detailed analysis of this exhibition, see Manuela Ammer, "In Engineering There Is Always the Other—the Other: Nam June Paik's Television

Experiment in *Exposition of Music, Electronic Television*, Galerie Parnass, Wuppertal 1963," in *Nam June Paik: Exposition of Music Electronic Television Revisited* (Vienna: MuMOK, 2009), 63–76.

15 Nam June Paik, "Afterlude to the Exposition of Experimental Television," in *Theories and Documents of Contemporary Art: A Sourcebook of Artists' Writings*, ed. Kristine Stiles and Peter Selz (Berkeley and Los Angeles: University of California Press, 1996), 431.

16 Paik quoted in Grace Glueck, "The World Is So Boring," *New York Times*, May 5, 1968, D31. Paik displayed twelve prepared TVs, one referencing McLuhan in its title. For more on the exhibition, see John Canaday, "Paik's TV Sets on View at Galeria Bonino," *New York Times*, December 4, 1965, 27. McLuhan knew about Paik by this time. The USCO member Gerd Stern sent him the program for the New Cinema Festival I, which took place at the Film-Makers' Cinematheque in New York on November 2, 1965, and included Paik's "electronic video projections." In the program, Paik writes: "It is the historical necessity, if there is historical necessity in history, that a new decade of electronic television should follow to the past decade of electronic music** Variability & Indeterminism is underdeveloped in optical art as parameter Sex is underdeveloped in music*** As collage technique replaced oil paint, the cathode ray tube will replace the canvass**** Someday artists will work with capacitators, resistors & semiconductors as they work today with brushes, violins & junk." Stern made special mention of Paik in his attached note. Marshall McLuhan Fonds, vol. 37, file 79.

17 John Cage, "Nam June Paik: A Diary," in *Electronic Art* (New York: Galeria Bonino, 1965), n.p., reprinted in John Cage, *A Year from Monday: New Lectures and Writings* (Middletown, CT: Wesleyan University Press, 1969), 89–91.

18 Cage and McLuhan first corresponded in 1960. Cage's diary is laced with McLuhan's aphorisms. See John Cage, *Diary: How To Improve the World (You Will Only Make It Worse)*, ed. Joe Biel and Richard Kraft (Los Angeles: Siglio, 2015). So too is John Cage, "Seriously Comma," in *A Year from Monday*, 26–29. In 1975, David Antin described the discourse of video art as "a kind of enthusiastic welcoming prose peppered with fragments of communications theory and McLuhanesque media talk." David Antin, "Video, the Distinctive Features of the Medium," in *Radical Coherency: Selected Essays on Art and Literature, 1966 to 2005* (Chicago: University of Chicago Press, 2011), 78.

19 Cage, "Nam June Paik: A Diary," 90. For more on Paik's relationship to

Cage, see John Cage, "McLuhan's Influence," in *John Cage*, ed. Richard Kostelanetz (New York: Praeger, 1970), 170–71.

20 The italicized portions of Cage's text come from Paik's writings.

21 McLuhan touched on Wiener's work: "Professor Wiener assures us that the new electronic brains dwarf the human performance in all utility operations. In the immediate prospect, as he sees it, the only functions left for the human mind are pure speculation, on one hand, or the manufacture of ever greater mechanical brains, on the other. Those who are not fitted for either of these arduous pursuits—the great majority of men—will inevitably sink into a serfdom for they have already been very well conditioned." *The Mechanical Bride*, 92. Finding Wiener's thesis technocratic and antihumanist, McLuhan wanted a theory that would give more people more to do.

22 Nam June Paik, in *Manifestos: A Great Bear Pamphlet* (New York: Something Else, 1966), 24.

23 Paik, "Norbert Wiener and Marshall McLuhan," n.p. For more on intermedia, see Dick Higgins, "Intermedia" (1965), in *Horizons: The Poetics and Theory of the Intermedia* (Carbondale: Southern Illinois University Press, 1983), 18–28. "Much of the best work being produced today seems to fall between media," Higgins wrote, mentioning both Paik and Cage. Ibid., 18. Higgins believed intermedia was crucial in creating a more open and fluid society.

24 Norbert Wiener, *The Human Use of Human Beings: Cybernetics and Society* (1950), rev. ed. (New York: Da Capo, 1954), 40.

25 Fred Turner, *The Democratic Surround: Multimedia and American Liberalism from World War II to the Psychedelic Sixties* (Chicago: University of Chicago Press, 2013), 161.

26 Of course, the hero of Poe's "A Descent into the Maelstrom" is a kind of helmsman, too.

27 Turner, *The Democratic Surround*, 131, 98.

28 David Riesman with Nathan Glazer and Reuel Denney, *The Lonely Crowd: A Study of the Changing American Character* (New Haven, CT: Yale University Press, 1950).

29 The exhibition ran from April 17 to May 11, 1968. Paik explained the origin of the work as follows: "There was an important program about Marshall McLuhan, made by NBC in 1967 or early 1968. Charlotte Moorman and I were on that program. By that time, I had developed various colorizing techniques, with the magnet inside the set. So I thought I might make an electronic movie of Marshall McLuhan, and I videotaped the program while it was on the air. I put various electromagnets on the set and turned

McLuhan right and left. What I wound up with was a McLuhan videotape loop that can be played around and around." Quoted in Douglas Davis, *Art and the Future: A History/Prophecy of the Collaboration between Science, Technology and Art* (New York: Praeger, 1973), 149–50.

30 Many years later, Paik made a work that literalized this idea, *Cage in Cage* (1993), which placed various television sets with recordings of John Cage in a birdcage-like structure.

31 Otto Piene, "Mother, Turn Off the Picture," *Artscanada*, June 1968, 15.

32 John Canaday, "Art: Serene Squares and Tortured TV," *New York Times*, April 20, 1968, 29.

33 Jane Holtz Kay, "Painting with Television," *TV Guide*, August 31–September 6, 1968, 6–9.

34 Photographs of the work appear in the catalog. Footage, shot off a television, appears in Paik's 1972 video *Waiting for Commercials*, made with Jud Yalkut for a performance by Charlotte Moorman. Spliced with Japanese TV ads, the video, as McLuhan explains, draws the viewer inside the TV while his image twitches, torques, twists, and finally breaks up into a field of static.

35 In her critique of Paik, which is also a critique of McLuhan, Martha Rosler claims that the artist never moved beyond formal concerns. His works, she writes, "formalize the TV signal and replicate viewer passivity, replacing messages of the State and the marketplace with aestheticized entertainment." Martha Rosler, "Video: Shedding the Utopian Moment," in *Illuminating Video: An Essential Guide to Video Art*, ed. Doug Hall and Sally Jo Fifer (New York: Aperture, 1990), 45. As late as 1991, Fredric Jameson could write of Paik's work: "Only the most misguided museum visitor would look for the 'art' in the content of the video images themselves." Fredric Jameson, *Postmodernism; or, The Cultural Logic of Late Capitalism* (Durham, NC: Duke University Press, 1991), 162.

36 Nam June Paik, "Utopian Laser TV Station," in *Manifestos*, 25. Paik goes on to offer a hypothetical schedule for his utopian TV station: "Chess lesson by Marcel Duchamp" airs at 7:00 A.M.; "Guided tour of Kurdistan, Turkistan and Kazakstan, by Dick Higgins" goes on at 3:00 P.M. Ibid.

37 McLuhan first appeared on the CBC in 1960. In 1967, NBC aired the documentary *This Is Marshall McLuhan: The Medium Is the Massage*, which included footage of Paik and the cellist Charlotte Moorman. Perhaps McLuhan's most infamous "television appearance," however, is as inspiration for Professor Brian O'Blivion in David Cronenberg's 1983 film *Videodrome*.

38 Two years before, in 1966, Kaprow sent McLuhan a poster for *A 3 Country Happening*, which was to be performed between New York, Berlin, and Buenos Aires with Wolf Vostell and Marta Minujín. Marshall McLuhan Fonds, vol. 27, file 75.

39 Paik later expanded on these ideas. See Nam June Paik, "Expanded Cinema for the Paperless Society" (1968), https://www.radicalsoftware.org/volume1nr1/pdf/VOLUME1NR1_art02.pdf. See also Tom Holert, "'A live feedback of You in the Now, alternating with broadcast in the central monitor': Video, Television, Self-Awareness, and Education around 1970," in *Changing Channels: Art and Television, 1963–1987* (Köln: Walther König, 2010), 37–52. McLuhan was interested in the educational potential of TV as early as 1954. After conducting an experiment with students, he wrote: "It is quite certain that the so-called mass media are not necessarily ordained to be channels of popular entertainment only." "Sight, Sound and Fury," 494.

40 For one example, see Nicolás Guagnini, "Cable TV's Failed Utopian Vision: An Interview with Dara Birnbaum," *Cabinet* 9 (Winter 2002–3): 35–39.

41 McLuhan, *Understanding Media*, 309.

42 "Marshall McLuhan: A Candid Conversation," 61.

43 Rick Bernstein, *Nixonland: The Rise of a President and the Fracturing of America* (New York: Scribner, 2009), 332. Yousuf Karsh, who photographed both McLuhan and Nixon, writes of the former: "Successful advertising campaigns, including even one for the presidency of the United States, have been based on [McLuhan's] message." Yousuf Karsh, *Faces of Our Time* (Toronto: University of Toronto Press, 1971), 74. Extracts from *Understanding Media* "distributed among the Richard Nixon staff" are included in Joe McGinnis, *The Selling of the President, 1968* (New York: Trident, 1969), 181–86.

44 McLuhan, *Understanding Media*, 309. Though typically imagined as a progressive strategy, focusing on process can be put to different political uses. Here is the video artist Dara Birnbaum writing in 1988: "To consider the action of editing is to reemphasize *process* over *product*, or the continuously shifting and uncertain event over the definitive object and statement. . . . The foregrounding of process still seems to provide the greater possibility for effecting change." Dara Birnbaum, "Out of the Blue," *Artforum*, March 1988, 117.

45 Rosenberg, "Philosophy in a Pop Key," 194. *Electronic opera* also updates Fernand Léger's 1924 film *Ballet mécanique*.

46 Paik quoted in *TV as a Creative Medium* (New York: Howard Wise Gallery, 1969), n.p.

47 See Jack Burnham, "Sacrament and Television," in *Video Art* (Philadelphia: Institute of Contemporary Art, 1975), 91–95.

48 For more on this history, see Deirdre Boyle, *Subject to Change: Guerilla Television Revisited* (Oxford: Oxford University Press, 1997).

49 Raymond Williams, *Television: Technology and Cultural Form* (Middletown, CT: Wesleyan University Press, 1974), 122. For a similar claim, see Douglas Davis, "The Decline and Fall of Pop: Reflections on Media Theory," in *Artculture: Essays on the Post-Modern* (New York: Icon Editions, 1977), 85–105.

## Chapter Five

1 Marshall McLuhan, "The Medium Is the Massage," in McLuhan and Staines, eds., *Understanding Me*, 77. McLuhan often claimed that the shift from an *e* to an *a*—from *message* to *massage*—was the result of a printer's error, though this story is likely apocryphal.

2 McLuhan, "Great Change-Overs for You," 114. The title of McLuhan's article plays on the fashion context: While seemingly announcing upcoming styles, the text discusses even more extreme shifts in behavior and comportment.

3 For more on McLuhan and Fiore's collaborations, see Jeffrey Schnapp and Adam Michaels, *The Electric Information Age Book: McLuhan/Agel/Fiore and the Experimental Paperback* (New York: Princeton Architectural Press, 2012).

4 Founded in 1965, *Aspen* offered a rebuke to the typical experience of reading a magazine. In a letter in the first issue, the publisher, Phyllis Johnson, enumerated some of the many possibilities for "the first three-dimensional magazine": "blueprints, a bit of rock, wildflower seeds, tea samples, an opera libretti [*sic*], old newspapers, [and] jigsaw puzzles." *Aspen*, no. 1 (1965), http://www.ubu.com/aspen/aspen1/letter.html.

5 *This Is Marshall McLuhan* was later released on sixteen-millimeter film for educational use.

6 McLuhan and Fiore, *The Medium Is the Massage*, 111.

7 Jerome Agel to Marshall McLuhan, April 28, 1967, Marshall McLuhan Fonds, vol. 18, file 10. The result is similar to John Cage's *Williams Mix* (1952), which creates a four-minute composition out of one-second-long bits of sound, though it also shares affinities with the cut-up experiments of William Burroughs and Brion Gysin. Not unlike the Beatles' *White Album*, which appeared a year later, the *Massage* record popularized avant-garde

experiments. Jumping between audio clips, it reminds one of changing channels or flipping through a radio dial.

8 McLuhan, *Understanding Media*, 22–32.

9 To advertise the *Massage* project, young women in New York, Los Angeles, Chicago, Boston, and San Francisco marched through the streets holding McLuhan signboards. Advertising here mimicked protest while also suggesting that there might be a politics in what McLuhan had to say. See "This Time the Medium Is the Mini," *New York Times*, July 20, 1967, 60.

10 The term belongs to Rosalind Krauss, who, following Fredric Jameson, seeks a way outside the regime of "postmodern sensation." See Rosalind Krauss, *"A Voyage on the North Sea": Art in the Age of the Post-Medium Condition* (New York: Thames & Hudson, 1999).

11 McLuhan, *Understanding Media*, 55.

12 This image also appeared on cover of the book's hardback edition. The photograph originally appeared in "SPEAKING OF PICTURES . . . These Show What 300MPH Wind Does to Human Faces," *Life*, May 2, 1949, 22–23. Over the years it has appeared in related corners of art history. The Scottish artist Eduardo Paolozzi included it in his 1972 *Bunk!* print portfolio, while the German artist Hans-Peter Feldmann made use of it many years later in his 1994 book *Voyeur* ([Germany]: OFAC Art Contemporain, 1994).

13 See Peter Moore, *Photographs* (Tokyo: Gallery 260, 1989). The book includes images of Charlotte Moorman, Nam June Paik, Robert Rauschenberg, and Carolee Schneemann, among others.

14 As mentioned earlier, McLuhan reviewed Moholy-Nagy's *Vision in Motion* in 1949. See "Encyclopaedic Unities." Moholy-Nagy's photograph also serves as a frontispiece to Marshall McLuhan, *Verbi-Voco-Visual Explorations* (New York: Something Else, 1967).

15 McLuhan and Fiore, *The Medium Is the Massage*, 26.

16 McLuhan and Fiore, *The Medium Is the Massage*, 25, 41.

17 McLuhan belonged to a midcentury cultural discussion about the "crisis of man," which was characterized by the fear that "human nature was being changed, either in its permanent essence or in its lineaments in the eyes of other men." Mark Greif, *The Age of the Crisis of Man* (Princeton, NJ: Princeton University Press, 2014), 3.

18 McLuhan and Fiore, *The Medium Is the Massage*, 68. "When printing was new, it created what was known as the Public," McLuhan wrote a year later. "In the 16th Century and after, Montaigne's phrase 'le publique,' came into use. . . . This completely altered politics and altered all social arrangements

in education, in work, and in every other area. Electric circuitry did not create the public; it created the mass, meaning an environment of information that involved everybody in everybody." McLuhan, "The Invisible Environment," 167.

19 Raymond Williams, *Politics of Modernism: Against the New Conformists* (London: Verso, 1989), 43.

20 "This stratum of 'bourgeois' was the real carrier of the public, which from the outset was a reading public." Jürgen Habermas, *The Structural Transformation of the Public Sphere: An Inquiry into a Category of Bourgeois Society*, trans. Thomas Burger (Cambridge, MA: MIT Press, 1991), 23. In time, of course, things would change. "The medium of print is now only a small part of our relation to what we understand as the public," Michael Warner writes. *Publics and Counterpublics* (New York: Zone, 2002), 169. In his reading, print gives way to "iconicity."

21 McLuhan and Fiore, *The Medium Is the Massage*, 68.

22 McLuhan, "Great Change-Overs for You," 114.

23 McLuhan, "The Emperor's Old Clothes," 95. McLuhan first formulated this idea as follows: "To prevent undue wreckage in society, the artist tends now to move from the ivory tower to the control tower of society." *Understanding Media*, 65. The art world quickly picked up the idea. In her December 12, 1968, *Village Voice* column, which surveyed an intermedia poetry program, the critic Jill Johnston wrote: "The ivory tower has become the control tower as the naked ape speeds toward the moon. . . . Presumably the control tower will continue to communicate with the astronauts as they speed toward infinity, sipping their final meals out of their final plastic bags. That might be the ultimate poetry." Jill Johnston, *Marmalade Me* (New York: E. P. Dutton, 1971), 23.

24 John McHale, "The Plastic Parthenon," *dot zero* 3 (Spring 1967): 11.

25 Jack Burnham, "Systems Esthetics," *Artforum*, September 1968, 30–35. Burnham emphasized his debt to McLuhan in this text, noting: "It is a legitimate extension of McLuhan's remark about Pop art when he said that it was an announcement that the entire environment was ready to become a work of art." Ibid., 34.

26 Allan Kaprow, in *Manifestos*, 23.

27 When Warhol released his *Index (Book)* (New York: Random House, 1967), replete with pop-up pages and an LP record, his publisher, Random House, claimed: "This is the book Marshall McLuhan has been waiting for. An experiment in total participation by the audience." Publicity material for *Andy Warhol's Index (Book)*, Random House Records, box 887, Rare

Book and Manuscript Library, Columbia University Library. On the connection between the *Index* book and the *Massage* book, see Branden W. Joseph, "White Light/White Noise," in *Andy Warhol: From A to B and Back Again*, ed. Donna DeSalvo (New York: Whitney Museum of American Art, 2018), 42–53.

28 Branden W. Joseph, "'My Mind Split Open': Andy Warhol's Exploding Plastic Inevitable," *Grey Room* 8 (Summer 2002): 89–90. Though the *EPI* offered the most explicit manifestation of the electric tendency in Warhol's work, McLuhan had long understood the artist's project to have similar implications. Writing to a friend about Warhol in 1964, McLuhan noted: "Any high definition image can be made environmental and involving by repetition." Marshall McLuhan to Wilfred Watson, March 31, 1964, in Molinaro, McLuhan, and Toye, eds., *Letters of Marshall McLuhan*, 297. It is not clear where McLuhan saw Warhol's work. In the letter, he writes: "An hour ago I was looking at Warhol's Pop Art show." Ibid. Warhol's first exhibition in Europe—at the Galerie Ileana Sonnabend in Paris—closed that February; his exhibition of Brillo boxes would open at the Stable Gallery in New York in April.

29 McLuhan and Parker, *Through the Vanishing Point*, 253. In a conversation published the same year, McLuhan and Parker took things further. "Well, of course, these light shows, the electric circus and all the rest of the things that are going on, are very indicative of this whole business, of the breakdown from lineality," Parker says. "I am not quite so sure that we need to foster them, as much as exploit them, in the hope that they will go away quickly." Conversation between Marshall McLuhan, Harley Parker, and Jacques Barzun, 6.

30 In its fun-house aspect, *Hon* echoed Marta Minujín's environment *La menesunda*, staged in Buenos Aires in 1965. One room featured a couple in bed reading McLuhan's *Understanding Media*.

31 At other moments, Saint Phalle referred to the work as "a factory" and "a whale." *Réalisations, et projets d'architectures de Niki de Saint Phalle* (Paris: Alexandre Iolas, 1974), n.p.

32 Saint Phalle had long traded in religious connotation. In an early essay the poet John Ashbery connected her to a tradition of cathedrals and religious art. John Ashbery in *Niki de Saint Phalle* (Paris: Galerie Rive Droite, 1963), n.p.

33 Arthur Secunda and Jan Thunholm, "Everyman's Girl," *Ramparts*, November 1966, 66. The previous issue of *Ramparts* featured a scathing review of McLuhan's *Understanding Media*. See Christopher Koch, "The Cool

Totalitarian or 'The McLuhan Megillah,'" *Ramparts*, October 1966, 55–58.

**34** *Hon* features prominently in McHale's "The Plastic Parthenon." The work later appeared in Hans Hollein, "Alles ist Architektur," *Bau* 1–2 (1968): 2–27. For more on this, see Craig Buckley, "From Absolute to Everything: Taking Possession in 'Alles ist Architektur,'" *Grey Room* 28 (Summer 2007): 108–22.

**35** Annika Öhrner, "Niki de Saint Phalle Playing with the Feminine in the Male Factory: *HON—en katedral*," *Stedelijk Studies*, no. 7 (2018), https://stedelijkstudies.com/wp-content/uploads/2018/11/Stedelijk-Studies-7-Niki-de-Saint-Phalle-Playing-with-the-Feminine-in-the-Male-Factory-Ohrner.pdf.

**36** McLuhan, "Great Change-Overs for You," 62. In this way, it also connected to McLuhan's conception of Pop art. Indeed, many reviews discussed the work's merits in relation to Pop.

**37** Secunda and Thunholm, "Everyman's Girl," 66.

**38** The exhibition *Claes Oldenburg: Skulpturer och teckningar* (Sculptures and drawings) ran from September 17 to October 30, 1966. The same year, on January 29, Al Hansen staged his *McLuhan Megillah* at New York's Third Rail Gallery. Amid an environment of painting and dance, Dick Higgins read from *Understanding Media*. See "Al Hansen's 'McLuhan Megillah,'" *Village Voice*, February 3, 1966, 11.

**39** Claes Oldenburg, untitled statement in *Hon—en historia* (Stockholm: Moderna Museet, 1967), 167.

**40** Claes Oldenburg, *Raw Notes* (Halifax: Press of the Nova Scotia College of Art and Design, 1973), 91.

**41** Claes Oldenburg, untitled statement, *Perspecta* 11 (1967): 53.

**42** Oldenburg, *Raw Notes*, 93.

**43** Kostelanetz, *The Theatre of Mixed Means*, 154.

**44** Oldenburg, *Raw Notes*, 96.

**45** McLuhan writes of the close connection between audience participation and corporate media: "From Life to General Motors, and from the classroom to the Executive Suite, a refocusing of aims and images to permit ever more audience involvement and participation has been inevitable." *Understanding Media*, 166.

**46** Oldenburg, *Raw Notes*, 96. A year later, Oldenburg wrote: "The 'happening' is one or another method of using *objects in motion*, and this I take to include people, both in themselves and as agents of object motion." Claes Oldenburg, "A Statement," in *Happenings: An Illustrated Anthology*, ed. Michael Kirby (New York: E. P. Dutton, 1965), 200.

47 Oldenburg, *Raw Notes*, 153, 126.

48 "In my Stockholm performance of *Massage*, the base was a recording I made of myself typing my notes," Oldenburg told Kostelanetz. "I became aware of how spatial and physical the sound of a simple thing like that could be, and I used it in the performance, highly amplified. The sound really took possession of the space. That was the first time I ever used tape." Kostelanetz, *The Theatre of Mixed Means*, 161.

49 Oldenburg, *Raw Notes*, 141. Discussing the typewriter, McLuhan writes: "That the typewriter, which carried the Gutenberg technology into every nook and cranny of our culture and economy, should, also, have given out these opposite oral effects is a characteristic reversal." *Understanding Media*, 262.

50 An interest in synesthesia, a rewiring of the senses, is suggested by a headline in Oldenburg's notes—"How to 'See' through the Ears"—which also include an idea for a film of his ear being massaged, both of which recall Peter Moore's photograph of the switched eye and ear in the *Massage* book. Oldenburg, *Raw Notes*, 94, 110.

51 Suzi Gablik, "Take a Cigarette Butt and Make It Heroic," *Art News*, May 1967, 30.

52 Oldenburg, *Raw Notes*, xiv. Oldenburg staged a subsequent happening, *The Typewriter*, in New York in 1968.

53 Oldenburg, *Raw Notes*, 109, 101, 99.

54 Claes Oldenburg, *Writing on the Side, 1956–1969* (New York: Museum of Modern Art, 2013), 256.

55 Oldenburg, *Raw Notes*, 151. Since *The Medium Is the Massage* had not yet been published, Oldenburg must have learned of McLuhan's use of the term through "Great Change-Overs for You."

56 Oldenburg, *Raw Notes*, 150. Gerard Malanga also performed S-M-inspired dances in Warhol's *Exploding Plastic Inevitable*.

57 Oldenburg, *Raw Notes*, 153.

58 Robert Pincus-Witten, "The Transformation of Daddy Warbucks: An Interview with Claes Oldenburg," in *Claes Oldenburg*, ed. Nadja Rottner (Cambridge, MA: MIT Press, 2012), 122.

59 Kostelanetz, *The Theatre of Mixed Means*, 145.

60 Susan Sontag, "One Culture and the New Sensibility," in *Against Interpretation and Other Essays* (New York: Picador, 1966), 302. For more on Sontag and performance, especially the work of Jim Dine, see Judith Rodenbeck, "Car Crash," in *Radical Prototypes: Allan Kaprow and the Invention of Happenings* (Cambridge, MA: MIT Press, 2011), 175–206.

61 Sontag, "One Culture and the New Sensibility," 301.

62 Gablik, "Take a Cigarette Butt and Make It Heroic," 30.

## Chapter Six

1 The work is featured in the catalog and early checklists for the exhibition, but at some point the artist appears to have switched it out for a work titled *Lindsay Caged*, a reference to John Lindsay, who was then mayor of New York.

2 Hultén also organized *Hon* and Oldenburg's exhibition at the Moderna Museet.

3 According to Hugh Kenner, Vaucanson's mechanical duck "could waddle and splash, beat the air with detailed feathered wings, wag its head, quack, pick up grain, ingest this with swallowing movements, and eventually excrete the residue." Hugh Kenner, *The Counterfeiters: An Historical Comedy* (1968; Baltimore: Johns Hopkins University Press, 1985), 29.

4 For a discussion of this work, see Jack Burnham, "The Aesthetics of Intelligent Systems," in *On the Future of Art* (New York: Viking, 1970), 106–7. A later painting by Dupuy, *Cone Pyramid* (1990), explains *Heart Beats Dust* in further detail: "Here, the viewer makes by means of a stethoscope, placed successively upon the temple, the neck, the heart. The organic vibrations of one person will be electronically ampliefied [*sic*] and will set in motion an organic red pigment (density 1.56), placed upon a membrane stretched across a loudspeaker attached beneath a transparent sealed rectangular box. The sound activates the pigment by its vibrations which form a cone pyramid. A sculpture which originates from the beam of the light projector, at the top of the box. The nature of this beam is to be a cone at the top and a pyramid at the bottom."

5 The Brooklyn exhibition ran from November 25, 1968, through January 5, 1969. See *Some More Beginnings: An Exhibition of Submitted Works Involving Technical Materials and Processes* (New York: Experiments in Art and Technology, 1968).

6 Max Kozloff, "Men and Machines," *Artforum*, February 1969, 29.

7 Pontus Hultén, *The Machine as Seen at the End of the Mechanical Age* (New York: Museum of Modern Art, 1968), 197.

8 Hultén, *The Machine as Seen at the End of the Mechanical Age*, 6.

9 Harold Rosenberg, *The De-Definition of Art* (Chicago: University of Chicago Press, 1972), 162 ("Past Machines/Future Art").

10 The exhibition ran from July 2 through September 20, 1970. For Rosen-

berg's take, see Harold Rosenberg, "The Art World: Dilemmas of a New Season," *New Yorker*, October 10, 1970, 149–56.

11 McLuhan's idea that pattern recognition helps negotiate information overload proved particularly instructive for McShine's exhibition. See Eve Meltzer, *Systems We Have Loved: Conceptual Art, Affect, and the Antihumanist Turn* (Chicago: University of Chicago Press, 2013), 45–46.

12 McLuhan, *Understanding Media*, 9.

13 McLuhan, "Great Change-Overs for You," 63.

14 Dan Graham, "Information," in *Articles* (Eindhoven: Van Abbemuseum, 1978), 15–19. See also Dan Graham, "The Artist as Bookmaker: The Book as Object," *Arts Magazine* 41, no. 8 (Summer 1967): 23.

15 For more on the exhibition's political dimensions, see Julia Bryan-Wilson, *Art Workers: Radical Practice in the Vietnam Era* (Berkeley and Los Angeles: University of California Press, 2009). The Art Workers Coalition emerged out of a protest at MoMA during the *Machine* exhibition: The Greek artist Takis physically removed his *Tele-Sculpture* (1960) because he had not been consulted about its inclusion. The *Information* exhibition can, in part, be seen as the museum's response to the debacle.

16 Kynaston McShine, *Information* (New York: Museum of Modern Art, 1970), 138.

17 McLuhan, "Sight, Sound, and the Fury," 490.

18 A number of artists, including Joseph Beuys, Bill Bollinger, Marta Minujín, and Yoko Ono, contributed to the catalog but did not participate in the exhibition.

19 In other words, it is *Machine* deindustrialized, geared toward finance capital and the service economy.

20 McShine, *Information*, 138.

21 McLuhan, "The Emperor's Old Clothes," 95. For more on Xerography, see Marshall McLuhan in *Do Books Matter?*, ed. Brian Baumfield (Leeds: Dunn & Wilson, 1973), 31–41, and "The Future of the Book," in *Understanding Me*, 173–86. For Jovanovich's take on Xerography, see William Jovanovich, "The Universal Xerox Life Compiler Machine," *American Scholar* 40, no. 2 (Spring 1971): 249–55.

22 McLuhan, "The Emperor's Old Clothes," 94.

23 Ironically, owing to cost issues, the book was printed by means of offset lithography. See Alexander Alberro, "The Xerox Degree of Art," in *Conceptual Art and the Politics of Publicity* (Cambridge, MA: MIT Press, 2003), 130–51.

24 Ian Burn, "The 'Sixties: Crisis and Aftermath (or the Memoirs of an Ex-Conceptual Artist)" (1981), in *Conceptual Art: A Critical Anthology*, ed. Alexander Alberro and Blake Stimson (Cambridge, MA: MIT Press, 1999), 404. For more on artist books, see Germano Celant, *Book as Artwork, 1960–1972* (London: Nigel Greenwood, 1972). Celant points out: "With the emergence of McLuhan . . . the media were understood as entities with their own meaning, messages in their own right, no longer devices in subjectivity." Ibid., 5.

25 Anne Wagner, "At Tate Britain," *London Review of Books*, July 14, 2016, 20.

26 Lev Manovich has argued that the computer was a blind spot in McLuhan's thought: "Even such a visionary as Marshall McLuhan—who seemed to predict with precision most features of contemporary cyberculture about three decades before they came into existence—ignored computers. In *Understanding Media*, which presents a systematic analysis of all key historical and modern media technologies, McLuhan does devote the very last section to data processing, but in general computation plays no role in his theories. This is so, probably, because McLuhan was thinking of media as above all a means of communication and/or representation. In the 1960s computers were not yet involved in any of these functions in a way that would be visible to the public." Lev Manovich, "Introduction to Info-Aesthetics," in *Antinomies of Art and Culture: Modernity, Postmodernity, Contemporaneity*, ed. Terry Smith, Okwui Enwezor, and Nancy Condee (Durham, NC: Duke University Press, 2008), 334.

27 McLuhan, *Counterblast: 1954 Facsimile*, n.p.

28 McLuhan, *Counterblast* (1969), 12.

29 Marshall McLuhan and Eric McLuhan, *The Lost Tetrads of Marshall McLuhan* (New York: O/R, 2017), 99.

30 Jean-François Lyotard, *The Postmodern Condition: A Report on Knowledge*, trans. Geoff Bennington and Brian Massumi (Minneapolis: University of Minnesota Press, 1984), 4.

31 McLuhan, "The Invisible Environment," 165.

32 The exhibition ran from September 16 to November 8, 1970.

33 Jack Burnham, "Alice's Head: Reflections on Conceptual Art," in *Great Western Salt Works: Essays on the Meaning of Post-Formalist Art* (New York: George Braziller, 1974), 47. The essay originally appeared as Jack Burnham, "Alice's Head: Reflections on Conceptual Art," *Artforum*, February 1970, 37–43.

34 Burnham, "Systems Esthetics," 14.

35 Negroponte would later go on to found MIT's famed Media Lab in 1985.

36 Grace Glueck, "Jewish Museum's 'Software' Confusing," *New York Times*, September 26, 1970, 25.

37 Douglas Huebler, *Variable Piece 4: Secrets* (1978; reprint, New York: Primary Information, 2017), n.p.

38 This material is available in the uncataloged archives of the Jewish Museum.

39 *Software: Information Technology: Its New Meaning for Art* (New York: Jewish Museum, 1970). With Ned Woodman, Nelson also contributed a hypertext exhibition catalog, *Labyrinth: An Interactive Catalogue*.

40 For more on this, see Max Kozloff, "The Contemporary Museum: Under the Corporate Wing," in *Museums in Crisis*, ed. Brian O'Doherty (New York: George Braziller, 1972), 145–60. Kozloff dismisses *Software*: "The aim of such currently bandied terms as software and information art is partially to introduce a variety of strains and breeds in a field, rather than to highlight what might be the salient esthetic intentions that distinguish it." Ibid., 149.

41 *Software*, 3. "This exhibition encourages artists to use the medium of electronic technology in challenging and unconventional ways," Chapin continued. "The link between art and science, which the artists in *Software* are examining, is the same link we must explore and strengthen in our automotive styling and engineering. Because of our continuing interest in people, in technological achievement, and in the advancement of modern art forms, our involvement in *Software* has been both rewarding and stimulating." Ibid.

42 McLuhan claims that automobiles were becoming obsolete, that, in a decade, "electronic successors to the car will be manifest." *Understanding Media*, 225 ("Motorcar: The Mechanical Bride").

43 Acconci first performed his work, which had him following a person until he or she entered a private space, as part of the exhibition *Street Works IV* at the Architectural League in New York in 1969. Haacke's work first appeared in the exhibition *Prospect 69* in Düsseldorf. In New York, Haacke's work received information from five international news sources: ANSA (Italian), dpa (German), the New York Times News Service, Reuters, and UPI. See *Hans Haacke: Unfinished Business*, ed. Brian Wallis (Cambridge, MA: MIT Press, 1986), 74.

44 Burnham, "Alice's Head," 55. In 1970, Barry wrote: "I think that artists will be using language to make their work for a long time." Quoted in David Lamelas, *Publication* (London: Nigel Greenwood, 1970), 4.

**45** McLuhan and Fiore, *Medium Is the Massage*, 84–85. That same year Barry published an artist book, empty save for a sentence on each page—English on the verso, Italian on the recto. "It cannot be known through the senses," we read. "It is not tangible." We never learn what *it* refers to. See Robert Barry, *Robert Barry* (Torino: Sperone Editore, 1970).

**46** *Recording Conceptual Art: Early Interviews with Barry, Huebler, Kaltenbach, LeWitt, Morris, Oppenheim, Siegelaub, Smithson, and Weiner by Patricia Norvell*, ed. Alexander Alberro and Patricia Norvell (Berkeley and Los Angeles: University of California Press, 2001), 89. Other artists at the time pursued similar questions. In 1967, Les Levine, who also exhibited in *Software*, created *Electric Shock* from TV sets and electric waves. "I was interested in how you can energize an empty space," he wrote, "how you can make a work of art out of nothing visible, nothing to see—just sensation." Quoted in Jack Burnham, "Les Levine: Business as Usual," *Artforum*, April 1970, 40.

**47** In 1965, Sontag made a similar point: "Art, which I have characterized as an instrument for modifying and educating sensibility and consciousness, now operates in an environment which cannot be grasped by the senses. But, of course, art remains permanently tied to the senses." Sontag, "One Culture and the New Sensibility," 301.

**48** As Gene Youngblood wrote: "Artistic activity during the last five years, known variously as land art, earthworks, conceptual art, process art, environmental art, has been characterized, however tentatively, by a common concern with interacting ecologies, whether social, biological or geosocial. . . . It is clear that art is tending toward that point at which all phenomena on Earth will constitute the artist's palette." Gene Youngblood, "World Game: The Artist as Ecologist," *Artscanada*, August 1970, 46.

**49** McLuhan, "The Agenbite of Outwit," 44.

**50** See György Kepes, *The New Landscape in Art and Science* (Chicago: Paul Theobald, 1956). See also György Kepes, ed. *Arts of the Environment* (New York: George Braziller, 1972), which chronicled the most recent spate of artistic activity. For more on *Parallel of Life and Art*, see my "The Brutalism of Life and Art," *October* 136 (Spring 2011): 63–86.

**51** Marshall McLuhan and Barrington Nevitt, *Take Today: The Executive as Dropout* (New York: Harcourt Brace Jovanovich, 1972), 6.

**52** Philipp Kaiser and Miwon Kwon, "Ends of the Earth and Back," in *Ends of the Earth: Land Art to 1974* (Munich: Prestel, 2012), 27.

**53** Marshall McLuhan, "The Relation of Environment to Anti-Environment," in *Media and Formal Cause* (Houston: NeoPoeisis, 2011), 24.

54 McLuhan, "The Invisible Environment," 165. At times, mainstream politics took a similar position, as when, e.g., President John F. Kennedy announced: "Never before has man had such capacity to control his own environment." "Address Before the 18th General Assembly of the United Nations, September 20, 1963," https://www.jfklibrary.org/archives/other-resources/john-f-kennedy-speeches/united-nations-19630920#:~:text=Never%20before%20has%20man%20had,to%20make%20it%20the%20last.

55 *Asphalt Rundown* was Smithson's contribution to the catalog. He displayed eight photo panels of *Spiral Jetty* in the exhibition.

56 Smithson owned both *Understanding Media* and *The Medium Is the Massage*. He also possessed a copy of Wyndham Lewis's *Time and Western Man*. *Robert Smithson* (Los Angeles: Museum of Contemporary Art, 2004), 256.

57 In a 1967 dialogue with Allan Kaprow, Smithson contrasted his ideas with "an attitude that tends toward McLuhanism." Where McLuhan sought work that would engage the environment outside the museum or, conversely, transform the museum into "a kind of specialized entertainment," Smithson focused on the museum's tendency to "exclude any kind of life-forcing position." "What Is a Museum? A Dialogue between Allan Kaprow and Robert Smithson," in *Robert Smithson: The Collected Writings*, ed. Jack Flam (Berkeley and Los Angeles: University of California Press, 1996), 43–51.

58 These works offer examples of *entropy*, another key term in Smithson's lexicon. In a film made to accompany *Asphalt Rundown*, Smithson cites the Watergate scandal as another example: "There is no way you can really piece it back together again."

59 For more on Smithson and cinema, especially *Spiral Jetty*, see George Baker, "The Cinema Model," in *Robert Smithson: Spiral Jetty*, ed. Lynne Cooke and Karen Kelly (Berkeley and Los Angeles: University of California Press, 2005), 79–113.

60 For more on Smithson and American history, see Jennifer Roberts, *Mirror-Travels: Robert Smithson and History* (New Haven, CT: Yale University Press, 2004).

61 The spiral is "the form taken by a destructive or overpowering nature—the form of the whirlpool and the tornado." The whirlpool is also at the center of the Poe story that McLuhan held so dear. Lucy Lippard, "Breaking Circles: The Politics of Prehistory," in *Robert Smithson: Sculpture*, ed. Robert Hobbs (Ithaca, NY: Cornell University Press, 1981), 35.

62 Robert Smithson, "A Tour of the Monuments of Passaic, New Jersey," in Flam, ed., *Robert Smithson: The Collected Writings*, 70.

63 Robert Smithson, "A Museum of Language in the Vicinity of Art," in Flam, ed., *Robert Smithson: The Collected Writings*, 91.

64 Robert Smithson, "A Sedimentation of the Mind: Earth Projects," in Flam, ed., *Robert Smithson: The Collected Writings*, 100–101.

## Chapter Seven

1 Diamond, "The Message of Marshall McLuhan," 54.

2 Theodor Adorno and Max Horkheimer, "The Culture Industry: Enlightenment as Mass Deception," in *Dialectic of Enlightenment*, ed. Gunzelin Schmid Noerr, trans. Edmund Jephcott (Stanford, CA: Stanford University Press, 2007), 94–136. In 2002, Fredric Jameson offered a similar formulation, arguing: "Culture has become the economic, and economics has become cultural." Quoted in Joshua Clover, *1989: Bob Dylan Didn't Have This to Sing About* (Berkeley and Los Angeles: University of California Press, 2010), 8.

3 "John Lennon and Yoko Ono Interview with Marshall McLuhan" (1969), YouTube (posted June 27, 2019), https://www.youtube.com/watch?v=knsi_gnTHoU. Bob Dylan took a similar position, claiming: "Museums are cemeteries. Paintings should be on the walls of restaurants, in dime stores, in gas stations, in men's rooms." Quoted in Thomas Crow, *The Long March of Pop: Art, Music, and Design, 1930–1995* (New Haven, CT: Yale University Press, 2015), 1. McLuhan wrote briefly about the Beatles two years prior: "The Beatles are trying to tell us by the anti-environment they present just how we have changed and in what ways." "The Invisible Environment," 166.

4 In his 1975 work *On Social Grease*, Hans Haacke quoted David Rockefeller about the nature of this relationship: "From an economic standpoint, such involvement in the arts can mean direct and tangible benefits. It can provide a company with extensive publicity and advertising, a brighter public reputation, and an improved corporate image."

5 Alvin Toffler, *The Culture Consumers: Art and Affluence in America* (New York: Pelican, 1965), 106. According to Toffler, corporate interests no longer patronized cultural activities but entered into partnership with them.

6 William Whyte, *The Organization Man* (New York: Simon & Schuster, 1956).

7 For more on McLuhan's relationship with Gossage, see Randall Rothen-

berg, *Where the Suckers Moon: An Advertising Story* (New York: Knopf, 1995), 187–89. Gossage went so far as to crib ad copy from *Understanding Media*.

8 As Tom Wolfe wrote in his 1965 profile of McLuhan: "There are currently hundreds of studs of the business world, breakfast food package designers, television network creative department vice-presidents, advertising 'media reps,' lighting fixture fortune heirs, smiley patent lawyers, industrial spies, we-need-vision board chairmen, all sorts of business studs who are all wondering if this man, Marshall McLuhan . . . is right." Wolfe, "The New Life Out There," 15.

9 *The Meaning of Commercial Television: The Texas-Stanford Seminar, 1966*, ed. Stanley T. Donner (Austin: University of Texas Press, 1967); Marshall McLuhan, *Sharing the News: Friendly Teamness, Teaming Friendness* (n.p.: American Broadcasting Companies/McLuhan Associates, 1971).

10 For a discussion of artists engaging "the North" of Canada, see Charity Mewburn, *Sixteen Hundred Miles North of Denver* (Vancouver: Morris and Helen Belkin Art Gallery, 1999).

11 McLuhan and Nevitt's *Take Today* offers another of the thinker's inversions: just as culture became business, the executive assumed the mantle of the dropout. A person who previously belonged to the faceless crowd, the so-called man in the gray flannel suit, now pushed against the grain of culture in order to sense its contours.

12 McLuhan, *Culture Is Our Business*, n.p., 129.

13 McLuhan, "The Agenbite of Outwit," 41–44.

14 McLuhan, *The Gutenberg Galaxy*, 275. McLuhan continues: "Art has become as total in its mandate for human order as the mass markets that created the plateau from which all can now share the awareness of new scope and potential for everyday beauty and order in all aspects of life at once." Ibid.

15 That said, painting and sculpture also absorbed corporate strategies. In a section of his "Other Criteria" titled "The Corporate Model of Developing Art," Leo Steinberg wrote that the formalist problem-solving that drove modernist painting created a "streamlined efficiency image" not unlike that of a Detroit automobile. Leo Steinberg, "Other Criteria," in *Other Criteria: Confrontations with Twentieth-Century Art* (New York: Oxford University Press, 1972), 79.

16 See Jack Burnham, "Corporate Art," *Artforum*, October 1971, 66–71; and David Antin, "Art and the Corporations," in *Radical Coherency*, 61–77.

17 Dan Graham, "Editorial Statement," *Aspen*, no. 8 (1970–71), quoted in

Gwen Allen, *Artists' Magazines* (Cambridge, MA: MIT Press, 2011), 65.

18 Jud Yalkut, "Art and Technology in Nam June Paik," *Arts Magazine* 42, no. 6 (April 1968): 51. Paik continued: "For example, John Cage as artist in residence at I.B.M., Allan Kaprow in the Chase Manhattan Bank, Mary Baumeister in Helena Rubinstein, Christo in the United Packing Company, Otto Piene in Polaroid, USCO in General Motors, Nam June Paik in Something Else Concern." Ibid.

19 In some cases, it was difficult to tell. Les Levine, whose art played the stock market, called himself a "corporate type with interests in all areas of management." Burnham, "Les Levine," 41. For more on Levine, see Sophie Cras, *The Artist as Economist: Art and Capitalism in the 1960s*, trans. Malcolm DeBevoise (New Haven, CT: Yale University Press, 2019), 128–34.

20 Quoted in Youngblood, "World Game," 47. For more on VanDerBeek, see Gloria Sutton, *The Experience Machine: Stan VanDerBeek's Movie-Drome and Expanded Cinema* (Cambridge, MA: MIT Press, 2015).

21 McLuhan, *Understanding Me*, 223 ("Art as Survival in the Electric Age").

22 Daniel Bell, *The Cultural Contradictions of Capitalism* (New York: Basic, 1976), 73. Dwight Macdonald wrote: "I predict a brisk sale for the book on Madison Avenue." Macdonald, review of *Understanding Media*, 207. The literary critic John Fekete went further, calling McLuhan "an ideologue of neocapitalist integration." John Fekete, *The Critical Twilight: Explorations in the Ideology of Anglo-American Literary Theory from Eliot to McLuhan* (London: Routledge & Kegan Paul, 1975), 144.

23 Marshall McLuhan, "Electronics and the Changing Role of Print," *Audiovisual Communication Review* 8, no. 5 (1960): 76.

24 McLuhan, *Understanding Media*, 23, 82.

25 McLuhan and Fiore, *Medium Is the Massage*, 125.

26 In 1969, the Canadian artists Iain and Ingrid Baxter incorporated their collaboration, N. E. Thing Co., as a business venture and operated a restaurant and a Cibachrome lab. They also transformed the National Gallery in Ottawa into an office space. According to Nancy Shaw, the Baxters "occupied the form of business in order to transform it" and "were extremely engaged with the McLuhanesque notion of artists as educators who expand perception through humour and perception." Nancy Shaw, "Expanded Consciousness and Company Types: Collaboration since Intermedia and the N. E. Thing Company," in *Vancouver Anthology: The Institutional Politics of Art*, ed. Stan Douglas (Vancouver: Talonbooks, 1991), 91–92. The Vancouver collective Image Bank also explored the potential of corporate forms. See *Image Bank: 1969–1977* (Berlin: Hatje Cantz, 2020).

27 While claiming 1968 as its birth year, General Idea formed in 1969.

28 McLuhan referred to *Life* as a mixture of "pictorial violence," "strip tease," and "a wodge of pseudo-science." *The Mechanical Bride*, 11 ("The Ballet Luce"). For more on FILE, see Diedrich Diederichsen, "Glad Rag," *Artforum*, April 2002, 104–8. While FILE was certainly inspired by Warhol's *Interview*, which at the time still functioned primarily as a magazine about film, it distinguished itself from the New York artist's enterprise with its strange sense of belatedness.

29 General Idea, "Homely Details of Everyday 'LIFE,'" *FILE* 1, no. 4 (December 1972): 5.

30 For more on this, see Noë Goldwasser, "Time-Life Files a Suit," *Village Voice*, March 15, 1976, 24.

31 "Performance," *FILE*, December 1973, n.p.

32 At this point, Zontal still went by the name Jorge Saia. See Willoughby Sharp, "The Gold-Diggers of '84: An Interview with General Idea," *Avalanche* 7 (Winter–Spring 1973): 15.

33 *FILE* 1, nos. 2–3 (May/June 1972): 62.

34 General Idea and Robert Cumming, "Borderline Research Project," *FILE*, September 1973, n.p. For a discussion of the concept of the borderline, see Philip Monk, *Glamour Is Theft: A User's Guide to General Idea* (Toronto: Art Gallery of York University, 2012), 75–79.

35 Participants were given the following charge: "The head is separate; the hand is separate. Body and mind are separate. The hand is a mirror for the mind—wrap your arm over your head, lodging your elbow behind and grabbing your chin with your hand. The act is now complete. Held, you are holding. You are object and subject, viewed and voyeur." General Idea, *Manipulating the Self* (Toronto: Coach House, 1971), n.p.

36 "Hans Ulrich Obrist in conversation with AA Bronson," in *Ziggurat: General Idea, 1968–1994* (New York: Mitchell-Innes & Nash, 2017), 57. "This venetian blind represents the borderline," Bronson explains. Ibid.

37 McLuhan, *Understanding Me*, 119. The year 1967 also marked Canada's centenary, which saw, among other events, the staging of Expo 67 in Montreal.

38 Hezy Leskly, "Conversation with General Idea," *Artzien: A Monthly Review of Art in Amsterdam* 2, no. 1 (November 1979): n.p. Bronson continues: "We learned about [McLuhan] in university. I went to university in '61, '62, '63 and he was being taught at that point in the schools." When asked about a common style between McLuhan and General Idea, he notes: "Canadians are definitely humour- and irony-prone."

39 Elke Town, *Fiction* (Toronto: Art Gallery of Ontario, 1982), n.p.

40 Gary Michael Dault, "3 Trendy Young Men Market Themselves," *Toronto Star*, November 3, 1975, D8.

41 Andy Warhol, *The Philosophy of Andy Warhol (From A to B and Back Again)* (New York: Harcourt Brace Jovanovich, 1975), 92.

42 For more on this genealogy, see Caroline Jones, *Machine in the Studio: Constructing the Postwar American Artist* (Chicago: University of Chicago Press, 1996), 203.

43 As Miriam Felton-Dansky has noted: "The beauty pageant offered a form ripe for subversion: partially for its strict dramaturgy of contest and results, partially for its association with hokey mainstream ideas of power, and partially because beauty pageants were at the epicenter of new thinking about gender at the time. . . . Inhabiting the beauty pageant, for General Idea, was a means of subverting from within, infiltrating and redirecting the aims of a product of mainstream culture, rendering an avatar of normativity delightfully queer." Miriam Felton-Dansky, *Viral Performance: Contagious Theaters from Modernism to the Digital Age* (Evanston, IL: Northwestern University Press, 2018), 102.

44 The question of myth is central to many cultural thinkers confronting modernity. See, e.g., Roland Barthes, *Mythologies*, trans. Annette Lavers (New York: Hill & Wang, 1972).

45 General Idea, "Editorial," *FILE* 3, no. 4 (Fall 1977): 11.

46 AA Bronson, "Copyright, Cash, and Crowd Control: Art and Economy in the Work of General Idea," in *General Idea: Haute Culture: A Retrospective, 1969–1994*, ed. Frédéric Bonnet (Zurich: JRP-Ringier, 2011), 118–19.

47 General Idea's connection to West Coast alternative culture, such as the Intermedia Society of which AA Bronson was a part, contributed to this view.

48 Mike Kelley and AA Bronson, "Excerpts from a Conversation," in *General Idea: Editions, 1969–1994* (Mississauga, ON: Blackwood Gallery, 2003), 283.

49 In 1974, John Bentley Mays wrote: "i think i've discovered how general idea plans to take over the world, & i've learned that the hard way, by becoming a victim in the germ-warfare of images." John Bentley Mays, "General Idea," *Open Letter* 2, no. 8 (Summer 1974): 30. For an important reading of the *Imagevirus* project, see Gregg Bordowitz, *General Idea: Imagevirus* (London: Afterall, 2010).

50 Philip Marchand, "The General Idea behind General Idea," *Toronto Life*, November 1975, 31.

51 *Shut the Fuck Up* was produced in Amsterdam as part of the project *Talking Back to the Media*.

52 A transcript of *Test Tube* is included in Elke Town, ed., *Video by Artists 2* (Toronto: Art Metropole, 1986), 59–66.

53 "Interview with AA Bronson, Felix Partz, and Jorge Zontal by Louise Dompierre (New York City, Friday July 26, 1991)," in Bonnet, ed., *General Idea: Haute Culture*, 158. Other artist collectives, such as Bernadette Corporation, have subsequently used the format of the corporation to similar ends. For more on this, see *Corporate Mentality*, ed. John Kelsey and Aleksandra Mir (New York: Sternberg, 2003).

54 McLuhan opened Appel's exhibition at the Art Gallery of Hamilton, in Ontario, in 1977.

55 Marshall McLuhan, foreword to *Karel Appel: Works on Paper* (New York: Abbeville, 1980), 9.

56 See Peter Selz, *New Images of Man* (New York: Museum of Modern Art, 1959), 16–21.

57 McLuhan, *Karel Appel*, 10.

58 Erasmus, *Praise of Folly* (New York: Penguin, 1971), 7.

## Postscript

1 Already in the 1990s, McLuhan served as a kind of inverse inspiration for the dystopian visions of cyberpunk writers. For more on this, see Hal Foster, *The Return of the Real: The Avant-Garde at the End of the Century* (Cambridge, MA: MIT Press, 1996), 218.

2 See Alexander Galloway, *Protocol: How Control Exists After Decentralization* (Cambridge, MA: MIT Press, 2004).

3 Emily Nussbaum called the spa industry a "new service economy" and a "new type of labor." Emily Nussbaum, "A Stranger's Touch," *New York*, November 23, 2007, https://nymag.com/beauty/features/41280/.

4 In 2011, I curated an exhibition featuring the artists Sean Paul, Pamela Rosenkranz, Georgia Sagri, and Antek Walczak at Andrew Roth Gallery that focused on these themes.

5 The critic Mark Fisher sees the call center as an emblem for the "centerlessness of capitalism." Mark Fisher, *Capitalist Realism: Is There No Alternative?* (London: Zero, 2009), 63.

6 This connects to the art world's fascination at this time with "materialisms." While some artists turned to these questions critically, others embraced raw materials therapeutically, as if they were desperate for touch. See my contribution to "A Questionnaire on Materialisms," *October* 155 (Winter 2016): 64–66.

7 The term was coined in Gene McHugh, *Post-Internet: Notes on the Internet and Art* (Brescia: LINK Editions, 2011). Ostensibly it was meant to refer to art made just after using the Internet.

8 Boris Groys, "From Image to Image File—and Back: Art in the Age of Digitalization," in *Art Power*, 83.

9 For more on this, see Julian Stallabrass, *Internet Art: The Online Clash of Culture and Commerce* (London: Tate Publishing, 2003).

# Bibliography

Alberro, Alexander. *Conceptual Art and the Politics of Publicity*. Cambridge, MA: MIT Press, 2003.

Allan, Ken. "Understanding *Information*." In *Conceptual Art: Theory, Myth, and Practice*, ed. Michael Corris, 144–68. Cambridge: Cambridge University Press, 2004.

———. "Marshall McLuhan and the Counterenvironment: 'The Medium Is the Massage.'" *Art Journal* (Winter 2014): 22–45.

Antille, Benoît. "'HON—en katedral': Behind Pontus Hultén's Theatre of Inclusiveness." *Afterall* 32 (Spring 2013): 72–81.

Antin, David. *Radical Coherency: Selected Essays on Art and Literature, 1966 to 2005*. Chicago: University of Chicago Press, 2011.

Battcock, Gregory. "Humanism and Reality: Thek and Warhol." In *The New Art*, ed. Gregory Battcock, 13–20. New York: E. P. Dutton, 1973.

———. "The Warhol Generation." In *The New Art*, ed. Gregory Battcock, 21–28. New York: E. P. Dutton, 1973.

Brown, Carolyn. "McLuhan and the Dance." *Ballet Review* 1 (1966): 13–20.

Burnham, Jack. "Systems Esthetics." *Artforum*, September 1968, 30–35.

———. "Real Time Systems." *Artforum*, September 1969, 49–55.

———. "Alice's Head: Reflections on Conceptual Art." *Artforum*, February 1970, 37–43.

———. "Les Levine: Business as Usual." *Artforum*, April 1970, 40–43.

———. *Software: Information Technology: Its New Meaning for Art*. New York: Jewish Museum, 1970.

Cage, John. "Nam June Paik: A Diary." In *Nam June Paik: Electronic Art*, n.p. New York: Galeria Bonino, 1965.

Carpenter, Edmund. *Oh, What a Blow That Phantom Gave Me!* New York: Bantam, 1972.

Carpenter, Edmund, and Marshall McLuhan, eds. *Explorations in Communication: An Anthology*. Boston: Beacon, 1960.

Carroll, Noël. *A Philosophy of Mass Art*. Oxford: Oxford University Press, 1998.

Cavell, Richard. *McLuhan in Space: A Cultural Geography*. Toronto: University of Toronto Press, 2002.

*Exploration of the Ways, Means, and Values of . . . MUSEUM COMMUNICATION with the viewing public: A SEMINAR with Marshall McLuhan, Harley Parker, and Jacques Barzun*. New York: Museum of the City of New York, 1969.

Fekete, John. *The Critical Twilight: Explorations in the Ideology of Anglo-American Literary Theory from Eliot to McLuhan*. London: Routledge & Kegan Paul, 1977.

*Forward through the Rearview Mirror: Reflections on and by Marshall McLuhan*, ed. Paul Benedetti and Nancy DeHart. Scarborough, ON: Prentice-Hall, 1996.

Foster, Hal. *The First Pop Age: Painting and Subjectivity in the Art of Hamilton, Lichtenstein, Warhol, Richter, and Ruscha*. Princeton, NJ: Princeton University Press, 2012.

Gablik, Suzi. "Take a Cigarette Butt and Make It Heroic." *Art News*, May 1967, 30–31, 77.

Galloway, Alexander, Eugene Thacker, and McKenzie Wark. *Excommunication: Three Inquiries in Media and Mediation*. Chicago: University of Chicago Press, 2013.

Giedion, Sigfried. *Mechanization Takes Command: A Contribution to Anonymous History*. New York: Oxford University Press, 1948.

Gilman, Richard. "The Doors McLuhan Opens." In *The Confusion of Realms*, 22–28. New York: Random House, 1969.

Goldin, Amy. "McLuhan's Message: Participate, Enjoy!" In *Art in a Hairshirt: Art Criticism, 1964–1978*, ed. Robert Kushner, 42–49. Stockbridge, MA: Hard Press, 2011.

Graham, Dan. "Information." In *For Publication*, n.p. Los Angeles: Otis Art Institute, 1975.

Hamilton, Richard. *Collected Words, 1953–1982*. London: Thames & Hudson, 1983.

Holert, Tom. "Information Society: The Art of Les Levine." *Artforum*, May 2013, 288–95.

Hultén, Pontus. *The Machine as Seen at the End of the Mechanical Age*. New York: Museum of Modern Art, 1968.

Huyssen, Andreas. "In the Shadow of McLuhan: Jean Baudrillard's Theory of Simulation." *Assemblage* 10 (December 1989): 6–17.

Innis, Harold A. *The Bias of Communication*. With an introduction by Marshall McLuhan. Toronto: University of Toronto Press, 1973.

Joseph, Branden. "'My Mind Split Open': Andy Warhol's Exploding Plastic Inevitable." *Grey Room* 8 (Summer 2002): 80–107.

Kaiser, Philipp, and Miwon Kwon. "Ends of the Earth and Back." In *Ends of the Earth: Land Art to 1974*, 17–31. Munich: Prestel, 2012.

*Karel Appel*. New York: Abbeville, 1980.

Kenner, Hugh. *Wyndham Lewis*. New York: New Directions, 1954.

———. *The Pound Era*. Berkeley: University of California Press, 1971.

———. *The Mechanic Muse*. Oxford: Oxford University Press, 1988.

Kostelanetz, Richard. *The Theatre of Mixed Means: An Introduction to Happenings, Kinetic Environments, and Other Mixed Means Performance*. New York: Dial, 1968.

———. "Marshall McLuhan: High Priest of the Electronic Village." In *Master Minds: Portraits of Contemporary American Artists and Intellectuals*, 82–114. New York: Macmillan, 1969.

Kracauer, Siegfried. *The Mass Ornament: Weimar Essays*. Translated by Thomas Y. Levin. Cambridge, MA: Harvard University Press, 1995.

Kroker, Arthur. *Technology and the Canadian Mind: Innis/McLuhan/Grant*. Montreal: New World Perspectives, 1984.

Lee, John M. "M'Luhan's Views Reshape Museum." *New York Times*, February 26, 1967, 32.

Lee, Pamela M. *Chronophobia: On Time in the Art of the 1960s*. Cambridge, MA: MIT Press, 2004.

Lewis, Wyndham. *The Art of Being Ruled*. 1926. Santa Rosa, CA: Black Sparrow, 1989.

———. *Time and Western Man*. London: Chatto & Windus, 1927.

———. *Men without Art*. 1934. Santa Rosa, CA: Black Sparrow, 1987.

———. *The Hitler Cult*. 1939. New York: Gordon, 1972.

———. *America and Cosmic Man*. Garden City, NY: Doubleday, 1949.

Linde, Ulf, and Öyvind Fahlström. "Claes Oldenburg at the Moderna Museet, Stockholm: Two Contrasting Viewpoints." *Studio International* 172, no. 884 (December 1966): 326–29.

Lyotard, Jean-François. *The Postmodern Condition: A Report on Knowledge*. Translated by Geoff Bennington and Brian Massumi. Minneapolis: University of Minnesota Press, 1984.

Marchand, Philip. *Marshall McLuhan: The Medium and the Messenger*. New York: Ticknor & Fields, 1989.

Marcus, Greil. "Twentieth-Century Vox: Marshall McLuhan and the Mechanical Bride." *Artforum*, September 2012, 458–67.

Mastin, Catherine, Robert Stacey, and Thomas Dilworth. *The Talented Intruder: Wyndham Lewis in Canada, 1939–1945*. Windsor, ON: Art Gallery of Windsor, 1992.

McHale, John. "The Man from Mascom." *Progressive Architecture*, February 1967, 170, 172, 176, 188, 199.

McLuhan, Marshall. "American Advertising." *Horizon* 93–94 (October 1947): 132–41.

———. "TIME, LIFE, and FORTUNE." *View*, Spring 1947, 33–37.

———. "The Folklore of Industrial Man." *Neurotica* 8 (Spring 1951): 3–20.

———. *The Mechanical Bride: Folklore of Industrial Man*. New York: Vanguard, 1951.

———. *Counterblast*. Toronto: self-published, 1954.

———. "Notes on the Media as Art Forms." *Explorations* 2 (April 1954): 6–13.

———. "Sight, Sound and Fury." In *Mass Culture: The Popular Arts in America*, ed. Bernard Rosenberg and David Manning White, 489–95. Glencoe, IL: Free Press, 1957.

———. "Electronics and the Changing Role of Print." *Audio Visual Communication Review* 8, no. 5 (1960): 74–83.

———. *The Gutenberg Galaxy: The Making of Typographic Man*. Toronto: University of Toronto Press, 1962.

———. *Understanding Media: The Extensions of Man*. New York: Signet, 1964.

———. "Culture and Technology." In *Astronauts of Inner-Space: An International Collection of Avant-garde Activity*, n.p. San Francisco: Stolen Paper Review Editions, 1966.

———. "The Emperor's Old Clothes." In *The Man-Made Object*, ed. György Kepes, 90–95. New York: George Braziller, 1966.

———. "Great Change-Overs for You." *Vogue*, July 1966, 62–63,114–17.

———. "The Invisible Environment: The Future of an Erosion." *Perspecta* 11 (1967): 162–67.

———. *Counterblast*. New York: Harcourt, Brace & World, 1969.

———. *The Interior Landscape: The Literary Criticism of Marshall McLuhan, 1943–1962*. Edited by Eugene McNamara. New York: McGraw-Hill, 1969.

———. *Culture Is Our Business*. New York: Ballantine, 1970.

———. "Lewis's Prose Style." In *Wyndham Lewis: A Revaluation*, ed. Jeffrey Meyers, 64–67. Montreal: McGill-Queen's University Press, 1980.

———. *Understanding Me: Lectures and Interviews*. Edited by Stephanie McLuhan and David Staines. Cambridge, MA: MIT Press, 2003.

McLuhan, Marshall, and Quentin Fiore. *The Medium Is the Massage: An Inventory of Effects*. New York: Bantam, 1967.

———. *War and Peace in the Global Village*. New York: Bantam, 1968.

McLuhan, Marshall, and Eric McLuhan. *Media and Formal Cause*. Houston: NeoPoiesis, 2011.

McLuhan, Marshall, and Harley Parker. *Through the Vanishing Point: Space in Poetry and Painting*. New York: Harper Colophon, 1968.

McLuhan, Marshall, with Wilfred Watson. *From Archetype to Cliché*. New York: Viking, 1970.

McShine, Kynaston. *Information*. New York: Museum of Modern Art, 1970.

Meyers, Jeffrey. *The Enemy: A Biography of Wyndham Lewis*. London: Routledge & Kegan Paul, 1980.

Michaud, Eric. *The Cult of Art in Nazi Germany*. Translated by Janet Lloyd. Stanford, CA: Stanford University Press, 2004.

Miller, Jonathan. *Marshall McLuhan*. New York: Viking, 1971.

Monk, Philip. *Glamour Is Theft: A User's Guide to General Idea*. Toronto: Art Gallery of York University, 2012.

Oldenburg, Claes. *Raw Notes*. Halifax: Press of the Nova Scotia College of Art and Design, 1973.

———. *Writing on the Side, 1956–1969*. New York: Museum of Modern Art, 2013.

Rauschenberg, Robert. "Random Order." *Location* 1 (Spring 1963): 27–31.

Richards, I. A. *Principles of Literary Criticism*. New York: Harcourt Brace & World, 1925.

Robbins, David, ed. *The Independent Group: Postwar Britain and the Aesthetics of Plenty*. Cambridge. MA: MIT Press, 1990.

Rosebush, Judson, ed. *Nam June Paik: Videa 'n' Videology, 1959–1973*. Syracuse, NY: Everson Museum of Art, 1974.

Rosenberg, Harold. *The De-Definition of Art*. New York: Collier, 1972.

Rosenquist, James, and David Dalton. *Rosenquist: Painting below Zero: Notes on a Life in Art*. New York: Knopf, 2009.

Ross, Andrew. "Candid Cameras." In *No Respect: Intellectuals and Popular Culture*, 102–34. New York: Routledge, 1989.

Ross, David. "Nam June Paik's Videotapes." In *Transmission: Theory and Practice for a New Television Aesthetics*, 151–63. New York: Tanam, 1985.

Roth, Moira. "The Aesthetic of Indifference." *Artforum*, November 1977, 46–53.

Schnapp, Jeffrey, and Adam Michaels. *The Electric Information Age Book: McLuhan/Agel/Fiore and the Experimental Paperback*. New York: Princeton Architectural Press, 2012.

Shanken, Edward A. "In Forming Software: Software, Structuralism, Dematerialization." In *Mainframe Experimentalism: Early Computing and the Foundations of the Digital Arts*, 51–62. Berkeley and Los Angeles: University of California Press, 2012.

Smithson, Robert. "A Museum of Language in the Vicinity of Art." In *Robert Smithson: The Collected Writings*, ed. Jack Flam, 78–94. Berkeley and Los Angeles: University of California Press, 1996.

———. "A Tour of the Monuments of Passaic, New Jersey." In *Robert Smithson: The Collected Writings*, ed. Jack Flam, 68–74. Berkeley and Los Angeles: University of California Press, 1996.

Sontag, Susan. *Against Interpretation*. New York: Farrar, Straus & Giroux, 1966.

Tomkins, Calvin. "Outside Art." In *Pavilion*, ed. Billy Klüver, Julie Martin, and Barbara Rose, 105–65. New York: E. P. Dutton, 1972.

Turner, Fred. *The Democratic Surround: Multimedia and American Liberalism from World War II to the Psychedelic Sixties*. Chicago: University of Chicago Press, 2013.

Wagner, Anne. "Acconci and the Senses." In *Cornerstones*, 116–31. Rotterdam: Witte de With, 2011.

Warhol, Andy, and Pat Hackett. *POPism: The Warhol '60s*. New York: Harcourt Brace Jovanovich, 1980.

Whiteley, Nigel. *Reyner Banham: Historian of the Immediate Future*. Cambridge, MA: MIT Press, 2002.

Wigley, Mark. "Network Fever." *Grey Room* 4 (Summer 2001): 82–122.

Williams, Raymond. *Television: Technology and Cultural Form*. Middletown, CT: Wesleyan University Press, 1974.

Williamson, Judith. *Decoding Advertisements: Ideology and Meaning in Advertising*. London: Marion Boyars, 1978.

Willmott, Glenn. *McLuhan, or Modernism in Reverse*. Toronto: University of Toronto Press, 1996.

Yalkut, Jud. "Art and Technology of Nam June Paik." *Arts Magazine* 42, no. 6 (April 1968): 50–51.

# Index